■ BUILDING WORDS

RELATED TITLES

Best Books for Building Literacy for Elementary School Children
Thomas G. Gunning
ISBN: 0-205-28625-9

Phonological Awareness and Primary Phonics
Thomas G. Gunning
ISBN: 0-205-32323-5

Vocabulary in the Elementary and Middle School
Dale D. Johnson
ISBN: 0-205-29862-1

Phonogram Poems for Teaching Phonic Rimes
Timothy V. Rasinski and Belinda S. Zimmerman
ISBN: 0-205-30909-7

■ BUILDING WORDS

A RESOURCE MANUAL FOR TEACHING WORD ANALYSIS AND SPELLING STRATEGIES

THOMAS G. GUNNING

Professor Emeritus, Southern Connecticut State University
Adjunct Professor, Central Connecticut State University

Illustrated by Norma Kable

Allyn and Bacon

Boston ■ London ■ Toronto ■ Sydney ■ Tokyo ■ Singapore

Series Editor: Arnis E. Burvikovs
Vice President, Editor-in-Chief: Paul A. Smith
Series Editorial Assistant: Patrice Mailloux
Marketing Manager: Stephen Smith
Manufacturing Buyer: David Repetto

Library of Congress Cataloging-in-Publication Data

Gunning, Thomas G.
    Building words: a resource manual for teaching word analysis and spelling strategies /
Thomas G. Gunning
        p.   cm.
    Includes bibliographical references (p.).
    ISBN 0-205-30922-4
    1. Reading—Phonetic method—United States.   2. English language—Orthography and
spelling—Study and teaching (Elementary)—United States.   I. Title.
LB1573.3.G83   2001
372.46'5—dc21

                                                                    00-020579

Printed in the United States of America
10   9   8   7   6   5   04   03

Contents

■ Preface

Building Words is a resource manual designed to provide step-by-step suggestions for assessing and instructing students in grades 1 through 4 in key word analysis and spelling skills and strategies. Major word analysis and related areas explored include emergent literacy, phonics, sight words, syllabic analysis, contextual analysis, and spelling.

In addition to providing an overview of word analysis skills and strategies and the role they play in a literacy program, the text presents virtually everything—except actual books—that a teacher might need in order to implement a high-quality, effective word analysis program. Major elements include:

- Instructions for quickly and efficiently assessing students in word analysis and spelling. All assessment devices are available on reproducible masters.
- Sample lessons for teaching key skills and strategies.
- Resource sections that spell out which phonics or multisyllabic patterns to teach. For each pattern there is a listing of words to be presented, related spelling words, possible writing topics, and reinforcement and application activities. These activities include games, puzzles, riddles, songs, rhymes, real-world materials, and children's books that contain the pattern.
- Illustrations that can be duplicated by the teacher and used for sorting or other activities.
- More than 200 copyright-free verses, songs, and riddles that the teacher can use to reinforce patterns.
- A series of fold-and-read books that can be used to reinforce patterns at the beginning levels.

Building Words was created as a way of sharing rhymes, children's books, teaching techniques, and other resources for strengthening students' word analysis and spelling skills. However, the teacher is the key element. A word analysis program is only as good as the teacher who implements it. Adapt the program to fit the needs of your students and your teaching style.

■ ACKNOWLEDGMENTS

My sincere appreciation goes to Virginia Lanigan and Arnis Burvikovs of Allyn & Bacon for their timely and encouraging support of this text. My thanks also go to Bridget Keane, editorial assistant, for her efficient help in moving this text from unedited manuscript to bound book. I would also like to express my appreciation to Norma Kable, the artist who created most of the illustrations for the text. Her illustrations have added greatly to the appeal of the text's suggested activities and fold-and-read booklets. I would also like to extend my appreciation to the following reviewer for his thoughtful comments and many valuable suggestions: Dr. Mahmoud Suleiman, California State University, Bakersfield.

■ Prologue

Building Words has been designed as a practical, hands-on resource guide. This prologue has been created in order to provide a rationale and research base for the program. The prologue provides a description of the events involved in the creation of *Building Words*. It also provides a brief history of phonics instruction and an overview of key research in the area. If you are well informed about the theory and research behind the program, you will be in a better position to implement the program and make appropriate adjustments. Understanding the "why" of a program leads to more confident and committed implementation.

Personal experiences, more than research, led to the creation and revision of *Building Words,* so this prologue is a personal account. In many instances, research verified what I had concluded based on my own experience with phonics. Much of the initial foundation and subsequent revisions to the program were dictated by my work with students who were learning to read, especially those who were struggling.

My initial professional experience with phonics occurred during my first year of teaching. As a new secondary English teacher, I was assigned to teach the lowest-achieving students, many of whom were struggling with basic reading skills. Prepared as a teacher of literature and writing, I sought help from more experienced colleagues. It was suggested that I teach phonics. The English Department chairperson provided me with a brief handbook on phonics and helped me find student books that were relatively easy to read.

Based on the handbook's suggestions, I had the class spend time noting whether vowels were long or short and telling how many syllables were in a word and marking accented syllables. I found the lessons to be challenging—not for the class, but for me. I had a great deal of difficulty telling whether a vowel was long or short until the class told me that the long vowels said their own name. That helped a great deal. They also explained the rules in easy-to-understand terms, so that I learned that "when two vowels go walking, the first one does the talking," which means that the *oa* in *goat* and *boat* is pronounced as a long *o*—that is, it says its own name. As challenging as it was to learn these rules, I couldn't help noticing that my students didn't apply them.

Despite the expert help given to me by my students, I decided that I should take a course in reading at Loyola College in Baltimore. There I learned that reading teachers were upset by a book entitled *Why Johnny Can't Read,* by Rudolph Flesch (1955), which had been published several years before. For a number of years, children had been taught through the look–say method. They learned words by memorizing them. Children were taught to use configuration clues—the shapes of the words—to help them memorize the words. Thus, the word *camel*, with its two-humped *m*, had the shape of a camel. After memorizing 50 to 100 high-frequency words, they were introduced to phonics. Consonant sounds were never to be spoken in isolation because this distorted them. Rather, they were to be pronounced within the context of a whole word. The sound represented by *m* was referred to as the sound that you hear at the beginning of *man*. Flesch advocated a more vigorous, synthetic approach to teaching phonics in which sounds in isolation were presented and then blended. To teach *man*, the teacher presented $m = /m/$, $a = /a/$, $n = /n/$, and then blended the sounds. This was criticized by reading teachers as being tedious and leading to a mindless sounding out of words. While taking Flesch to task for oversimplifying the reading process, the professor at Loyola did admit that maybe we should be teaching more phonics. Apparently, teaching phonics was frowned upon in many schools. My classmates told tales of teachers who closed their doors before teaching phonics. Fortunately, for me and my students, most of the children I taught had some grasp of basic word analysis skills.

Meanwhile, intrigued by reading, I continued to take courses and enrolled in a doctoral program at Temple University in Philadelphia, where I obtained a position as the reading teacher in the lowest-achieving junior high school in the city. Using a group reading inventory, I located fifty students operating on a beginning reading level. Never having taught beginning readers, I decided to try a new method of teaching word analysis skills, the linguistic approach. The rationale behind the Merrill Linguistics (Fries, Wilson, & Rudolph, 1996) program was straightforward: students would be taught decodable words first, and these would be taught in pattern form using a linguistic technique known as minimal contrast. There was to be no sounding out of words. Students would discriminate between printed words the same way we discriminate between spoken words—by contrasting them. Thus they would learn *hat* by contrasting it with *cat* and would learn *sat* by contrasting it with *hat* and *cat*. The books had no pictures, so that students would be forced to focus on the print rather than guess at the words by using picture clues. For me, the absence of pictures had a more important advantage: my seventh and eighth graders couldn't tell that the books had been written for primary-grade children.

Teaching the students in groups of ten, I was relieved and gratified to see that they made progress. In analyzing the program, I could see why this was so. The students were being instructed on the appropriate level, they were taught new words before encountering them in a story, the stories incorporated the patterns they had been taught, and there was a great deal of reinforcement. The entire first book of the program was devoted to short *a*. Unfortunately, because the stories were restricted to patterns that had been taught and a few high-frequency words, the stories were contrived and didn't allow for the use of context clues or the flow of natural language. A few years later, when I became aware of Ken Goodman's (1967) theory on the importance of using a three-pronged cueing system, graph-phonemic, syntactic, and semantic, I realized that word-level decoding had been overemphasized and syntactic and semantic cues badly neglected.

Meanwhile, Jeanne Chall's *The Great Debate* (1967) was published. Jeanne Chall had reexamined the research on phonics and concluded that students taught through a phonics approach did better than those who weren't. The message was similar to Flesch's. Whereas Flesch could be dismissed because he was not an expert in the field and had overstated the value of phonics, Jeanne Chall's book was a work of careful, courageous scholarship. The profession took note.

In 1973 I took a job as a reading consultant in Hartford, Connecticut. It was the era of the open classroom. The school where I was assigned was using a half-dozen approaches to teaching reading. Many of the teachers were using a highly programmed, step-by-step phonics approach in which students worked at their own level and at their own pace. Because students were working at their own level and their own pace, there was little direct instruction. The program advocated grouping the students for instruction, but the teachers were used to working one on one with students. Mostly they checked mid-book and end-of-book tests. Most students learned, but a sizable percentage needed more teacher help than they were getting. For me, it dramatized the importance of direct, systematic instruction, especially for struggling readers, and the important role that the teacher plays. The program would probably have been highly effective if the teachers had provided more guidance.

At home, my wife was complaining about the reading program that my daughter, a first grader, was using. The school had adopted *Reading Systems*, a holistic basal reading program co-authored by Ken Goodman (Aaron et al., 1971).

In this program students were introduced to reading through predictable texts in which they used picture clues and repeated text to read selections. My wife wanted to know how our daughter was supposed to read when she hadn't been taught phonics. Later, our daughter's teacher supplemented *Reading Systems* with *Programmed Reading* (Buchanan & Sullivan, 1973). Thus the program that had the least phonics was combined with the program that had the most phonics. The result? My daughter acquired outstanding decoding skills and became an avid reader. This reinforced my belief in instruction in systematic decoding skills, combined with the use of context, and lots of reading of interesting material.

Meanwhile, as a reading consultant I was seeking ways to improve the school's reading program. Not entirely happy with any of the commercial approaches available, I decided to construct my own. Searching for the easiest way to introduce phonics, I attempted to build on what students know. Since students knew the names of the letters, and the vowel letter names are the same as their long-vowel sounds, I presented long *o* and had them build words by adding consonants (*go, no, so*) or long *e* (*he, me, we, she, see*). After they learned a few long-*o* and long-*e* high-frequency words, we built words using short-vowel patterns. I adopted a pattern approach based on the success I had had with Merrill Linguistics (Fries, Wilson, & Rudolph, 1966). To find out which patterns were most useful, I analyzed the 1,500 most frequently used words in printed English (Gunning, 1975). I also created or sought stories that reinforced the patterns but were less contrived than those in the linguistics program. Subsequent research by Juel and Roper/Schneider (1985) verified the importance of providing students with opportunities to meet in print the phonics elements they have been taught. Juel and Roper/Schneider found that students who read selections in which patterns were reinforced performed better than those who read traditional basals.

The approach, which I dubbed "Word Building," worked well, but an essential element was missing: it lacked a satisfactory technique for teaching students a strategy for decoding words that they had difficulty with in their reading. Influenced by Pat Cunningham's (1978) research in which she had students compare unknown words with known words, I incorporated that strategy. In a compare/contrast or analogy strategy, a student compares the unknown word *flat* to the known word *hat*. The strategy worked, but I sometimes had difficulty thinking of a suitable prompt. If the student had difficulty with the word *brought* or *grudge,* I had to think of familiar words that were analogous to them. Ultimately, in order to become an independent reader, the student would have to think of analogous words.

Remembering an article I had read by Glass and Burton (1973), in which they suggested teaching pronounceable word parts such as *at* or *est*, I decided to undertake some research to see how students actually attempt to decode unknown words. I tested forty-one second graders. Twenty-one had been taught using an intensive phonics program that presented a series of rules. The others had been taught using traditional basal approaches. The results were dramatic and surprising. Just as Glass and Burton (1973) had reported, I found that when encountering unfamiliar words, many students sought out a familiar word part and used that to reconstruct the whole word. Although half the students had been taught through a synthetic rule-based approach, I saw no evidence that they decoded words sound by sound, and the only rule used was the final-*e* generalization, in which the *e* marks the vowel as being long (*hope*). Although half the students had been taught to use context or context plus initial consonant, I saw no evidence of this strategy. Based on the results of the research, I incorporated the pronounceable word part strategy into Word Building. If a student balks at a difficult word, the teacher simply asks, "Is there any part of that word that you can say?" or "Is there any part of that word that you know?" This simple prompt worked beyond all expectations. When it didn't work, I used an analogy strategy prompt ("Is this word like any word you know?") or a contextual prompt ("What word would fit here?") (Gunning, 1988, 1999).

The pronounceable word part strategy works because it fits with the way students naturally decode words. As Cunningham (1992) notes, children are able to decode an unfamiliar word successfully when the spelling patterns that make up that word are stored in memory. Encountering the word *brand* for the first time, the child recognizes the *and* because she has seen *and* by itself and in *sand* and *hand*. The student also has seen *br* in *bring* and *break*. Recognizing the *and*, the student adds *br* and says the word *brand*. If the student had only limited experience with words containing *br* or *and*, then she might not recognize *and* or *br* as familiar spelling patterns. She would then use an analogy strategy. She might note that the word *brand* is like the known word *sand* and the known word *break*. The student would decode the unfamiliar word *brand* by comparing it to known words such as *and* and *break*.

Later, I observed that for some students the pronounceable word part and analogy strategies don't happen automatically. One novice reader with whom I was working could read *us* with ease but could not read *Gus* in the sentence, "Get on the bus, Gus." Students seem to need a certain familiarity with words before they can use patterns from them as a pronounceable word part or analogy. Although many students pick up these strategies on their own, others need systematic instruction and lots of prompting.

As I supervised graduate students working with struggling readers and worked with struggling readers myself, I made additional discoveries about word analysis. Tremain's (1992) research suggested that the rime (the rhyming part of words: the *oat* in *goat*, the *et* in *net*) was a natural unit of language and easier for students to learn than the individual sounds and letters that make up words. However, I found that some of the struggling readers I encountered needed to work through words sound by sound, but, in time, were able to work with larger units. This fit with research by Gibson (1969) suggesting that students learn initial consonants, then final consonants, then medial vowels, and eventually higher units of language. It also fits with Ehri's (Ehri & McCormick, 1998) stage theory of the acquisition of decoding skills. Children first use a letter or two to decode words, later use all the letters in the words, and eventually use patterns. To incorporate these findings, I changed Word Building so that students decode both rimes or patterns and individual sounds.

Struggling readers also taught me that it was important to match each sound in a word with the letter or letter combination that represents the sound. According to Gaskins, Ehri, Cress, O'Hara, & Donnelly (1996–1997), the sounds of words must be fully realized so that the letters of *goat* are matched with its three sounds: $g = /g/$, $oa = /\bar{o}/$, and $t = /t/$. This allows students to store words in memory so that when the letters are seen, the reader retrieves the sounds that they represent. Instruction begins on the auditory level. Students first identify the sounds in a word and then learn which letters or letter combinations represent those sounds.

At the reading clinic, I also noticed that the time-honored practice of having students memorize a store of high-frequency words wasn't working. Without any systematic way to attach sounds to letters, the students quickly forgot the words they memorized. Once they were taught to use phonics to help them remember the words, their performance improved significantly. Most of these high-frequency words were fully or partially predictable. Only a few, such as *of* and *once*, were highly irregular.

As an elementary-school reading consultant, I had encountered a number of students, including some in second grade, who were making no progress in reading and had difficulty with such foundational tasks as rhyming or detecting initial consonant sounds. Just up the road at the University of Connecticut, Isabelle Liberman and her colleagues (Liberman, Shankweiler, Fischer, & Carter, 1974) were making landmark discoveries about the importance of phonemic awareness. Their findings supported those of the Russian psychologist Elkonin (1973), who stated that being able to analyze a word into its component sounds "is the most important prerequisite for the successful learning of reading and writing" (p. 571).

In working with struggling readers who were having a particularly difficult time learning to read and write, I found that they didn't make much progress until they could identify the beginning sounds of words, something Stahl, Stahl, and McKenna (1998) also found in their research. Seeing the importance of phonemic awareness, I modified Word Building so that more stress would be placed on noting sounds in words, thus fostering phonemic awareness. Phonemic awareness is reciprocal: although a certain amount is needed before students can grasp the alphabetic principle that letters represent sounds, working with words and sounds fosters phonemic awareness.

From Adams's (1990) review of the research and her model of reading, I was reminded that decoding is a parallel process that involves four processors: orthographic, phonological, meaning, and context. The orthographic processor perceives the sequences of letters in words. The phonological processor translates the letters into their spoken equivalents. "The meaning processor contains one's knowledge of word meanings, and the context processor is in charge of constructing a continuing understanding of the text" (Stahl, Osborne, & Lehr, 1990, p. 21). The processors work simultaneously and both receive information and send it to the other processors; however, the orthographic and phonological processors are always key elements in the process. Context might speed the interpretation of orthographic and phonological information but does not take its place. When information from one processor is weak, another may be called on to give assistance. For instance, when a word such as *read* is encountered, the context processor assists the meaning and phonological processors in assigning the correct meaning and pronunciation.

Although systematic instruction in phonics is important, it must be conducted within the context of real reading so that systems are fully developed. To provide more reinforcement for Word Building, I sought out rhymes, songs, riddles, stories, and children's books that would provide practice with elements that had been presented. Noting the research on invented spelling (Clarke, 1988) and the reading–writing connection, I added a writing component.

In 1995 I attended a workshop given by Donald Bear of the University of Nevada. His session convinced me of the value of sorting or categorizing printed words. Not only does sorting help students make discoveries about letter–sound relationships, it is also an active, highly motivating activity. Both Morris (1999) and Santa (Santa & Høien, 1999) used sorting extensively in their highly successful programs. I added sorting as a key reinforcement activity to Word Building.

And so Word Building is, in part, a product of my research and experience and that of my colleagues. However, the key contributors were the achieving and struggling readers who helped me see which elements were working and which needed revising. These students also provided the motivation for the program. It is my belief that, if implemented carefully, Word Building will help students achieve their highest level of competency and will help correct and prevent reading difficulties.

Chapter 1

TEACHING WORD ANALYSIS

Created in the classroom and refined in the reading clinic, Word Building is a functional word analysis program that presents a full array of phonics and spelling skills but stresses strategies that will enable students to decode words independently. A functional, strategic program, it is based on the premise that students should be taught only those concepts, skills, and strategies that will enable them to become better readers, so that if they encounter words that are in their listening vocabularies but not known in print, they will be able to decode them. Along with being taught the sounds that consonant letters and vowel patterns such as *-at* and *-en* represent, it is also essential that students learn strategies that will enable them to use this knowledge to decode unfamiliar words.

In phonics, a little instruction goes a long way. Instruction in a pattern should be followed by many opportunities to meet that pattern in real reading and to write words using that pattern. This is not to imply that phonics instruction should be catch-as-catch-can. Instruction should be systematic and thorough, especially when working with students who are struggling to learn to read. Although some children might pick up phonics through informal contacts with print, many students need a carefully planned, well-implemented program. The key is to create a balanced, functional program that is reinforced by numerous opportunities to read and write. It is also essential that instruction be provided in the context of real reading and writing. Students should be taught the *-oon* pattern, for instance, in preparation for reading or writing about the moon or a magic spoon. The best way to reinforce the *-oon* pattern is for students to read *Yoo Hoo, Moon!* (Blocksma, 1989), or another book or selection that contains *-oon* words.

THE NATURE OF WORD ANALYSIS STRATEGIES

In addition to being presented functionally, phonics should be integrated with other word analysis strategies. Recently, while reading an article on the brain, I encountered the word *agonal.* Not having seen the word before, I used both phonics and syllabic analysis to reconstruct what I thought was the word's pronunciation: /uh-GON-uhl/. However, even after working out the pronunciation of the word, I didn't recognize it. Since there was no match between *agonal* and an item in my mental store of words, I attempted to use context. It didn't help. So I tried morphemic analysis, which is the use of meaning-bearing elements such as prefixes, suffixes, and roots. "Could the *gon* be the *gon* that means "sides" as in *polygon*? Could the *a* be the *a* that means "not" as in *aliterate?*" I asked myself. The suffix *al*, of course, made the word an adjective. Putting all the elements together suggested that *agonal* had something to do with angles or sides, but this meaning didn't fit the context in which the word appeared, so I used the word analysis strategy of last resort: the dictionary. To my surprise, I found that *agonal* was pronounced /AG-uh-nul/, meaning "pertaining to agony." My hypothesis about *agonal* being formed from the element *-gon* was wrong. It was actually formed from *agony.* Part of being an effective reader is having a command of a full range of word analysis strategies: sight words, phonics, syllabic analysis, morphemic analysis (working with prefixes, suffixes, and roots), contextual analysis, and dictionary skills. Having a command of the strategies is not enough, however. You have to know when and where to use them. You also need to know what to do if a particular strategy does not work. After trying phonics, syllabic analysis, and context to derive the meaning of *agonal*, I resorted to morphemic analysis and looked at what I thought were the word's root and affixes. To check the tentative meaning I derived, which didn't seem to fit the context in which the word was used, I went to the dictionary and was able to correct my misperception. Given the fallibility of strategies, it is frequently necessary to use one strategy to verify or cross-check another. For instance, I used context to verify the appropriateness of the definition I selected from the dictionary.

This is a brief overview of the strategies used by an experienced reader. (In this text, all of the major word analysis strategies, except morphemic analysis and dictionary skills, are presented.) Strategy use is determined in part by the reader's experience. Novice readers, for instance, might use picture clues to help them identify an unknown word. Although both novice and experienced readers have the construction of meaning as their overall goal, the nature of reading is somewhat different for expert readers than it is for novices. When I encounter an unknown word, it is because the word is not in my store of words whose meanings I know. Meaning is primary. Pronunciation is secondary. There are many words that I recognize in print but cannot pronounce correctly. Novices have the opposite concern. Generally, they know the meanings of the words they encounter in print. However, they may not recognize the printed form of the word. Unable to supply the pronunciation of the printed form, they cannot match it with an item in their store of known words.

STAGES OF LITERACY

In order to understand how strategy use might vary as students move from novice to expert, it is helpful to look at the stages of literacy and the kinds of strategies that each stage demands. Growth in literacy is continuous and complex, so the stages are a bit artificial. However, they help focus attention on essential tasks faced by readers at various points.

EARLY EMERGENT STAGE

The emergent stage includes all those behaviors that lead up to conventional reading. Children learn to handle books, learn that one reads print and not pictures, and that one reads from left to right, and from top to bottom. Students also begin to learn where printed words begin and end. When they "read" a book, children at this stage are usually constructing meaning from pictures. When students do learn to read a few words, their reading is generally logographic (Ehri, 1994). They make associations between a nonverbal visual aspect of a word and the spoken equivalent of that word. The visual aspect is not a letter–sound relationship. For instance, to identify a "McDonald's" sign, they don't sound out the *M*; they use the golden arches. To identify Crest, they use the overall design of the label and their knowledge of what is in the tube. However, since they are not reading letter–sound cues, they may "read" a Crest label as "toothpaste." Sometimes they seem to be using letter–sound cues but are not. Donald may recognize his name when he sees it because it starts with a *D*. However, Donald is not aware that *d* represents the sound /d/. If he encountered the word *dog* or *doughnut*, he would not be able to sound out the first letter. Unable to use letter–sound relationships, students in this stage are limited to the use of picture clues, context, or memory of word forms.

TABLE 1.1   Spelling Stages

Age	Stage	Example
18 months	Random scribbling	*mw*
3 years	Wordlike figures	*lⲟⲅ I Λ*
4–5 years	Early emergent (prephonemic)	NVT
4–6+	Early alphabetic (early letter name)	RD
5–7+	Alphabetic (letter name)	RID
6–7	Word pattern (within-word)	ride
8–10+	Syllabic (syllable juncture)	riding
10–20+	Morphemic (derivational constancy)	equestrian

In writing, Donald may draw pictures, scribble, use wordlike figures, or use actual letters, but again, the letters do not represent sounds (see Table 1.1). Donald may even spell his name and a few other words correctly, but this will be because he has memorized the spellings of the words. The emergent stage flows into the alphabetic stage as children discover and begin to use the alphabetic principle.

ALPHABETIC STAGE

The hallmark of the alphabetic stage is the use of letter–sound relationships to decode words. Typically, students first use initial consonants, then initial and final consonants, and finally all the elements in a word. Because decoding skills are limited at this stage, students rely heavily on picture clues or picture clues in combination with the initial consonant, especially in the beginning of the stage. Reading a story that has an illustration of a dog and a cat and encountering the word *dog*, the students can use their knowledge of initial *d* to figure that the word is *dog* and not *cat*. Of course, if there are also a duck and a deer in the illustration, they will be in trouble, unless they are able to decode final consonants.

As students progress through this stage, they use more parts of the word to decode it. Students also begin to notice patterns in words. They begin to notice that the *-e* at the end of words like *hate* changes the vowel sound so the word is *hate*, not *hat*. At some point, students begin using elements longer than a single letter or sound. Instead of decoding *hat*, /h/, /a/, /t/, they see natural patterns and decode /h/, /at/. As students begin using chunks of words rather than individual letters, they move into the word pattern stage.

Students' progression through the alphabetic stage is often reflected in their writing, especially if they use invented (developmental) spelling. Increasingly, the child's writing incorporates the alphabetic principle (Bear, Invernizzi, Johnston, & Templeton, 1996). In the earliest stages, a single letter may represent a whole word: *K* for *car*. Later, the child represents the first and last consonant sounds: *KR* for *car*. As the child progresses, she or he begins using vowels. Long vowels are spelled with letter names: *FET* for *feet*. Fortunately for the inventive speller, the names of the long vowels incorporate their sounds. Because short vowels do not have letter names, many inventive spellers use the long-vowel letter name that is made in approximately the same place in the mouth as the short vowel they are attempting to spell. Thus, short *e* is articulated in the same place as long *a* so a student spells *bed* as *BAD*. This is known as the "close to" tactic. Other "close to" spellings include spelling short *i* with an *E* (*HEM* for *him*), short *o* with an *i* (*HIP* for *hop*), and short *u* with an *O* (*MOD* for *mud*) (Read, 1971). Short *a* is generally spelled with an *a*.

For some consonant spellings, the spelling–sound connection is not apparent at first glance. For instance, *tr* is frequently spelled *ch*, as in *chain* for *train*; and *dr* may be spelled *JR* as in *JROM* for *drum*. To see why these spellings are logical from the child's point of view, listen carefully as you say *chain* and *train*. Did you notice that the beginning sound of *train* is very similar to the beginning sound of *chain*? And if you say *tree,* it sounds like *chree.* (Temple, Nathan, Temple, & Burris, 1993). In similar fashion, the *d* in *dr* has a /j/ sound, so *drop* may be spelled *JRUP* or simply *JUP.* During this stage, spellings with nasal sounds such as /m/ and /n/ are omitted when they occur before a consonant, so that *bump* may be spelled *BUP* and *bunk* might be spelled *BUK.* In general, students have difficulty with both initial and final clusters. The major characteristic of this stage is that students write what they hear (Gentry, 1997). As students get ready to move into the word pattern stage, they begin spelling short vowels and also begin correctly spelling consonant sounds that they had misspelled. They also begin using double consonants to represent sounds, such as *ll* in words like *hill* and *ck* in words like *pick* (Hughes & Searle, 1997).

■ WORD PATTERN STAGE

In the word pattern stage, which is generally reached by the end of first or the beginning of second grade, students begin using final *e* markers (*cape*) and vowel digraphs (*creep*) to decode words. They realize that *cap,* because it has a CVC pattern, is an article of clothing worn on the head, and that *e* at the end of *cape* marks its pronunciation as an article of clothing worn over the shoulders. They also use patterns such as *at, ip, ight* to decode words. Instead of decoding *ship* as "sh-i-p—ship," they use the word's pattern and decode it "sh-ip—ship." Having mastered most short vowels in the alphabetic stage (*hop, cut*), students learn short-vowel patterns with clusters or digraphs (*drop, shut*), final-*e* long-vowel patterns (*ride, hope*), digraph long-vowel patterns (*boat, steam*), *r*-vowel patterns (*fear, chair, store*), and other-vowel patterns (*coin, hour, soon*).

Through encountering standard spelling in books and environmental print, children begin to notice certain spelling conventions: *train* is spelled with *tr;* the *ai* in *train* and *e* at the end of a word is a marker for a long vowel (*rake*). They begin to use visual features in addition to sound features to spell words. Although their spelling is not always correct—in the early stages *rain* might be spelled *RANE* and *rake* might be spelled *RAIK*—spelling is becoming more standard and incorporates such features as final-*e* markers and double vowel letters to spell long-vowel sounds. They are also able to spell *r*-vowel (*chair, here, bear, fir, turn*) and other-vowel patterns (*tall, claw, caught, fruit, boot, noise, brook*). The major characteristic of this stage is that students visualize spellings rather than relying strictly on what they hear (Gentry, 1997). By the end of this stage, they are able to spell most single-syllable words correctly. As they master single-syllable patterns, students begin encountering a greater proportion of multisyllabic words that incorporate these patterns and move into the multisyllabic stage. Although students show increasing ability to write single-syllable words, they experience difficulty with multisyllabic words, especially those that drop final *e* (*hoping*) or have double final consonants (*stopping*).

■ MULTISYLLABIC STAGE

Even the easiest materials contain some multisyllabic words. However, as reading material becomes more difficult, the proportion and complexity of multisyllabic patterns increases. In this stage, which usually begins in grade 3, students show gradually improving ability to decode increasingly complex multisyllabic patterns. Student progress through easy inflectional syllable patterns (*jumping, helping*), compound word patterns (*sunset, baseball*), and a variety of multisyllabic patterns that incorporate single-syllable patterns they already know (*butter, carpet*), plus patterns that occur only in multisyllabic words (*action, impression*).

In spelling, students show increased awareness of syllable junctures (the points such as *hop(e)ing, drop ped* where syllables are joined.) Students learn when to double the final consonant or drop the final *e* when an ending such as *-ing* is added (*dropping, taking*). They learn that syllables that end in a consonant often have a short vowel (*runner*) and those that end in a vowel often contain a long vowel (*local*), so that the *a* in *baby* is long, but the *a* in *babble* is short. Students also apply their knowledge of the spellings of single-syllable words so that they spell *remain* with an *ai* rather than an *a* and final *e* (*remane*). During this stage, students show some initial awareness of prefixes, suffixes, and roots and gradually move into the morphemic analysis stage.

■ MORPHEMIC ANALYSIS STAGE

As reading begins to incorporate a significant number of new concepts, students encounter an increasing number of words that are not in their listening/speaking vocabularies. The ability to use knowledge of prefixes and suffixes and root words to derive the meanings of unfamiliar words becomes more important. In both their reading and spelling, students apply the principle of meaning. They discover that words that have similar meanings have similar spellings even though the pronunciations may be different. From a phonemic point of view, a better way to spell *sign* would be *SINE*. However, *g* is retained to maintain the semantic connection between *sign* and *signature*, so *sign* and *signature* both contain "sign" (Venezky, 1965). Although the *g* is not articulated in *sign*, it is sounded in *signature*. In spelling, students learn how to use the meanings of words to guide their spelling. Students are more likely to spell words such as *composition* and *contribution* correctly if they realize that the affixed forms are based on *compose* and *contribute*. At this stage students might have difficulty knowing whether to add *able* or *ible* to words such as *reason, adapt,* or *break* to form *reasonable, adaptable,* or *breakable*. Average students enter this stage at about the fourth-grade level and stay in it for the rest of their lives. You and I are in the morphemic analysis stage.

■ THE NATURE OF THE SPELLING SYSTEM

In order to teach phonics, it is important to know something about the nature of the writing system. At first glance, English spelling may seem to be chaotic. For instance, the vowel sound /ē/ can be spelled in the following ways: *ee* (*keep*), *ae* (*Caesar*), *ay* (*quay*), *e* (*equal*), *e . . . e* (*precede*), *ei* (*receive*), *eo* (*people*), *ey* (*key*), *i* (*machine*), *ie* (*field*), *is* (*debris*), *oe* (*amoebae*), *y* (*city*). However, the truth is that long *e* is most often spelled *ee, ea, ie, e . . . e,* or *y*. The other spellings are derived from foreign words or are rare. In fact, English spelling is fairly regular. In about 80 percent of English words, pronunciation can be predicted from spelling (Hanna, Hodges, Hanna, & Rudorf, 1966).

A number of so-called irregularities have historical causes. Up until the seventeenth century, *gn* represented a cluster of two sounds in words such as *gnat* and *gnaw* (Venezky, 1965). A number of other seeming irregularities form a marking function. They help indicate the pronunciation of a preceding letter. The *u* after *g* marks the *g* as a /g/ rather than a /j/ sound, as in *guess* and *guide*. Without the *u*, these words have a /j/ pronunciation. Similarly, the *e* following *g* as in *age* and *c* as in *face* marks *g* and *c* as having a /j/ or /s/ rather than a /g/ or /k/ pronunciation (Venezky, 1965).

By knowing and using the regularities of English spelling, you can help students come to a deeper understanding of the system and make better use of it in both reading and spelling. For instance, knowing that *compose* and *composition* are related in meaning even though their pronunciation differs could help students learn to read and spell the word *composition*. The key would be to present pairs of related words such as *compose–composition* and *sign–signal* and help students see the relationships between the members of each pair.

THE CONTENT OF PHONICS

The American English sound system is composed of approximately 41 sounds: 25 consonant and 16 vowel sounds. When discussing consonants and vowels, it is important to distinguish between sounds and spellings. For instance, the statement that "*y* is sometimes a vowel" is confusing. A more precise way to describe *y* is to say that the letter *y* is sometimes used to spell a vowel sound or phoneme as in *why*. To prevent confusion, vowel and consonant sounds will be presented between slashes (/b/). Vowels and consonants referred to as letters will be italicized.

CONSONANTS

Consonant spellings are more regular than those of vowels. The sound /b/, for instance, is almost always spelled *b* (**B**ob). Some consonants are spelled with two letters (**sh**op, **ch**air). These are known as digraphs. A list of consonant correspondences frequently taught to emergent readers is presented in Table 1.2. The last four correspondences, *c* = /s/, *g* = /j/, *qu* = /kw/, and *x* = /ks/, are usually taught after the preceding correspondences have been introduced. A list of consonant digraph correspondences frequently taught to beginning readers is presented in Table 1.3.

Variable Consonant Correspondences.   Both the letters *c* and *g* can represent two sounds. The letter *c* stands for /k/ and /s/, as in *cup* and *city*; the letter *g* represents /g/ and /j/, as in *go* and *giant*. The letter *c* represents /k/ far more often than it stands for /s/ (Gunning, 1975), and this is the sound students usually attach to it (Venezky, 1965); the letter *g* more often represents /g/. In teaching the consonant letters *c* and *g*, the more frequent sounds (*c* = /k/, *g* = /g/) should be presented first. The other sound represented by each letter (*c* = /s/, *g* = /j/) should be taught sometime later. At that point, you might want to teach the following generalizations:

- The letter *g* usually stands for /j/ when followed by *e* or *y*, as in *gem* and *gym*. (There are a number of exceptions: *geese, get*.)
- The letter *c* usually stands for /k/ when it is followed by *a*, *o*, or *u*, as in *can, cold*, or *cup*.
- The letter *c* usually stands for /s/ when followed by *e, i*, or *y*, as in *cent, circus*, or *cycle*.
- The letter *g* usually stands for /g/ when followed by *a, i, o*, or *u*, as in *gave, girl, got*, or *guppy*. (There are some exceptions: *giant, giraffe*.)

TABLE 1.2   Consonant Correspondences Taught to Beginning Readers

b = /b/	ball	*p* = /p/	pen
c = /k/	cat	*r* = /r/	ring
d = /d/	dog	*s* = /s/	sun
f = /f/	fish	*t* = /t/	ten
g = /g/	goat	*v* = /v/	vase
h = /h/	hat	*w* = /w/	wagon
j = /j/	jar	*y* = /y/	Yo-Yo
k = /k/	king	*z* = /z/	zebra
l = /l/	lion	*c* = /s/	city
m = /m/	man	*g* = /j/	giraffe
n = /n/	nail	*x* = /ks/	fox

TABLE 1.3   Digraph Correspondences Taught to Beginning Readers

ch = /ch/	chair
sh = /sh/	shoe
th = /th/	thumb
th = /<u>th</u>/	the
wh = /w/	wheel

When teaching the *c* and *g* generalizations, have students sort *c* = /k/ and *c* = /s/ words and, later, *g* = /g/ and *g* = /j/ words and discover the generalizations for themselves. An alternative to presenting the *c* and *g* generalizations is to teach students to be prepared to deal with the variability of the spelling of certain sounds. Students need to learn that, in English, letters can often stand for more than one sound. After learning the two sounds for *c* and *g*, students should be taught to use the following variability strategy when they are unsure how to read a word that begins with *c* or *g:*

1. Try the main pronunciation—the one the letter usually stands for.
2. If the main pronunciation gives a word that is not a real one or does not make sense in the sentence, try the other pronunciation.
3. If you still get a word that is not a real word or does not make sense in the sentence, try using context clues, skip it, or ask for help.

CONSONANT CLUSTERS

Consonants often appear in clusters. Consonant clusters (*stop, best, strap*), which are sometimes known as blends, are spelled with two letters or more and consist of two or more sounds. Because their separate sounds are difficult to distinguish, clusters pose special decoding problems for struggling readers. Major clusters are presented in Table 1.4.

VOWELS

In reading, twenty-one vowels are taught. These include short vowels (*cat, pet, hit, hot, but*), long vowels (*late, meet, life, hope, use*), other vowels (*paw, cow, boy, book, moon*), *r*-vowels (*her, hear, fire, where, four*), and schwa (*sofa*). Technically, there are only 16 vowels. Linguistically, *r*-vowels are not a separate category. However, in reading instruction, *r*-vowels are traditionally listed separately. Vowels and their major spellings are presented in Table 1.5.

Onset and Rimes.   Vowel correspondences may be taught in isolation, but in Building Words they are taught as part of rimes. Words are composed of two parts: the onset and the rime. The onset is the initial consonant, digraph, or cluster (*s, sh, st*). The rime is the rhyming part of the word, the vowel or the vowel plus consonant(s) coming after the vowel (*-o, -ag, -eet*). Rimes, which are also referred to as word patterns, word families, and phonograms, are more stable than vowels appearing alone. Theoretically, the letter *a* can represent more than a dozen

TABLE 1.4   Consonant Clusters

L clusters

bl (**bl**anket), *cl* (**cl**oud), *fl* (**fl**ower), *gl* (**gl**ass), *pl* (**pl**ane), *sl* (**sl**ed)

R clusters

br (**br**ead), *cr* (**cr**ab), *dr* (**dr**um), *fr* (**fr**og), *gr* (**gr**apes), *pr* (**pr**etzel), *tr* (**tr**ee)

S clusters

sc (**sc**arecrow), *sch* (**sch**ool), *scr* (**scr**eam), *shr* (**shr**ink), *sk* (**sk**unk), *sl* (**sl**ed), *sm* (**sm**ile), *sn* (**sn**ake), *sp* (**sp**oon), *spl* (**spl**ash), *spr* (**spr**ing), *st* (**st**ar), *str* (**str**ing), *squ* (**squ**irrel), *sw* (**sw**ing)

Other clusters

tw (**tw**elve), *qu* (**qu**een)

TABLE 1.5   Vowel Spellings

Vowels	Examples	Model Word
Short vowels		
/a/	hat, batter, have	cat
/e/	ten, better, bread	bed
/i/	fit, little, remain	hit
/o/	hot, bottle, father	mop
/u/	cup, butter	bus
Long vowels		
/ā/	made, nail, radio, hay, flavor	cake
/ē/	he, see, seal, sunny, turkey, these, neither	tree
/ī/	smile, night, pie, spider	bike
/ō/	no, hope, grow, toad, gold, roll, local	goat
/ū/	use, music	mule
Other vowels		
/aw/	ball, walk, paw, song, caught, thought, off	saw
/oi/	joy, join	boy
/o͞o/	zoo, blue, grew, fruit, group, two	moon
/oo/	took, could, push	book
/ow/	owl, south	cow
/ə/	ago, telephone, similar, opinion, upon	banana
R-vowels		
/ar/	car, charge, heart	star
/air/	fair, bear, care, there	chair
/eer/	ear, cheer, here	deer
/ir/	sir, her, earth, turn	bird
/or/	for, four, store, floor	door

sounds. However, in the following rimes the sound of *a* is highly predictable: *-at, -an, -ap, -ain, -ay, -ate.* Because rimes or patterns are highly predictable, they are the core of phonics instruction in Building Words. Rimes that appear with a high degree of frequency and which are presented in this program are listed in Table 1.6.

■ VOWEL GENERALIZATIONS

Although vowels can be spelled in many ways, their spellings generally fall into one of four patterns. The most frequent pattern is the vowel–consonant–vowel, or closed syllable pattern (*sat, sit, set*), in which the word or syllable ends in a vowel and the vowel is short. Long vowels have three major patterns: open syllable, digraph, and final *e*. In an open syllable, the syllable or word ends with a vowel and is usually long (*no, he, o-pen*). A final *e* frequently indicates that the preceding vowel is long: *pane, hope.* Long vowels can also be spelled with digraphs: *pain, sheep, goat.* However, digraphs are also used to spell other vowel sounds: *paw, boil;* and a few digraphs represent a number of pronunciations: *beat, steak, bread.*

"When two vowels go walking, the first one does the talking" is one of the most frequently recited of the vowel generalizations or rules. It refers to the tendency of the first vowel in a vowel digraph to have a long sound, as in words like *beast* and *goat.* Unfortunately, as stated, it is virtually worthless. About one word out of every five has a double vowel, or digraph; however, the generalization does not apply equally to each situation. For some spellings—*ee,* for example—it applies

TABLE 1.6   High-Frequency Rimes

Short Vowels		Long Vowels		r-Vowels		Other Vowels	
-ack	tack	-ace	race	-air	hair	-al(l)	ball
-ad	sad	-ade	made	-are	square	-alk	walk
-ag	bag	-age	page	-art	cart	-aught	caught
-am	ham	-aid	paid	-ear	bear	-aw	saw
-an	pan	-ail	nail	-ar	star	-ew	new
-ap	map	-ain	train	-ard	card	-ong	song
-at	cat	-ait	wait	-ark	shark	-oss	boss
-ed	bed	-ake	cake	-arm	arm	-ost	lost
-ell	bell	-ale	whale	-art	chart	-ought	bought
-en	ten	-ame	name	-ear	ear	-oice	voice
-end	send	-ane	plane	-eer	deer	-oil	boil
-ent	went	-ate	gate	-er	her	-ong	song
-est	nest	-ave	wave	-ir	stir	-oin	coin
-et	net	-ay	hay	-ird	bird	-oo	zoo
-ick	stick	-e	me	-ire	tire	-oon	moon
-id	lid	-ea	sea	-oor	door	-oy	toy
-ig	pig	-ead	bead	-or	for	-ound	round
-in	pin	-eak	beak	-ore	score	-our	hour
-ing	ring	-eal	seal	-orn	corn	-ouse	house
-ip	ship	-eam	dream	-ort	fort	-out	shout
-ish	fish	-ean	bean	-ur	fur	-ow	cow
-it	hit	-eat	eat	-urn	burn	-own	clown
-ob	Bob	-ee	bee			-ood	wood
-ock	lock	-eed	seed			-ould	could
-op	mop	-eel	wheel			-ook	book
-ot	pot	-een	green			-ool	school
-ub	tub	-eep	jeep			-oom	broom
-uck	duck	-eet	feet			-oon	spoon
-ug	rug	-ice	mice			-oot	boot
-um	gum	-ide	ride			-oud	cloud
-ump	jump	-ie	tie			-ound	round
-unk	skunk	-ife	knife			-ull	pull
-up	cup	-ike	bike			-ue	blue
-us(s)	bus	-ile	smile				
-ut	cut	-ime	dime				
		-igh	high				
		-ight	night				
		-ine	nine				
		-ite	kite				
		-o	no				
		-oad	road				
		-oak	oak				
		-oat	goat				
		-oke	smoke				
		-old	gold				
		-ole	mole				
		-oll	roll				
		-one	bone				
		-ope	rope				
		-ote	note				
		-ose	rose				
		-ow	crow				
		-y	cry				

nearly 100 percent of the time. The letters *ea*, however, represent at least four different sounds (*bean, bread, earth, steak*). Moreover, the generalization does not apply to such vowel–letter combinations as *au, aw, oi, oy*, and *ou* (Gunning, 1975).

Instead of being taught as a blanket generalization, vowel digraphs should be taught as patterns, such as *feet, meet*, and *street*, or *boat, coat, goat*, and *float*. Emphasis should be on providing ample opportunities to meet the double vowels in print. Providing exposure is the key to learning phonics. Generalizations and patterns draw attention to regularities in English spelling, but actually meeting the elements in print is the way students' decoding skills become automatic.

Like the two-vowel rule, most vowel generalizations are not worth teaching because they have limited usefulness, too many exceptions, or are difficult to apply. However, the following generalizations are relatively useful (Gunning, 1975, 1999):

- **Closed syllable generalization.** A vowel is short when followed by a consonant: *let, letter*. This is known as the closed syllable rule because it applies when a consonant "closes," or ends, a word or syllable.
- **Open syllable generalization.** A vowel is usually long when it is found at the end of a word or syllable: *no, notice*. This generalization is known as the open syllable rule because the word or syllable ends with a vowel and so is not closed by a consonant.
- **Final *e* generalization.** A vowel is usually long when it is followed by a consonant and a final *e: fine, hope*. Of all the vowel generalizations, final *e* is the one that students find most useful. Perhaps, because it appears at the end of a word and so stands out, it is the easiest to apply.

If vowel generalizations are taught directly, they should be taught inductively. For example, after encountering many words that end in *e* preceded by a consonant, students should conclude that words ending in a consonant plus *e* often have long vowels. Students might also discover this by sorting words that end in final *e* and words that don't.

Because none of the vowel generalizations applies all the time, students should be introduced to the variability principle. They need to learn that digraphs and single vowels can represent a variety of sounds. If they try one pronunciation and it is not a real word or does not make sense in context, then they must try another. A student who read "breeth" for *breath* would have to try another pronunciation, because *breeth* is not a real word. A student who read "deed" for *dead* would need to check to see if that pronunciation fits the context of the sentence in which the word was used. Although *deed* is a real word, it does not make sense in the sentence, "The flowers were dead," so the student would need to try another pronunciation. Students should use the same variability strategy that was presented earlier for decoding words such as those containing initial *c* or *g:*

1. Try the main pronunciation—the one the letters usually stand for.
2. If the main pronunciation gives a word that is not a real one or does not make sense in the sentence, try the other pronunciation. (If there is a chart of spellings available, students can use it as a source of other pronunciations.)
3. If you still get a word that is not a real word or does not make sense in the sentence, try using context clues, skip it, or ask for help.

The variability strategy is a simpler procedure than the application of rules. Rather than trying to remember a rule, all the student has to do is try the major pronunciation, and, if that pronunciation does not work out, try another.

Chapter 2

GETTING STARTED: ASSESSING STUDENTS' LITERACY DEVELOPMENT

The first step in a word analysis program is to find out where students are in their reading and writing development. To learn where students are in their literacy development, administer the Emergent Literacy Survey, Word Pattern Survey, or Syllable Survey, which can be found later in this chapter, or a similar instrument. If you know that students are at the very beginning stages of reading, administer the Emergent Literacy Survey. If students can read at least a few words but have not mastered single-syllable phonics, administer the Word Pattern Survey. If students have mastered single-syllable phonics, administer the Syllable Survey. If you are not sure where to begin, start with the Word Pattern Survey. Also administer the Benchmark Passages Inventory to all students except those in the emergent literacy stage. The Benchmark Passages Inventory, which is given in Appendix A at the back of the book, assesses word analysis skills in context. It also assesses comprehension.

ASSESSING EMERGENT LITERACY

Emergent literacy includes literacy knowledge and skills that form a foundation for formal reading and writing instruction: phonemic awareness, alphabet knowledge, and concepts of print. All students, no matter how low they may be functioning, have some degree of emergent literacy. Typically, young students are in the emergent literacy stage. However, some older students who have serious reading problems may be operating on an emergent level. To assess emergent literacy, use the following measures: Letter Names, Rhyming Sounds, Beginning Sounds, Beginning Consonant Correspondences, and Concepts of Print. An Emergent Literacy Assessment Survey is also included.

LETTER NAMES

One of the best indicators of how well youngsters will do in a formal reading program is letter recognition. To administer the Letter Names Survey, make two copies of the Letter Names Survey. Show the student the survey and say, "I want to see how many letters you know. Look at this paper. You will see rows of letters. Tell me the names of the letters as I point to them." On a separate copy of the survey, note which letters the student can name. Discontinue testing if the student misses five letters in a row, or if it is obvious that he or she does not know the letters. Record students' performance on the Emergent Literacy Assessment Survey. Generally,

Letter Names Survey

Name _____ Date _____ Uppercase score ____ Lowercase score ____

S O A X

R E M U

C F B I

D H W G

Y T J L V

Z K N P Q

s o a x

r e m u

c f b i

d h w g

y t j l v

z k n p q

Emergent Literacy Assessment Survey

Name _____ Age _____

Dates of observations _____

Concepts about Reading

Knows the parts of a book. _____

Understands that print is read. _____

Understands that print is read from left to right and from top to bottom. _____

Can identify separate words in a line of print. _____

Can identify letters in a word. _____

Can read words. _____

Assessment Scores

Letter Name Survey   Uppercase ____/26   Lowercase ____/26

Rhyming ____/7

Beginning sounds ____/7

Consonant correspondences ____/20

Writing Development

Writing own name

____ Writes first and last names accurately.

____ Writes first name accurately.

____ Writes most of the letters of first name.

____ Writes one or two letters.

____ Scribbles or uses random letters.

____ Would not attempt to write name.

Story about picture

____ Writes a story and uses spacing to indicate separate words. Uses invented or conventional spelling.

____ Writes a story and uses spacing to indicate separate words. Uses random letters or letter-like forms.

____ Story is not composed of separate words. Uses random letters, letterlike forms, or scribbles.

____ Draws instead of writing.

____ Does not attempt task.

---

students do better with uppercase letters. If a student has difficulty identifying letters, block off three letters and ask him to point to the letter that you name. Then block off a second set of three letters, a third set, etc. This easier task will indicate whether the student knows the letters on a recognition level.

A score of 20 out of 26 uppercase letters is adequate. Eventually, of course, students will need to learn all the letters. As you assess students' performance, in addition to determining how many letters they are able to recognize, compare their performance on uppercase versus lowercase letters. Also note any confusion of similar letters, and consider opportunity to learn. If a student recognizes very few letters but has not been in a program in which letters were taught, she may have no difficulty learning letters once she is provided with instruction. However, if a student has completed a program in which letters were taught but knows few letters, then she may need special help.

▨ RHYMING SOUNDS SURVEY

In addition to being able to recognize the letters of the alphabet, the beginning reader must acquire phonemic awareness. Phonemic awareness is the ability to detect separate phonemes (speech sounds) in words. A lack of phonemic awareness is a primary cause of reading difficulty. The ability to detect rhyme is an indicator of phonemic awareness. To administer the measure, distribute copies of the Rhyming Sounds Survey in Figure 2.1. Explain to the students the purpose of the measure and give them directions. Say, "I want to see if you can tell when words rhyme. Words rhyme if they have the same ending sound. For example, *Bill* and *Jill* rhyme because they both have an *ill* sound. *Book* and *look* rhyme because they both have an *ook* sound. I'm going to point to three pictures. Here are pictures of a man, a shoe, and a pan. Now say the name of each picture. Which two rhyme? Which two have the same sounds at the end?" (If students are unable to answer or give an incorrect response, say, "If you listen carefully, you can tell that *pan* and *man* rhyme. They both have an *an* sound.") Administer the remaining sets of pictures in the same way: *cake, rake, bus; fish, bee, tree; horse, car, star; goat, boat, saw; bell, cat, hat; ring, king, deer; whale, nail, spoon.* An adequate performance is 5 out of 7. Record students' performance on the Emergent Literacy Assessment Survey.

Scores lower than the criterion suggest the need for additional work in this area. Students may do poorly because of limited experience with rhyme, or they may find the terminology confusing. You might try working on rhyme with the lowest-scoring youngsters to determine how readily they learn this concept. Although most youngsters will learn rhyme naturally through listening to nursery rhymes and participating in shared reading, some will need direct instruction.

▨ BEGINNING SOUNDS SURVEY

The ability to detect beginning sounds, which is also a measure of phonemic awareness, is a prerequisite for beginning reading. To administer this assessment, distribute copies of the Beginning Sounds Survey in Figure 2.2. Explain to students the purpose of the measure and then give directions. Say, "I want to see if you can tell whether two words begin alike. Words begin alike if they begin with the same sound. The words *tie* and *ten* begin alike because they begin with the same sound: /t/. The words *pen* and *pet* begin alike because they begin with the same sound: /p/. Look at these pictures: *saw, cake, sun.* Say the name of each picture. See if you can tell which two pictures have names that begin with the same sound: *saw, cake, sun.* Which two begin with the same sound: *saw, cake, sun*?" (If students are unable to answer or give an incorrect response, say, "If you listen carefully, you can tell that *saw* and *sun* both begin with the same sound. The sound they both begin with is /s/." Administer the remaining sets of pictures in the same way: *deer, fork, fish; man, monkey, star; hat, bus, horse; dog, bell, boat; ring, nail, rake; goat, cat, car; lion, shoe, lock.*

Record students' performance on the Emergent Literacy Assessment Survey. A score of 5 out of 7 indicates an adequate grasp of beginning sounds. Lower scores suggest the need for additional work in this area. Students may do poorly because they have little experience with beginning sounds or find the terminology unfamiliar. You might further probe low scores in this area by teaching beginning sounds to low-scoring youngsters and noting how they respond to instruction. Also check the performance of low-scoring students in the rhyming subtest. Low scores in both Rhyming and Beginning Sounds indicate a need for intensive work in phonemic awareness.

FIGURE 2.1   Rhyming Sounds Survey

From the *Teacher's Guide for Word Building: Beginnings* by T. Gunning, 1994. New York: Phoenix Learning Resources. Reprinted by permission of Galvin Publications.

FIGURE 2.2 Beginning Sounds Survey

From the *Teacher's Guide for Word Building: Beginnings* by T. Gunning, 1994. New York: Phoenix Learning Resources. Reprinted by permission of Galvin Publications.

BEGINNING CONSONANT CORRESPONDENCES SURVEY

The ability to match letters and sounds grows out of letter knowledge and phonemic awareness. If students have done poorly on the previous subtests, omit this assessment, because it will most likely be too difficult for them.

Distribute copies of the Beginning Consonant Correspondences Survey, which is found in Figure 2.3. Explain the purpose of the measure to the students and then give them directions. Say, "I want to see if you can tell which letters are used to spell the beginning sounds of words. I'm going to show you some pictures. I want you to say the name of the picture and then tell me what letter the name of the picture begins with. Then I want you to write that letter. For instance, this is a picture of a fish. The letter *f* is used to spell the sound /f/ that you hear at the beginning of *fish,* so I write an *f* next to the picture of the fish. This is a picture of a horse. The letter *h* is used to spell /h/, the sound that you hear at the beginning of *horse,* so I write an *h* next to the picture of the horse. Now say the name of this picture (*sun*). What letter does *sun* begin with?" (If students are unable to answer or give an incorrect response, say, "If you listen carefully, you can tell that *sun* begins with /s/. The sound /s/ that you hear at the beginning of *sun* is made with the letter *s,* so I write an *s* next to the picture of the sun." Administer the remaining sets of pictures in the same way: *man, ring, dog, hat, nail, goat, fork, zebra, watch, lion, bus, jar, key, pen, queen, table, violin, car, saw, Yo-Yo.*

Record students' performance on the Emergent Literacy Assessment Survey. A score of 10 out of 20 shows that students have begun to master initial consonant correspondences. Ultimately, of course, they need to know all of the initial consonant correspondences. However, if students know at least half of the beginning consonant correspondences, they are ready for instruction with easy short-vowel patterns.

ASSESSMENT OF CONCEPTS OF PRINT

Concepts of print are basic understandings about the nature and purpose of print. Concepts of print include knowing that words can be written down and read, words are composed of letters, one reads words rather than pictures, and one reads from left to right and from top to bottom. A key concept of print is being able to identify separate words in a line of print. The first fold-and-read booklet in Appendix B can be used to assess students' concepts about print. Hand the student the booklet and ask the following series of questions: "Where should I start reading? What tells me what to say? Where are the words on the page? How many words are on this page?" Pointing to a word, ask, "How many letters are in this word? Can you read any of the words?" On the Emergent Literacy Survey, note the child's overall level of development.

Then read the story to the student. Explain, "As I read the story, point to each word. Point to each word as I read it." Note the student's ability to point to each word. Read the story a second time. Invite the student to read along with you. Again, ask the student to point to each word as you read it. Note the student's performance. Then invite the student to read the story. Ask the student to point to each word as she reads it. Note the student's ability to read each sentence accurately and to point to each word as it is being read. Asking the student to point to each word assesses the student's concept of word, a key concept in emergent literacy (Johnston, Juel, & Invernizzi, 1998). Until students have a sense of where a word begins and ends, they will be hampered in their ability to memorize words that they see in print or learn initial consonant correspondences. After finishing this portion of the assessment, fill in the Concepts about Reading section of the Emergent Literacy Assessment Survey.

FIGURE 2.3　Beginning Consonant Correspondences Survey

From the *Teacher's Guide for Word Building: Beginnings* by T. Gunning, 1994. New York: Phoenix Learning Resources. Reprinted by permission of Galvin Publications.

■ DRAWING/WRITING SAMPLE

Ask the student to draw a picture of herself. If the student is reluctant, encourage her to do her best. If necessary, model the process of drawing a picture of oneself. After the student has drawn her picture, ask her to write her name under it. Then ask her to write a story that tells what she likes to do. Encourage the student to write any way that she can. This would include drawing, scribbling, writing random letters, using invented spelling, or using conventional spelling. Note the maturity of the student's writing and drawing. Record results on the Writing Development section of the Emergent Literacy Assessment Survey.

■ INTERPRETING RESULTS

After entering the results of the various emergent literacy tasks on the Emergent Literacy Assessment Survey, analyze each student's performance. If students know at least 10 of the initial consonant correspondences or are judged to have some reading ability, assess their ability to read single-syllable words. This can be done quickly and efficiently by administering the Word Pattern Survey, which is explained in the next section. Otherwise, use the assessment results to determine each student's major strengths and needs. If students are able to detect rhyme and beginning sounds but not correspondences, they are ready for instruction in beginning consonant correspondences. If they are able to detect rhyme but have difficulty with beginning sounds, they may need some more work with phonemic awareness. If they have difficulty with both beginning sounds and rhyme, then they probably need fairly extensive work with phonemic awareness. Note, too, how well they do with letter knowledge. Also analyze their drawing and writing. Generally, the more detailed the drawing, the more mature the students are intellectually. If they draw, scribble, or simply use random letters, they have probably not yet discovered the alphabetic principle. Use of invented spelling, on the other hand, indicates that they are becoming aware of letter–sound relationships.

■ ASSESSING ABILITY TO DECODE SINGLE-SYLLABLE WORDS

To assess students' ability to read single-syllable words, administer the Word Pattern Survey. The survey consists of 80 words that include most of the major word patterns found in single-syllable words. The words are arranged in four levels of difficulty: easy long vowels and short vowels, long vowels, *r*-vowels and other vowels, and infrequent vowel patterns. There are 20 words at each level. The mastery standard at each level is 80 percent. If students can read orally 16 out of 20 words at a level, they are considered proficient at that level. The first level at which students' performance falls below 80 percent is the level at which students need instruction. However, if students get fewer than five words correct, they should be given the Emergent Literacy Survey, if this has not already been administered. If students get 60 or more correct, administer the Syllable Survey.

Before administering the Word Pattern Survey, discuss with the student why she is being tested. Say, "I want to see how well you can read single words, so I'm going to ask you to read a list of words to me. Some of the words may be hard for you, but I want you to read as many as you can."

All students begin with the first word and continue reading until they miss five in a row. As the student reads each word, record her performance on your copy of the test with a plus or minus. You may also want to write out incorrect responses. Incorrect responses provide valuable insight into the student's method of approaching words. If the student makes no response, write a 0 in the blank. Be encouraging and supportive. If a student says, "I don't know," or gives no response, encourage her to try to read the word, or at least to read as much as she can.

Word Pattern Survey

Name _____   Total number correct _____

Date _____   Estimated level _____

1. go_____	21. game_____	41. spark _____	61. through _____
2. me_____	22. tree _____	42. stair _____	62. straight_____
3. see_____	23. wide _____	43. shore_____	63. enough_____
4. I_____	24. road_____	44. curl_____	64. clue _____
5. no _____	25. use _____	45. steer_____	65. edge _____
6. hat_____	26. goat _____	46. park_____	66. strong _____
7. wet_____	27. save _____	47. purse _____	67. suit_____
8. sit_____	28. wheel_____	48. clear_____	68. thought _____
9. hop_____	29. mine _____	49. storm _____	69. flood_____
10. fun _____	30. cute _____	50. charge_____	70. breathe_____
11. ran _____	31. chain_____	51. chalk_____	71. calm _____
12. men _____	32. speak _____	52. brook _____	72. clothes_____
13. win_____	33. slide_____	53. crown _____	73. knock_____
14. got_____	34. toast _____	54. join _____	74. soft _____
15. bug_____	35. blind _____	55. should_____	75. fault_____
16. drop _____	36. plane _____	56. stew_____	76. tough _____
17. jump_____	37. steel_____	57. bounce _____	77. height _____
18. sand _____	38. drive_____	58. crawl _____	78. laugh _____
19. ship _____	39. broke _____	59. broom _____	79. earth _____
20. lunch _____	40. price _____	60. pound _____	80. brought _____

Directions: Give one copy of the survey to the student and keep one for marking. Mark each response + or −. Start with the first item for all pupils. Say to the student, "I am going to ask you to read a list of words to me. Some of the words may be hard for you, but read as many as you can." Stop when the student gets five wrong in a row. The Survey tests four levels. Each level has 20 items as follows: 1–20, easy long-vowel and short-vowel patterns; 21–40, long-vowel patterns; 41–60, *r*-vowel and other-vowel patterns, /aw/, /o͞o/, /oo/, /ow/, /oy/; 61–80, irregular and low-frequency patterns. Students are proficient at a level if they get 80% or more correct at that level. Students should be instructed at a level if they get more than 4 out of 20 wrong at that level.

Syllable Survey

Name _____   Score _____ /50

Date _____

1. sunup_____
2. inside _____
3. ago _____
4. open_____
5. under _____
6. farmer _____
7. finish_____
8. mistake_____
9. thunder _____
10. morning_____
11. reward_____
12. famous _____
13. mumble _____
14. spider_____
15. chicken _____
16. rocket_____
17. magnet _____

18. distant_____
19. prevent_____
20. museum _____
21. several _____
22. building _____
23. probably_____
24. modern _____
25. monument _____
26. opposite _____
27. message_____
28. success _____
29. struggle_____
30. repeat_____
31. recognize _____
32. survive_____
33. appreciate_____
34. antelope _____

35. creature _____
36. audience_____
37. pleasant_____
38. spaghetti_____
39. information_____
40. voyage _____
41. confusion_____
42. neighborhood _____
43. studio _____
44. allowance _____
45. microphone_____
46. auditorium_____
47. available _____
48. disappointment_____
49. bulletin_____
50. moisture _____

Directions: Give one copy of the survey to the student and keep one for marking. Mark each response + or −. If possible, write down each incorrect response for later analysis. Start with the first item for all pupils. Say to the student, "I am going to give you a list of words to read. Some of the words may be difficult, but I want you to read as many as you can. Even if you can't read the whole word, read as many syllables as you can." Stop when the student gets five wrong in a row. A score of 45 or more indicates that the student is able to decode multisyllabic words. A score between 40 and 44 indicates some weakness in decoding multisyllabic words. A score below 40 indicates a definite need for instruction and practice in decoding multisyllabic words. A score of 5 or less suggests that the student may be deficient in basic decoding skills. Give the Word Pattern Survey.

■ INTERPRETING RESULTS

Use the figures at the bottom of the test page to determine students' levels and major needs. For instance, if a student reads most of the short-vowel words correctly but has difficulty with the long vowels, then teach long-vowel patterns. If the student gets only five or six long-vowel words wrong, then she might need just a review of patterns at that level to shore up a weak area. Look at the words that the student misread. The student might be able to read words that have single consonants but may have particular difficulty with initial or final clusters (blends) and so needs some supplementary instruction. If, on the other hand, the student got all or nearly all of the easiest items wrong, then she needs more extensive instruction and may need to work on phonemic awareness or beginning consonant correspondences.

As with any other assessment measure, the Word Pattern Survey is subject to error. As an additional check on decoding, have students read the Benchmark Passages Inventory in Appendix A, or have them orally reread passages from their daily work that have already been read silently. Note strengths and weaknesses. Also note students' use of strategies. When a student is facing a difficult word, ask, "What could you do to help you figure that word out?" After a student has read a hard word successfully, ask, "How did you figure that word out?"

■ ASSESSING ABILITY TO DECODE MULTISYLLABIC WORDS

If students score 60 or more on the Word Pattern Survey or if your observations suggest that they have a good grasp of single-syllable phonics, assess their ability to read multisyllabic words. This can be done by observing as they read passages containing multisyllabic words, or by administering the Syllable Survey, or by doing both.

■ ADMINISTERING THE SYLLABLE SURVEY

The Syllable Survey consists of 50 words that incorporate a variety of high-frequency multisyllabic patterns. The Syllable Survey is administered individually and should take no more than 5 to 10 minutes. The student being evaluated should be seated to your left, so that he has an unobstructed view of the words, and you can easily observe his performance. The student reads from one copy while you follow along using another copy.

Before administering the Syllable Survey, discuss with the student why he is being tested. Say, "I want to see how well you can read words that have more than one syllable, so I'm going to give you a list of words to read. Some of the words may be difficult, but I want you to read as many words as you can. Even if you can't read the whole word, read as many of its syllables as you can."

All students begin with the first word and continue reading until they miss five in a row. As the student reads each word, record his performance on your copy of the test using a plus or minus. You may also want to write out incorrect responses. Incorrect responses provide valuable insight into the student's method of approaching multisyllabic words. If the student makes no response, write a 0 in the blank. Be encouraging and supportive. If a student says, "I don't know," or gives no response, encourage him to try to read the word, or at least to read as much as he can. Note students' use of strategies. After a student has successfully decoded a difficult word, ask, "How did you figure that word out?"

■ INTERPRETING RESULTS

Tally the student's total score. A student who scores below 20 should be given the Word Pattern Survey, if this has not already been administered. A student who scores 46 or more has mastered the basics of decoding single-syllable and multi-syllabic words. She may benefit from occasional guidance with unusual or very difficult multisyllabic words and would probably benefit from advanced work in morphemic analysis and dictionary skills. A student who scores between 40 and 45 has some weakness decoding polysyllabic words and needs some instruction. A student who scores below 40 has a definite need for instruction.

The Syllable Survey provides information about each student's specific strengths and weaknesses in decoding multisyllabic words. Analyze both correct and incorrect responses. Note the kinds of words that were dealt with successfully and those that posed problems. You may find, for instance, that a student can handle two- and three-syllable words but has trouble with longer words. Certain kinds of syllable patterns, such as -*ture* and -*tion,* may pose problems. Also check the responses to make sure that they are all real words. Production of nonwords suggests that the student may not be reading for meaning. It also suggests that the student may have a limited vocabulary. If a multisyllabic word is not in a student's listening vocabulary, he won't be able to adjust pronunciation when reconstructing the word. Verify students' performance by observing them in their everyday reading. Note their strengths and weaknesses as they encounter multisyllabic words. Also administer the Benchmark Passages Inventory (Appendix A) to see how well they handle multisyllabic words in context. To gain insight into students' knowledge of phonics elements and use of decoding strategies, analyze their errors or miscues.

■ FINDING STUDENTS' INSTRUCTIONAL LEVELS

Just about the most important instructional decision that you will make is identifying the level of materials that your students should be reading. Giving students materials that are too hard fosters frustration. Giving them materials that are too easy leads to boredom and a lack of achievement. The Word Pattern and Syllable Surveys have been designed to provide information about students' level of decoding skills: short-vowel, long-vowel, other- and *r*-vowel, or multisyllabic level. However, the surveys also provide estimates of the level of material that students can handle. To use the surveys to obtain students' estimated instructional level, which is the level of material that students can handle if given some instruction, tally the total number of correct responses on the Word Pattern or Syllable Survey and then find the grade level that corresponds to the total number of words read correctly. Tables 2.1 and 2.2 provide estimated grade levels. Please keep in

TABLE 2.1   Placement Chart for Word Pattern Survey

Total Score	Estimated Instructional Level
0–5	Retest with Beginning Consonant Correspondences Survey
6–10	Sight word
11–20	Easy first grade
21–30	Middle first grade
31–45	Ending first grade
46–60	Grade 2
61–80	Grade 3; give Syllable Survey

TABLE 2.2   Placement Chart for Syllable Survey

Total Score	Estimated Instructional Level
1–20	Grade 2
21–39	Grade 3
40–45	Grade 4
46–50	Grade 4+

mind that the grade level obtained is an estimate and is based only on the student's ability to pronounce words in isolation. This procedure tends to overestimate the instructional level of students who are facile decoders but poor comprehenders, and to underestimate the levels of pupils who are especially adept at using context.

USING THE BENCHMARK PASSAGES INVENTORY

The best procedure for obtaining an instructional level is to administer an informal reading inventory, which is a series of graded passages. If time allows, administer the Benchmark Passages Inventory, which is presented in Appendix A and is a streamlined informal reading inventory. A summary of reading assessment devices is presented in Table 2.3. (Also see Chapter 10 for additional assessment suggestions.)

WORD ANALYSIS INTERVIEW

To obtain additional information about decoding processes, you might conduct an interview with students. These interviews can be informal. Possible interview questions include the following:

1. What is the hardest thing for you to do in reading?
2. What do you do when you come across a hard word?
3. How do you try to figure out hard words?
4. What makes it hard to figure out words?
5. If someone asked you how to figure out a hard word, what would you tell that person?

ASSESSING SPELLING

Spelling can be assessed by observing the kinds of spellings students create. To determine students' spelling stage, analyze samples of their writing. You might also use the Elementary Spelling Inventory shown in Table 2.4. The inventory pre-

TABLE 2.3   Assessing Reading Development

Student's Reading Ability	Assessment Measure
Knows fewer than 20 consonants	Emergent Literacy Survey Observation
Ranges from ability to read a few words to ability to read most single-syllable words	Word Pattern Survey Benchmark Passages Inventory Observation
Can read some multisyllabic words	Syllable Survey Benchmark Passages Inventory Observation
Has mastered multisyllabic words	Benchmark Passages Inventory Observation
Ability unknown	Word Pattern Survey

TABLE 2.4   The Elementary Spelling Inventory (with Error Guide)

Stage	Early Letter Name	Letter Name	Within-Word Pattern	Syllable Juncture	Derivational Constancy
1. bed	b bd	bad	bed		
2. ship	s sp shp	sep shep	sip ship		
3. drive	jrv drv	griv driv	drieve draive drive		
4. bump	b bp bmp	bop bomp bup	bump		
5. when	w yn wn	wan whan	wen when		
6. train	j t trn	jran chran tan tran	teran traen trane train		
7. closet	k cs kt clst	clast clost clozt	clozit closit		
8. chase	j jass cs	tas cas chas chass	case chais chase		
9. float	f vt ft flt	fot flot flott	flowt floaut flote float		
10. beaches	b bs bcs	bechs becis behis	bechise beches beeches beaches		

Stage	Within-Word Pattern	Syllable Juncture	Derivational Constancy
11. preparing	preparng preypering	preparing prepairing preparing	
12. popping	popin poping	popping	
13. cattle	catl cadol	catel cattel cattle	
14. caught	cot cote cout cought caught		
15. inspection	inspshn inspechin	inspecshum inspecsion inspection	
16. puncture	pucshr pungchr puncker	punksher punture puncturec	
17. cellar	salr selr celr seler	seller sellar celler cellar	
18. pleasure	plasr plager plejer pleser plesher	plesour plesure	pleasure
19. squirrel	scrl skwel skwerl	scqoril sqrarel squirle squirrel	
20. fortunate	forhnat frehnit foohinit	forchenut fochininte fortunet	fortunate

Stage	Within-Word Pattern	Syllable Juncture	Derivational Constancy
21. confident		confedent confedint confedent confedent conphident confiadent confident confedent confodent confident	confident
22. civilize		sivils sevelies sivilise cifillazas sivelize sivalise civalise civilise	civilize
23. flexible		flecksibl flexobil flexuble flecible flexeble flexibel flaxable flexibal flexable	flexible
24. opposition	opasion opasishan opozcison opishien opasitian	opasition oppasishion oppisition	oposision oposition opposition
25. emphasize		infaside infacize emfisize emfisize imfasize ephacise empasize emphasise	emphisize emphasize

Note: The Preliterate Stage is not presented here.

Adapted from *Reading Psychology 10* (3), 1989, pp. 275–292, by D. Bear and D. Barone.

25

sents 25 words that increase in difficulty and embody key elements of the stages. Start with the first word and continue testing until the words become too difficult. Ask students to spell as best they can, because even partially spelled words reveal important information about students' spelling. Before administering the inventory, explain to students that you want to see how they spell words. Tell them that some of the words may be hard, but they should do the best they can. Say each word, use it in a sentence, and say the word once more. After administering the inventory, use it to determine which stage students are in.

You can also give a placement test to assess students' spelling development. The Spelling Placement Assessment shown in Table 2.5 has five levels. Level 1 consists of easy sight words and short-vowel patterns and is equivalent to grade 1 spelling. Level 2 consists of long-vowel patterns and is equivalent to grade 2 spelling. Level 3 is comprised of *r*-vowels, other vowels, and some irregular short-vowel words and is equivalent to grade 3 spelling. Level 4 consists of multisyllabic words and is equivalent to grade 4 spelling. Level 5 also consists of multisyllabic words and is equivalent to grade 5 spelling.

To administer the Spelling Placement Assessment, explain to the students that you will be dictating some words. Tell them that some words may be hard to spell, but urge them to do their best. Tell them that even it they can't spell the whole word, they should spell as much as they can, even if it's just the first letter. Say each word in isolation, in a sentence, and then again in isolation. Start with the first list, unless you know that the students are advanced spellers. Stop when students are missing most of the words in a list.

The criteria for an instructional level for spelling are lower than for reading. Students are instructional at the level at which they are able to spell between 50 and 75 percent of the words correctly (Temple & Burris, 1993). After you have obtained students' levels, analyze the results to determine which stage they are in and also their major needs. Students who are unable to spell any of the

TABLE 2.5   **Spelling Placement Assessment**

Level 1	Level 2	Level 3	Level 4	Level 5
cat	name	star	happen	damage
the	what	guess	metal	happiness
sad	like	care	everyone	opposite
is	any	laugh	welcome	laughter
ten	read	school	between	adventure
one	want	build	holiday	passenger
not	show	farm	carried	caution
was	been	young	against	ninety
hop	train	turn	middle	voyage
you	from	touch	famous	president
sing	sleep	shook	question	magazine
on	put	learn	absent	government
get	use	south	weather	probably
do	once	sure	yesterday	mention
sun	place	cloud	thousand	separate
give	were	month	success	continue
fish	night	join	student	description
come	your	should	mountain	future
bug	smile	caught	neighbor	information
are	milk	warm	problem	electric

words are at the emergent stage. Those who are able at least to represent initial consonants are at the beginning alphabetic (letter name) stage. Those who are able to spell the short-vowel patterns are at the end of the alphabetic stage. Those who show some knowledge of long-vowel patterns, even if their spelling of long-vowel words is not always correct (may spell *train* as *TRANE*), are in the word pattern stage. Those who are able to spell most single-syllable words correctly are at the end of the word pattern stage. Students who are able to spell multisyllabic words and who know when to drop a final *e* (*hoping*) and when to double final consonants (*planning*) are in the multisyllabic (syllable juncture) stage. Spelling may lag behind reading. A student in the multisyllabic stage in reading may be in the word pattern stage in spelling.

It is important to know what stage students are in so that instruction can be geared to students' conceptual understanding of the spelling system. For instance, students in the early alphabetical stage do not have sufficient grasp of the spelling system to grapple with final *-e* words such as *hope* and *plane*. They still conceptualize spelling as being one letter for each sound. They might spell *eighty* as *A-T-E* (Gentry, 1997). They are not quite ready to spell by eye but will be ready to do so once they have encountered more final-*e,* long-vowel words in print.

Also note the kinds of words with which students had difficulty. Many words can be spelled auditorially. Words such as *hat, went,* and *stop* are spelled just the way they sound, so they can be spelled correctly if the students sound them out. Some words such as *mention* and *future* require advanced knowledge of phonics before they can be spelled correctly. And some words such as *money, do, where,* and *police* are only partially spelled the way they sound and so require students to memorize them visually as well as auditorially. Still other words such as *hopped* and *liked* can be spelled correctly if students apply the correct rules. Knowledge of roots, suffixes, and prefixes helps students spell words like *finally* and *actually.* Realizing that *final* and *actual* are the base words, the student adds *ly* to create an adverb and so spells the word correctly as *finally* and *actually.* In the first three levels of the Spelling Placement Assessment, the odd-numbered words are highly predictable and lend themselves to an auditorial spelling. The even-numbered words are less predictable spellings and so require the use of visual memory.

Also observe students as they attempt to spell words. Note the strategies that they use and the references they consult. Discuss with students strategies that they use to spell and study difficult words. Insights gained from observations, discussions, and interviews will help you in your planning. Possible discussion or interview questions are listed in Table 2.6.

Although the two processes differ somewhat—spelling requires producing letter sounds, reading requires only the recognition of letter sounds—students' spellings can offer insights into their knowledge of the phonics system, especially in the early stages. If a student is using only initial consonants to spell words, for instance, that suggests that he has not yet grasped vowels. This could be a good time to introduce short-vowel patterns, but teaching long-vowel patterns may be beyond the student's level of development. In general, spelling lags a bit behind reading. For example, students can usually read long-vowel words before they can spell them (Stahl, Stahl, & McKenna, 1998).

In addition to determining what stage students are in and what level they are operating on, it is important to know what strategies they are using. Are they using sound, visual, and meaning strategies in a balanced fashion, or are they are neglecting a particular area? What do they do when they are required to spell a new word? How do they go about learning to spell words? How do they go about proofreading their work? Chapter 9 provides additional suggestions for assessing students' use of strategies to spell words and also students' strategies for studying spelling words.

TABLE 2.6   Student Spelling Interview

Name _____   Date _____

Grade _____   Age _____

1. What kinds of words are easy for you to spell?

2. What words are hard for you to spell?

3. What makes a word hard to spell?

4. How do you do about spelling a hard word?

5. How do you go about studying spelling words? Show me how you might study a list of words for a test.

6. How do you check to see if the words are spelled correctly in a story that you have written?

7. What might you do to become a better speller?

Observations while student is writing:

Note what steps a student takes when trying to spell a difficult word. Does the student try several spellings?

Does the student use a reference, such as a word wall or dictionary?

Also note whether the student proofreads written work.

ONGOING ASSESSMENT

Assessment, of course, should be ongoing. Continue to observe students in their everyday reading and writing tasks, and also collect samples of their work. Anecdotal records are also an excellent way to collect helpful information. After witnessing a student cope with a difficult word in spelling or reading, write a brief description of the incident. Be sure to include successful encounters as well as unsuccessful ones, so that you get an accurate picture of the student's performance. A sample anecdotal record is presented in Figure 2.4. Note how the anecdotal record yields information about what the student can do on his or her own and what the student needs help with. On the basis of your ongoing assessment, make adjustments in instruction and materials as necessary.

Jay

student

Date	Comments
11/12/00	Was able to read, " Get on the bus" but struggled with the word Gus. Was unable to respond to pronounceable word part prompt, but was able to read us when I covered up G. And was then able to read Gus.

FIGURE 2.4 Sample Anecdotal Record

■ Chapter 3

FOSTERING EMERGENT LITERACY

If students can answer no more than three or four items on the Word Pattern Survey (see Chapter 2) and if specific needs are evidenced by the Emergent Literacy Assessment Survey (Chapter 2) and/or your observations, they may need to develop a foundation for phonics instruction. This foundation includes phonological awareness (rhyming and initial sounds), letter knowledge, and the following concepts of print:

> Book orientation concepts
> > Recognizing the function of the cover and title page
> > Recognizing the function of print and pictures
>
> Print direction concepts
> > Reading from left to right
> > Reading from top to bottom
>
> Print concepts
> > Understanding that words can be written down and read
> > Recognizing a letter, a word, and a sentence
> > Understanding that words are composed of letters
> > Understanding that words are composed of sounds
> > Understanding that letters represent sounds
> > Being able to point to separate words in print and match these with words
> > > that are being read by oneself or another

Above all, students should understand that reading is a meaningful act. Reading is not primarily a task of translating letters into sounds but is mainly a matter of constructing understanding. Beginning or emergent literacy concepts are best developed through immersion in reading and writing activities. Just about the best activity for developing literacy at all levels is to read to students. As you read books to children, point out the cover, the title, and the author's name. Discuss illustrations as you read. As you write messages or lists of names or schedules on the chalkboard, reinforce appropriate literacy concepts. Display and discuss labels, notes, letters, announcements, signs, and students' writing.

■ SHARED READING

Shared reading is also an excellent device for fostering literacy development. In shared reading, use enlarged text to convey initial concepts of print, letter knowledge, and phonological awareness. Enlarged text may take the form of commercially produced big books, big books that you create yourself, poems or songs written on the chalkboard, or experience stories written on large sheets of paper or on the chalkboard. Because the text is enlarged, the class can follow along as you read a selection. If you are working with just one student, you can use a regular-size text. This procedure can be used to introduce or reinforce nearly any skill or understanding in early reading, from the concept of going from left to right to the reading of words, phrases, and sentences or the reinforcement of initial consonant correspondences or vowel patterns. Listed below are procedures for conducting a shared reading activity.

▓ SHARED READING LESSON

Step 1: Preparing for the Reading.   Prepare students for a shared reading by discussing the cover illustration and the title and, if you wish, some illustrations from the text. Based on a discussion of the cover (and text illustrations) and the title, have them predict what the selection might be about. Set a purpose for reading. If students have made a prediction, the purpose might be to compare their predictions to what actually happens in the text.

Step 2: Reading the Selection.   As you read the selection, point to each word as you say it, so students get the idea of going from left to right and that there is a one-to-one match between the spoken and the printed word. Stop and clarify difficult words and concepts. Discuss interesting parts and have students evaluate their predictions, revising them if they see fit.

Step 3: Discussing the Selection.   After students have read the selection, discuss it with them. Begin by talking about their predictions. Also try to relate the selection to experiences that students may have had. Try to elicit responses to the characters and situations portrayed, asking such questions as, "Do you know anyone like the main character? Has anything like this happened to you?"

Step 4: Rereading the Selection.   During subsequent readings of the text, point out one or two concepts of print, such as words, letters, or punctuation marks, or focus on high-frequency words, or a phonics element, such as initial consonants. During these subsequent readings, also encourage students to join in and read parts that they can handle. This may be a repeated word or phrase or a whole sentence. If the book is a popular one, schedule several rereadings. Each time, the students should take more responsibility for the reading. As a follow-up, students may want to listen to taped versions of a big book, or read regular-size versions to a partner.

▓ STUDENTS' WRITING

To foster the development of literacy concepts further, encourage students to write. They should be encouraged to spell as best they can and to use invented spelling if they are unable to spell conventionally. Through invented spelling, students explore the nature of the spelling system and advance in their ability to spell and decode words (Gunning, 2000).

Daily writing activities in which invented spelling is encouraged foster development in both reading and writing. Initially, the writing activities might start with drawing a picture and writing a story about the picture. Other writing activities might include describing trips and memorable events, writing pieces telling about themselves and others, composing lists, writing notes and letters, creating fictional pieces, and keeping a journal.

■ EXPERIENCE STORIES

In addition to encouraging student-written pieces, you might arrange for youngsters to dictate experience stories. (Experience stories can be created by individuals or a group.) In this activity, students discuss an experience, such as a trip to a pumpkin farm or acquiring a new class pet, and dictate a story about the experience. The teacher scribes the story on the chalkboard or a large sheet of paper. As you scribe the story, you can spell out each word, so that students are exposed to letter names. The teacher then reads the story with the student or group in the same way as in a shared reading. Experience stories can be used to foster concepts of print, letter knowledge, and phonological awareness, and can be used to provide practice with initial consonant correspondences, short-vowel patterns, or other elements. For instance, after composing a story such as "The Seals," reproduced in Figure 3.1, you can talk over the words that begin with the same sound: *seals, saw,* and *sea.* Experience stories are especially useful when you lack appropriate materials, and they can be used with older as well as younger students.

■ EXPERIENCE STORY LESSON

Step 1: Discussing the Experience or Topic. Under the teacher's direction, the class discusses the experience or topic that is the basis of the piece to be written. For this story, the teacher discusses the trip that the class took to an aquarium. Through questioning, the teacher helps the class recall and organize information in preparation for writing a story.

Step 2: Scribing the Story. On their own or at the teacher's suggestion, the class decides to write a story. The teacher asks questions that help students shape the story: "What should we tell first in our story? Where did we go? How might we write a sentence that tells where we went? What did we see there? Which animal did you like best?" As the teacher scribes the story, she spells out each word so that students can see that talk can be written down and also are exposed to letter names. After writing a sentence, the teacher reads it back and asks the class if that is what they wanted to say.

Step 3: Reading the Story. The teacher reads the story to the class, pointing to each word as she says it. The teacher then rereads the story. Students are invited to read along with her.

Step 4: Teaching Elements in the Story. The teacher selects an element for instruction, such as reading from left to right, learning some high-frequency words, or an initial consonant sound. For this selection, the teacher reinforces the concept of beginning sounds. She discusses how *seal, sea,* and *saw* begin with the same sound and how *bounce* and *ball* begin with the same sound. The class then discusses other words that begin like *seal* or *ball.*

Step 5: Extending the Learning. The teacher may plan additional shared readings of the experience story to further reinforce beginning sounds or another skill or to provide students with added practice with the overall experience of reading.

FIGURE 3.1   Experience Story

The Seals

We went to Mystic Aquarium.
We saw lots of sea animals.
We liked the seals best.
Seals can clap their flippers.
And they can bounce a ball with their noses.

█ USING REAL-WORLD MATERIALS

One way to initiate an exploration of literacy concepts is to examine labels, signs, and other real-world materials that students encounter in their everyday lives. Holding up a box of corn flakes, encourage students to read the words *corn flakes*. Encourage them to use clues given on the box: an illustration of a bowl of corn flakes, for instance. Talk about the letters that are in the words *corn flakes*. Discuss other food packages. However, adapt your teaching to students' level of knowledge about print. If students have little knowledge of letters, stress the function of letters. Lead them to see that the words *corn flakes* are made up of letters and that these letters have names. Later, teach them letter names and, later still, the sounds that the letters represent.

When presenting labels, help students use clues on the package to identify the words on the carton: the shape of the package, the presence of an illustration on the package, and the contents of the package. Use brand names that are most likely to be familiar to students. Also bring in food packages that reflect all the cultures in your class. In time, you might group objects whose names begin with the same letter and talk about the sound that this letter represents. Also encourage students to play store and other games in which they explore the uses of reading and writing. Make sure that markers, crayons, and pads of paper are available so that students can create shopping lists, tally up bills, order stock, write ads, and take phone messages.

Display and discuss other signs that students are likely to encounter. You might take a walking tour around the school, noting the exit sign, signs marking the office, the nurse's suite, the lunchroom, and other areas. Discuss the letters that make up the signs and the sound that each beginning letter makes.

█ PHONOLOGICAL AWARENESS

In addition to knowing the functions and features of print, students must be able to manipulate the sounds of words. Most experts now agree that the ability to detect and manipulate sounds is the most essential prerequisite for learning to decode. As a practical matter, the relationship is probably reciprocal. Being able to detect and manipulate sounds makes it possible for students to learn phonics and spelling. As they learn phonics and spelling, their phonological awareness improves. Three key phonological skills are the ability to detect rhyme, the ability to segment words into individual sounds, and the ability to perceive beginning sounds in words. Once students can perceive beginning sounds, they should be able to grasp beginning phonics (Stahl, Stahl, & McKenna, 1998).

As part of your instruction in phonics, continue to build phonological awareness on a level that is commensurate with what students are required to do. If students are working with initial consonants, they only need to be able to perceive beginning sounds. However, when they move to final consonants and clusters, they will have to be able to perceive final sounds and the separate sounds in clusters—the /s/ and the /t/ in *stop,* for instance. As they move into vowels they will need to be able to perceive rimes or patterns—for example, *-at, -ent*—and the sounds that make up the rime /a/ and /t/ for *-at* and /e/, /n/, /t/ for *-ent*. These more advanced skills are best taught when students need to use them.

█ RHYME

One of the most effective ways to teach rhyming is to recite or read aloud nursery rhymes, verses, and rhyming tales. At first, just read or recite the rhymes. Focus on providing students with an enjoyable experience. As students become familiar with rhyming pieces, stress the rhyming elements. As you develop a concept of rhyme, also build the language used to talk about rhyme: *same, sounds, rhyme, words*. Stress the concept that rhyming words end with the same sound(s). Also encourage students to think of other words that might have the same sound(s) as the rhyming pair. For instance, lead them to see that there are many words that rhyme with *hat* and *cat: bat, mat, sat, fat, that*. Books that might be used to reinforce rhyme include the following:

Cameron, P. (1961). *"I can't," said the ant*. New York: Coward. With the help of some other creatures, an ant repairs a broken teapot: " 'Push her up,' said the cup. 'You can,' said the pan. 'You must,' said the crust."

Fox, M. (1993). *Time for bed*. San Diego: Harcourt. Mother animals and a human mother put their babies to sleep.

Hague, M. (1993). *Teddy bear, teddy bear*. New York: Morrow. In this action rhyme, Teddy Bear is asked to do such things as turn around, touch the ground, and show your shoe.

Hutchins, P. (1976). *Don't forget the bacon*. New York: Greenwillow. Distracted as he heads toward the grocery store, a boy distorts his memorized grocery list—with humorous results. Can be read aloud to illustrate rhyme and substitution of sounds.

Lobel, A. (1986). *The Random House book of Mother Goose*. New York: Random House. Features more than 300 traditional rhymes.

McMillan, B. (1991). *Play day, A book of terse verse*. New York: Holiday House. With color photos and two-word verses, depicts children at play: bear chair, fat bat.

Raffi. (1989). *Down by the bay*. New York: Crown. Celebrates silly rhymes: "Did you ever see a whale with a polka-dot tail/Down by the bay?"

Shaw, N. (1986). *Sheep in a jeep*. Boston: Houghton Mifflin. Sheep have a series of misadventures. Part of a series.

Building Rhymes.   To extend the concept of rhyme, build rhymes with students. Using the element *an*, here is how a rhyme might be built. Say "an." Have students say "an." Tell students that you are going to make words that have *an* in them. Say "c-an," emphasizing the *an* portion of the word. Ask students if they can hear the *an* in *c-an*. Holding up a picture of a can, have them say *can* and listen to the *an* in *c-an*. Hold up a picture of a pan. Have students tell what it is. Tell students that *p-an* has an *an* in it. Ask them if they can hear the *an* in *p-an*. Introduce *man, fan*, and *van* in the same way. Ask students if they can tell what sound they can hear in *can, pan, man, fan*, and *van*. Stress the *an* in each of these words. Explain that *can, pan, man, fan* and *van* rhyme because they all have *an* at the end. Invite students to suggest other words that rhyme with *can*.

Ask students if *hat* rhymes with *can*. Discuss the fact that *hat* ends with *at* and *can* ends with *an* so they don't rhyme. Ask if *Dan* rhymes with *can*. Discuss why these two words rhyme. Emphasize that they both end with *an*, so they rhyme.

Identifying Rhymes.   Have students tell whether word pairs such as the following rhyme: *cat–hat, hat–pan, mat–rat, can–man*. If students give correct responses, affirm their answers and explain why the answers are correct: "Yes, *cat* and *hat* do rhyme. They both end with an *at* sound. No, *hat* and *pan* do not rhyme. *Hat* ends with an *at* sound and *pan* has an *an* sound. *An* and *at* are different sounds." If students provide a wrong response, gently supply the correct response and an explanation, or rephrase the question so students have a better chance of getting it correct: "Do you hear the same sound at the end of *hat* that you hear at the end of *pan*?" From time to time, explain again what a rhyme is.

Sorting Rhymes. Sorting is also an effective way to teach and practice rhyming. In sorting, students group objects or pictures whose names rhyme. Start with objects, if you can. Objects are more concrete than pictures and less likely to be misinterpreted. Display two boxes, one with a toy cat in front of it and one with a toy goat in front of it. Tell students that they will be putting objects that rhyme with *cat* in the cat box and those that rhyme with *goat* in the goat box. Sort one or two objects as examples. Holding up a hat, say its name, emphasizing the *at* portion, then say, "*Hat* rhymes with *cat*. Both have an *at* sound, so I'll put it in the cat box." Once students understand what they are to do, have them sort the objects. Have them name the object, tell which of the two boxes it should be placed in, and why. After all the objects have been sorted, have students name the objects in each box and note that all the objects rhyme.

Also have students sort pictures. Some pictures that might be used in sorting rhymes include: bat, cat, hat, rat; bag, tag, rag, flag; nail, pail, sail, snail; cake, rake, snake; bed, bread, sled; hen, men, ten; car, jar, star; king, ring, spring, string; clock, lock, rock, sock; hose, nose, rose; stool, school, pool. (A number of rhyming pictures can be found at the end of the chapter. These can be photocopied and used in a variety of rhyming activities.) Pictures are sorted in much the same way as are objects. Select a picture to serve as a model for each rhyming pattern and have students place rhyming pictures underneath them as in Figure 3.2. Or have students sort piles of pictures that contain two or three sets of rhyming words. For instance, students might sort *at* and *ing* pictures. Each time a student sorts a picture, she should say the name of the picture and the name of the model picture so that she has a better chance of detecting rhyme. After completing a sort, the student should name all the pictures sorted, to make sure that they do rhyme and to reinforce the concept of rhyme.

Students can sort individually, in pairs, or in small groups. If students are slow or hesitant, discuss any questions they might have and ask them to sort again. If students have completed a sort under your guidance, have them sort the items a second time for additional practice.

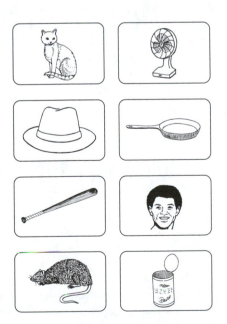

FIGURE 3.2 Rhyme Sort

Odd-One-Out.   Once students have become proficient at sorting rhymes, have them try odd-one-out. In odd-one-out, students are presented with three objects or pictures, only two of which have rhyming names. Students identify the items that rhyme and then tell what the rhyming element is. For instance, presented with the illustration of a cow, a rat, and a hat, the student selects the rat and the hat and explains that they both end with the *at* sound. The rhyming pictures presented at the end of the chapter, which were suggested for use with sorting activities, can also be used in odd-one-out exercises.

Extension and Application.   Since rhyme is a concept that may take a while to develop, continue reading rhyming tales to students and conducting other activities that will help develop their ability to detect rhyme. Additional reinforcement activities include the following:

  1. While reading a rhyming couplet, read all but the last word and have students supply the missing word:

> He was so tall, He tripped and had a long _____.
>
> Hurry up, Kate, Or you will be _____.
>
> Dad said that he would bake, A very big chocolate _____.
>
> Sitting in my chair, Was a big, furry _____.
>
> Do not stay in the park, After it gets _____.
>
> A cat with a hat, Is swinging a baseball _____.
>
> The tall man came to town, In a tan _____.
>
> There goes Dave, Give him a big _____.
>
> When she is hungry, Pam likes bread and _____.
>
> Don't be bad, Or dad will be _____.

  2. Using pairs of rhyming cards, have students play go fish or concentration. To play rhyming concentration, place 12 cards (six pairs of rhymes) face down. The student turns over a card, says its name, and then attempts to locate a picture that rhymes with it. Turning over another card, the player says its name, says the name of the card originally turned over, and tells whether they rhyme. If the player fails to locate a rhyme, he turns the original card face down and the next player takes a turn. If the player succeeds in making a match, he says the name of each card and says that they rhyme. The game ends when all the cards have been picked up. The winner is the person with the most rhyming pairs. The illustrations at the end of the chapter may be used to make rhyming cards.

  3. After reading one of Bruce McMillan's terse verse books (see p. 34), help the class create a book of terse verses: fat cat, goat boat, school pool, rag bag, nail pail.

▇ DETECTING INDIVIDUAL SPEECH SOUNDS IN WORDS

To speak and understand spoken language, it is not necessary to be aware of individual sounds in words. Indeed, if we needed to be aware of individual sounds in words, comprehension of speech itself would be extremely cumbersome. Imagine speaking or listening by saying or putting a string of separate sounds together. What we use instead is a highly efficient process known as coarticulation (Liberman & Mattingly, 1991). Through coarticulation, speech sounds are blended in such a way that it is difficult, if not impossible, to say when one sound stops and the next one begins. For instance, as we say the /k/ in /kat/, we are also articulating the /a/. And as we form the /a/, we coarticulate the /t/. Being relatively seamless, coarticulation speeds up the articulation of words and the processing of spoken language. However, coarticulation makes learning to read difficult. When our words seem like one continuous sound, it is difficult to detect separate speech sounds. However, both spelling and decoding demand an awareness of the individual sounds in words. Otherwise, students would be unable to match individual letters and the sounds they represent.

Introducing the Concept of Sounds in Words.   To introduce the concept of sounds in words or segmentation, play this game with students. Pointing to a picture of a goat, ask, "Is this a /g/?" When the class says no, agree and explain, "That's right. I didn't say all of the word's sounds. I said, 'Is this a /g/?' " Then say, "Is this a /gō/?" (emphasize each sound). Explain that no, this is not a /gō/. It doesn't have enough sounds. Next ask, "Is this a goat?" Once again, carefully enunciate all three sounds, /g/, /ō/, /t/. When the class says yes, explain that they are right. *Goat* has three sounds and you said all three of them. Present *sun* and *cat* in this same way.

To provide added instruction and practice in phonemic segmentation, use Elkonin blocks. Elkonin blocks are blocks drawn under an illustration of a word, as shown in Figure 3.3. One block is drawn for each sound. For the word *cat*, three blocks are drawn under the illustration of a cat, one each for /k/, /a/, /t/. Three boxes are also drawn for the word *goat*. Although *goat* has four letters, it has only three sounds: /g/, /ō/, /t/. Students indicate the number of sounds in a word by placing a marker in a box for each sound they hear. Demonstrate the procedure. Say the word, emphasizing each sound. As you say a sound, place a marker in the box. After demonstrating the procedure, walk students through it.

Duplicate the practice exercises in Figure 3.3. Direct students to the drawing of the sun at the top of the page. Ask the students to say the name of the picture. Urge them to stretch out each of the word's sounds so they can hear the separate sounds. If students have difficulty doing this, provide additional demonstrations. Explain to students that they are to put a marker in a box as they say each sound. As the students say /s/, they put a marker in the first box. As they say /u/, they put a marker in the second box; saying /n/, they place a marker in the final box and then say the whole word. Do several items cooperatively. Once students seem able to apply the procedure, let them finish the exercise independently, but check their responses.

At this level, the emphasis is on detecting sounds in words. That's why students put markers rather than letters in the boxes. Later, as students learn letter–sound relationships, they can put letters rather than markers in the boxes. (When a sound is represented by two letters, then both letters are placed in one box.) As students learn to read and spell words, you might use Elkonin boxes to aid them. If you are helping a student spell the word *can*, for instance, draw three boxes and fill in the letters that he would most likely be unable to supply. If he knows only initial consonants, fill in the *a* and *n* and encourage him to supply the initial consonant. If he knows initial and final consonants, fill in only the vowel, say the sound it represents, and have him complete the word. Along with or instead of using Elkonin boxes, model how you might stretch out a word so that you can hear how many sounds it has. Encourage students to do the same. For instance, if a student has difficulty spelling *sun*, encourage her to stretch it out, *s-u-n,* and to write a letter for each sound that she hears.

Extension and Application.   Because the ability to detect separate sounds in words may develop slowly and over an extended period of time, continue to present Elkonin boxes and other segmentation activities. Use naturally occurring opportunities to point out the sounds of words. As you write the day's date, messages, or students' names on the chalkboard, say each sound as you write the

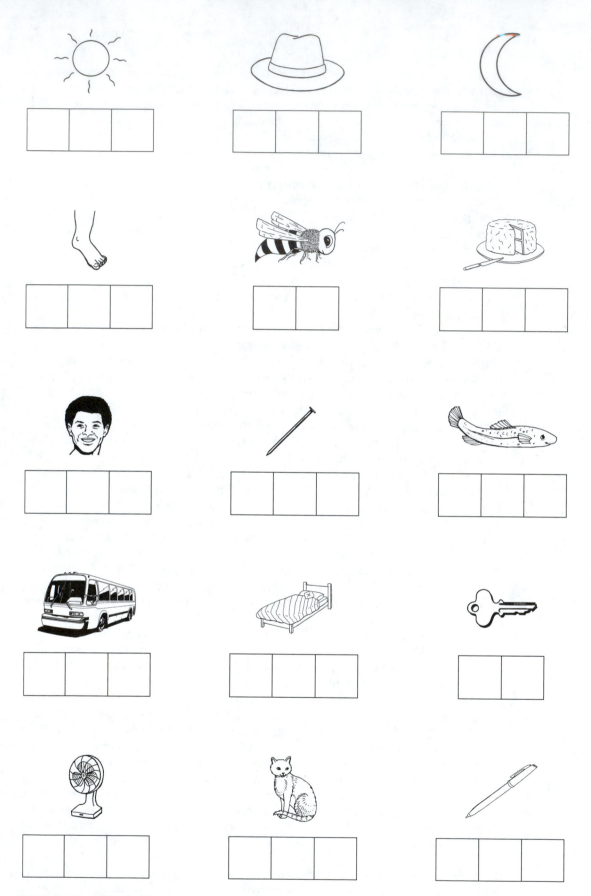

FIGURE 3.3   Elkonin Boxes

From *Word Building: Beginnings* by T. Gunning, 1994. New York: Phoenix Learning Resources. Reprinted by permission of Galvin Publications.

letter(s) that represents it. As you write the name *Bob,* for instance, say /b/, /o/, /b/. Then discuss the number of sounds in *Bob.* Also read books to students that focus on the sounds of language. Some possible titles include:

Degen, B. (1983). *Jamberry.* New York: Harper. Humorous poem features a number of words that end in "berry."

Geisel, T. S. (1965). *Fox in socks.* Uses rhyming words to create a humorous, tongue-twisting tale. New York: Random House.

Geisel, T. S. (1979). *Oh say can you say?* New York: Random House. Features a series of humorous tongue twisters.

▪ BEGINNING SOUNDS

Rhyming and segmenting words into their speech sounds prepares students for the perception of beginning consonant sounds. If students can't perceive beginning consonant sounds, then they will have difficulty learning letter–sound relationships. A fun way to introduce beginning consonant sounds is to read and discuss Dr. Seuss's *There's a Wocket in My Pocket* (New York: Beginner, 1974). In this rhyming tale, Dr. Seuss uses a number of nonsense words that were created by changing the beginning sounds of real words. Playing with words in this way calls students' attention to beginning sounds in a very natural fashion. Since students will probably enjoy this tale, it can be read to them many times.

To develop the concept of beginning sounds further, read and discuss alphabet books with your students. Focus on the sounds. Some alphabet books that might be used to reinforce initial consonant sounds include the following:

Base, G. (1987). *Animalia.* New York: Harry N. Abrams. Each letter is accompanied by a highly alliterative phrase using the target letter.

Chess, V. (1979). *Alfred's alphabet walk.* New York: Greenwillow. Scenes are described with alliterative phrases.

Eastman. P. D. (1974) *The alphabet book.* New York: Random House. Each letter is accompanied by alliterative phrases.

Geisel, T. S. (1973) *Dr. Seuss's ABC.* New York: Beginner. Each letter is accompanied by a humorous alliterative story.

Kellogg, S. (1987) *Aster Aardvark's alphabet adventures.* New York: Morrow. Each letter is accompanied by an alliterative story.

In addition to alphabet books, a number of other books highlight beginning sounds. These offer excellent opportunities for discussing beginning sounds. For instance, when the Hungry Thing in books by Slepian and Seidler asks for foods such as bellyjeans and hookies, you can ask students to guess what foods the Hungry Thing means and then encourage the class to listen as one of the characters in the book translates the Hungry Thing's requests. Some books that call attention to sounds in words include the following:

Koch, M. (1991). *Hoot howl hiss.* New York: Greenwillow. Depicts sounds that animals make, in words and illustrations. Highlights initial /h/.

Noll, S. (1992). *I have a loose tooth.* New York: Greenwillow. People misinterpret what Molly is saying because her speech is distorted by her loose tooth.

Ogburn, J. K. (1995). *The noise lullaby.* New York: Lothrop, Lee & Shepard. Little girl hears all sorts of noises just before she falls to sleep.

Slepian, J., & Seidler, A. (1967). *The hungry thing.* New York: Scholastic. One morning the Hungry Thing appears in town with a sign that says, "Feed Me." The creature demands shmancakes, tickles, and hookies. The townspeople and the reader have to figure what the Hungry Thing really wants.

Slepian, J., & Seidler, A. (1990). *The hungry thing returns*. New York: Scholastic. One morning Hungry Thing and Small Hungry Thing appear in the school yard with signs that say, "Feed Me" and "Me Too." The creatures ask for flambergers, bellyjeans, and crackeroni and sneeze. The headmaster, cook, students, and the reader have to figure out what Hungry Thing and Small Hungry Thing really want.

Alliterative Tongue Twisters.   Use alliterative tongue twisters such as the following to introduce and reinforce the concept of beginning sounds. Recite the tongue twisters to students and invite them to repeat some of the lines. Discuss the tongue twisters' beginning sounds. Additional tongue twisters are listed in the resource section at the end of the chapter.

Peter Piper

Peter Piper picked a peck of pickled peppers;
Did Peter Piper pick a peck of pickled peppers?
If Peter Piper picked a peck of pickled peppers,
Where's the peck of pickled peppers Peter Piper picked?

Betty Botter

Betty Botter bought some butter,
But, she said, this butter's bitter;
If I put it in my batter,
It will make my batter bitter,
But a bit of better butter will make my batter better.
So she bought a bit of butter
Better than her bitter butter,
And she put it in her batter,
And it made her batter better,
So 'twas better Betty Botter
Bought a bit of better butter.

Sorting by Initial Sound.   Just as sorting can be used to reinforce rhyming, it can also be used to foster awareness of beginning sounds in words. If possible, start with objects. Also sort consonants such as /s/, /m/, and /f/, which are relatively easy to distinguish and articulate. Display two boxes, one with a moon pasted on it and one with a sun attached to it. Tell students that they will be putting the objects that begin with /s/ as in *sssun* in the sun box and those that begin with /m/ as in *mmmoon* in the moon box. Sort one or two objects as examples. Holding up a sock, say its name, emphasizing the initial sound. Then say "Sock begins with /s/, the same sound that *sun* begins with, so I put sssock in the sssun box."

Once students understand what they are to do, have them sort the objects. Have them name the object, tell which of the two boxes it should be placed in, and why. After all the objects have been sorted, have students name the objects in each box and note that all the objects begin with the same sound.

Also have students sort pictures. Some pictures that might be used in sorting beginning sounds are presented at the end of Chapter 4. Pictures are sorted in much the same way as are objects. Select a picture to serve as a model for each beginning sound and have students place pictures that have that same beginning sound underneath the model picture. Before students begin to sort, it is important to discuss the names of the pictures or objects to make sure that these items are familiar. As students sort, it is also important that they say the model word and the word they are sorting. This helps them focus on the word's initial sound. After they sort, it is important that they tell why they sorted as they did and that they note what all the items had in common.

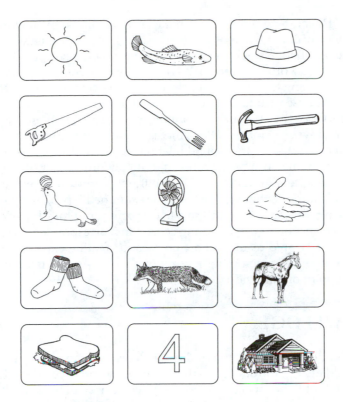

FIGURE 3.4   Beginning Sounds Sort

Students can work individually, in pairs, or in small groups. After a sort has been completed, have students say the name of each picture in a category. If students are slow or hesitant, discuss any questions they might have and ask them to sort again. If students have completed a sort under your guidance, have them sort the items a second time for additional practice. A sample sort is shown in Figure 3.4.

Games.   Games add interest to practice activities. One game that students enjoy playing is "I Spy." To play "I Spy," you provide one or more clues and the students guess the item that you spy. If the object you spy is a mirror, you might say, "I spy something on the wall that begins with 'mmm,'" or "I spy something on the wall that shows how you look and begins with 'mmm.'"

■ DEVELOPING THE CONCEPT OF WORD

One of the most important concepts of print is knowing what a word is and where a word begins and ends. Attaining a concept of word and being able to detect separate sounds in words are related skills. Students demonstrate their concept of separate words by pointing to each word of a sentence as you read the sentence. Morris (1992) provides a vivid description of a first grader who was having difficulty finger-point reading. The instructor slowly read to the student the sentence, "My little red wagon has four red wheels," pointing to each word as he pronounced it. When asked to finger-point read the sentence, the child moved his finger from left to right and said the words, but there was no connection between the word the child was reading and the word to which he was pointing. Although bright and more than halfway through first grade, the child was unable to match printed and spoken words and would make virtually no progress in reading until he learned to do so. Shared reading and experience stories are particularly effective techniques for developing a concept of word.

Developing the ability to match printed and spoken words fosters the development of knowledge of initial consonant correspondences and vice versa. Students are better able to learn initial consonant correspondence if they can track individual words. Moreover, it is easier for students to track words if they can use the beginning letters as signposts. Because most words begin with consonants, students can use their knowledge of initial consonants to help them note where words begin. Once they know the beginning letters, they are then able to explore other letters in a word (Morris, 1998). And as students note the letters within words, they learn more about letter–sound relationships. As Morris (1983) concluded, "Once a reader can match spoken words to written words, he or she can then begin to analyze the letters in the words. . . . the frame (word) has been established; now the parts (letters) within the frame can be examined" (p. 370). Students have difficulty tracking the separate words in a line of print until they have learned initial consonant correspondences (teaching consonant correspondences is covered in the next chapter). Shared reading of big books and creating experience stores are excellent devices for developing the concept of a word. As you read or create a story, carefully point out individual words.

LETTER KNOWLEDGE

As students develop the ability to detect rhyme and beginning sounds, they should also be introduced to the letters of the alphabet. If students don't know the identity of *t*, they will not be able to associate it with the sound it represents. If they confuse *t* and *p*, they may assign the sound of /t/ to /p/ and vice versa. In addition to preventing confusion, knowing the name of a letter aids memory. Students who know the names of the letters are better able to learn letter–sound relationships (Ehri, 1983). Many letters incorporate their sounds in their names. For instance, the names of the vowel letters *a, e, i, o,* and *u* are their long sounds. Students use this knowledge when they begin to spell. Many of the names of the consonants begin with the sound represented by the consonant letter: *bee, cee, dee, gee, jay, kay, pee, tee, vee, zee.* A number of the names of the remaining consonant letters incorporate the sounds in the middle or at the end of their names: *ef, el, em, en, es, ex.* As Durrell (1980) notes, only the letter names *h, q, w,* and *y* have no relationship to the phonemes that they spell.

TEACHING LETTER NAMES

Names are the first words that most children learn, so names form a natural basis for learning letters. To initiate a study of names and the letters used to spell them, write your name on the board, saying each letter as you write it. Discuss the fact that our names are made up of letters and that different names have different letters. Write the names of some students on the board. Discuss the letters that make up each name. Point out the longest and the shortest names and names that begin with the same letters. Help students write their names if they can't already do so. You might want to provide each child with a model of his or her name. Students can then learn the names of the letters in their first and last names.

If students have difficulty learning the letters of their names, use cut-out or magnetic letters to spell their names. Name each letter as you spell the child's name. Then mix up the letters and have the child reassemble the letters, saying each one as she moves it into place. Also play concentration with the letters in the child's name.

Use naturally occurring opportunities to reinforce children's recognition of their names: write their names on their cubbies, have them write their names on their papers, write students' names on the board when they have special assignments or need to report to another professional or when they are being recognized for a birthday or other reason. You might also set up a class mailbox and encourage students to send letters or drawings to each other. Show them how to "address" their mail.

One of the most effective ways to reinforce knowledge of letter names is to surround students with examples of letters and reasons to use them. Display a model alphabet and have available old typewriters, computers, stamp sets, letter stencils, magnetic and felt letters, and a wide assortment of writing instruments and paper. Encourage students to experiment with the alphabet and to play alphabet games. Also encourage the use of invented spelling and provide lots of opportunities for writing. Read and discuss alphabet books and encourage students to examine these texts. Other activities that might be used to reinforce letter knowledge include the following:

- Use environmental print. As suggested earlier, bring in cereal boxes, milk cartons, and other items with labels. Have students "read" the labels and identify the letters that make up the labels.
- Help students create alphabet books. You might give them sheets, one for each letter of the alphabet, which contain the letter in upper- and lowercase form. The sheet might also contain a picture showing an object that begins with the letter name being presented and the name of the picture. Thus the *b* page would contain *Bb* and a drawing of a bee.
- Develop letter knowledge as a natural part of your routines. As you list names or write messages on the board, spell out the words and names.
- Have students sing the alphabet song. As they sing it, they should touch the name of the letter that they are singing.
- Display an alphabet strip that shows how each letter is formed. Also provide each student with an individual alphabet card showing how the letters are formed.
- Sort letters with different fonts. Have students put all the *m*'s in one column and all the *t*'s in another and the *w*'s in a third.
- Provide students with a set of alphabet cards. Students can use the cards to match upper- and lowercase letters, to play concentration by matching upper- and lowercase letters, and for a variety of recognition activities. They might also put a scrambled set of letters in alphabetical order. They should say the letter's name as they put it in order. Spend about 10 minutes working with the alphabet on a daily basis. Working with groups of three letters, have students hold up the letter that you name: lowercase *b*, lowercase *c*, lowercase *s*, for instance. A set of alphabet cards is given in Figures 3.5 and 3.6. The cards can be duplicated in such a way that the lowercase letters appear on the reverse side of the uppercase letters.
- Have available and read to students alphabet books. Invite students to read alphabet books to themselves or to a partner.
- Have a meal of alphabet soup or Alphabits cereal.
- Sing songs such as "Old McDonald Had a Farm," in which alphabet letters are highlighted.

As part of your instruction, teach students how to form the letters of the alphabet. Once students have acquired some basic concepts of print, have developed some phonological awareness, and are familiar with most of the letters of the alphabet, they are ready for systematic instruction in phonics.

Technology.   Word processing programs can help students learn the names of alphabet letters. If you are using Dr. Peet's Talk/Writer (Edmark), which has an ABC Discovery module that introduces the alphabet, or another word processing program that has speech capability, the name of the letter will be pronounced when the child presses the key. Bailey's Schoolhouse (Edmark) features rhyming and other emergent literacy activities.

a	b	c	d	e
f	g	h	i	j
k	l	m	n	o
p	q	r	s	t
u	v	w	x	y
z				

FIGURE 3.5   Lowercase Alphabet Cards

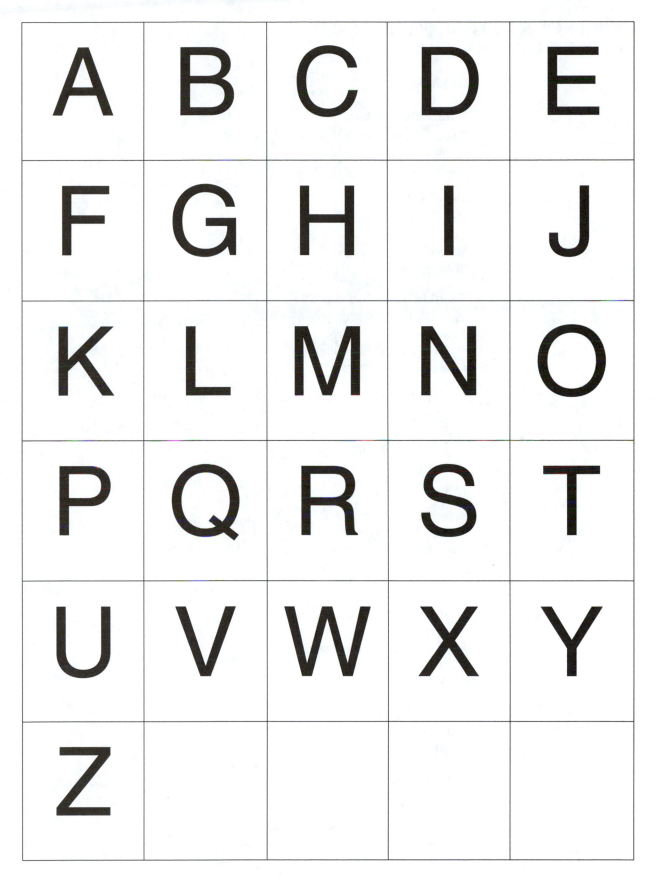

FIGURE 3.6   Uppercase Alphabet Cards

RESOURCES FOR FOSTERING EMERGENT LITERACY

RHYMES

Rain, Rain, Go Away

Rain, rain, go away,
Come again another day;
Little Robert wants to play.

I'm a Little Teapot

I'm a little teapot short and stout:
Here is my handle and here is my spout.
When I get all steamed up, I just shout:
"Just tip me over and pour me out!"

Twinkle, Twinkle, Little Star

Twinkle, twinkle, little star,
How I wonder what you are!
Up above the world so high,
Like a diamond in the sky.

Jack Hall

Jack Hall,
He is so small,
A rat could eat him,
Hat and all.

Rub-a-Dub-Dub

Rub-a-dub-dub,
Three men in a tub,
And who do you think they be?
The butcher, the baker,
The candlestick maker.

Garden Gate

Two, four, six, eight.
Meet me at the garden gate.
If I'm late, do not wait.
Two, four, six, eight.

Little Bo-Peep

Little Bo-Peep has lost her sheep,
And can't tell where to find them;
Leave them alone, and they'll come home,
And bring their tails behind them.

Little Boy Blue

Little boy blue, come blow your horn;
The sheep's in the meadow, the cow's in the corn.
Where's the little boy that looks after the sheep?
He's under the haystack fast asleep.
Will you wake him? No, not I;
For if I do, he'll be sure to cry.

Little Betty Blue

Little Betty Blue,
Lost her new shoe.
What will poor Betty do?
Why, give her another,
To match the other,
And then she will walk in two.

Mary's Lamb
Sara Josepha Hale

Mary had a little lamb,
Its fleece was white as snow,
And everywhere that Mary went
The lamb was sure to go.

It followed her to school one day—
That was against the rule;
It made the children laugh and play
To see a lamb at school.

Baa, Baa, Black Sheep
Baa, baa, black sheep,
Have you any wool?
Yes, sir, yes, sir,
Three bags full.

One for the master,
One for the dame,
But none for the little boy
Who cries in the lane.

Wee Willie Winkie
Wee Willie Winkie runs through the town,
Upstairs and downstairs in his nightgown,
Rapping at the window, crying through the lock,
Are the children all in bed, for now it's eight o'clock?

ALLITERATIVE SELECTIONS

Apples, peaches, pears, and plums,
    Tell me when your birthday comes.

A Sailor Went to Sea
A sailor went to sea
To see what he could see,
And all that he could see,
Was the sea, sea, sea.

Jack and Jill
Jack and Jill went up the hill,
To fetch a pail of water;
Jack fell down and broke his crown,
And Jill came tumbling after.

Dickery, Dickery, Dare
Dickery, dickery, dare,
The pig flew up in the air;
The man in brown
Soon brought him down,
Dickery, dickery, dare.

Rhyme Illustrations

Rhyme Illustrations

Chapter 4

TEACHING PHONICS

Phonics can be taught in a number of ways. It can be presented analytically, synthetically, or through patterns. In an analytic approach, elements are taught within the context of a whole word. For instance, the correspondence b = /b/ is presented as the sound heard at the beginning of *ball*. Since the element is not isolated, the student must abstract it from the word. In the synthetic approach, elements are presented in isolated fashion—for example, the student is told that b makes a "buh" sound. Saying speech sounds in isolation distorts them. However, struggling readers may find it difficult to abstract sounds from words, so having sounds presented in isolation is easier for them. In a pattern approach, students learn elements by noting that *at* in *cat*, *hat*, and *sat* are the same. Which approach works best? All three have their advantages and disadvantages. The synthetic approach breaks down phonics into its simplest elements. However, it distorts consonant sounds, which are not designed to be spoken in isolation. The analytic approach does not distort sounds, but is more roundabout. It refers to b = /b/ as the sound heard at the beginning of *ball*.

In a pattern approach, students learn a series of words that incorporate a common rime: *cat*, *hat*, *sat*, *rat*, *bat*, for example. Although economical because it combines sounds (/a/ + /t/), a pattern approach requires students to make fine discriminations, as in the difference between *cat* and *can* or between *pet* and *pit*. Some novice readers might also find it more difficult to deal with a combined element as in *-ig* or *-ap* rather than the single elements /i/ + /g/ or /a/ + /p/. In this text an approach known as Word Building, which combines the best features of all three, is advocated. Word Building starts with the easiest-to-learn, most readily perceived element in a pattern and involves students in building whole words.

WORD BUILDING

As a technique, Word Building presents the most basic pronounceable element in the pattern being taught and leads students to build words by adding to that core element. In presenting long e, for example, the teacher tells students that e represents /ē/ and helps them to build words like *he*, *me*, *we*, and *she*. On a more advanced level, Word Building helps students learn multisyllabic words by building on known elements. For instance, building on their knowledge of *at*, students learn multisyllabic words such as *batter*, *matter*, and *chatter*.

By showing how phonic elements are used to construct words, students acquire a more concrete understanding of the alphabetic spelling system. They are then shown how to use this knowledge to decipher unfamiliar words independently. When faced with a word that poses difficulty for them, students use the strategy of seeking a pronounceable word part and then using that pronounceable word part as the basis for reconstructing the word. A student who is unable to pronounce the printed word *ranch* might use the pronounceable word part *an* to reconstruct the word, saying "an," "ran," and finally "ranch." The pronounceable word part strategy is supported by practice and several research studies (Glass & Burton, 1973; Gunning, 1988, 1995, 1999; Hardy, Stennett, & Smythe, 1973).

If the pronounceable word part strategy does not work, the student would then try an analogy strategy. Unable to find a pronounceable word part in the unknown word *vet,* the student might compare it to the known word *pet* and work out the pronunciation through analogy. The analogy strategy is also supported by research and practice (Cunningham, 1978; Gaskins, Gaskins, & Gaskins, 1991; Goswami & Bryant, 1990). Context, of course, is emphasized. The overall sense of the selection and the immediate context in which the unfamiliar word appears are woven into the pronounceable word part and analogy strategies. Context, including picture clues, is also used when neither the pronounceable word part nor the analogy strategies works.

■ TARGET AUDIENCE

Word Building has been used with gifted, average, and poor readers, with excellent results. Even severely disabled readers have learned to read with Word Building when all other methods have failed (Gunning, 1998b). One such student was 8-year-old Marcia. Although Marcia has at least average intelligence and had been placed in a self-contained room for learning-disabled pupils, she was still operating on a beginning first-grade level. In addition to having difficulty learning and applying phonics, Marcia had acquired a condition known as learned helplessness. Repeated failure had convinced her that she was unable to decipher unfamiliar printed words, so she stopped trying. This belief became self-fulfilling. Feeling incompetent, Marcia stopped trying to figure out difficult words. Encountering an unknown word, she either skipped it or sought help from the teacher. Because of disuse, her limited deciphering skills failed to develop. Word Building helped extend Marcia's skills. The strategies that grew out of Word Building—pronounceable word parts and analogy—empowered Marcia by providing her with techniques that she could use to unlock unknown words on her own. Encouraged by her initial success and a feeling that she had some control over her reading, Marcia slowly grew in skill and confidence.

■ EASY TO TEACH

In addition to being highly effective, Word Building is easy to teach. Word Building is a very simple, natural approach that is based on the way students actually attack unfamiliar words (Glass & Burton, 1973; Gunning, 1988, 1999; Hardy, Stennett & Smythe, 1973). When faced with unfamiliar words, most youngsters seek out a familiar portion of the word and attempt to pronounce it. This portion is generally longer than a letter but often smaller than a syllable. It may be the *en* in *bench,* the *ar* in *farther,* or the *et* in *letter* that provides the reader with the phonological clue that enables her to reconstruct the entire word. Word Building emphasizes these natural units and presents them in such a way that students' ability to use them to decode unfamiliar words is fostered.

■ BASIC PRINCIPLES

Word Building is grounded in three basic principles. (1) Build on what students know. It is important to observe students carefully, so as to be aware of what their knowledge of phonics elements is and to see what kinds of strategies they use when they encounter difficult words in their reading. (2) Proceed from the simple to the complex. Word Building has been designed to start with the simplest, easiest-to-learn phonic elements and to use these as building blocks for more advanced elements. (3) Provide ample reinforcement. Children's books, real-world materials, writing, games, and other activities can be used to provide practice.

For struggling learners, added practice materials can be the great equalizer. In a traditional class situation, everyone in the group receives the same amount of practice, even those who are slow to catch on. In this program, you are urged to provide each student with as much practice as he or she needs. For instance, if a student has gone through the practice activities for the -*at* pattern and still hasn't mastered it, several suggestions for additional practice are provided. Best of all, three well-known children's books listed in the Vowel Pattern Resources section (Eric Carle's *Have You Seen My Cat?*, Brian Wildsmith's *Cat on the Mat*, and Alice Cameron's *The Cat Sat on the Mat*) can be used for extra reinforcement and application.

▪ STAGES OF THE PROGRAM

Word Building starts with instruction in initial consonant correspondences and leads to three-letter, short-vowel patterns (*cat, hat; wet, pet, set*). Single-syllable patterns of gradually increasing difficulty, including long-vowel patterns (*wait, late*), *r*-vowel patterns (*fear, fur*), and other-vowel patterns (*coin, how*), are presented until all major single-syllable patterns have been introduced. High-frequency multisyllabic patterns are presented last. Although consonants, consonant clusters, and vowel patterns are presented separately, their introduction should be integrated. It is not necessary or even desirable to present all the consonants, then the digraphs, and then the clusters before introducing vowel patterns. After teaching about 5 consonant correspondences, introduce a vowel pattern or two. This enables students to analyze and form whole words instead of just working with consonants. A suggested sequence of introduction is presented in Table 4.1.

▪ TEACHING CONSONANT CORRESPONDENCES

Once students are able to detect initial sounds, can identify most of the letters of the alphabet, and have begun acquiring the concept that letters represent sounds, begin presenting initial consonant correspondences. The first correspondences recommended for presentation are $s = /s/$, $m = /m/$, and $f = /f/$. These correspondences are continuants: they are articulated with a continuous stream of breath and so are easier to perceive. They also are among the most frequently occurring correspondences, but are very different from each other. They have very different pronunciations, and their letters have very different shapes, so students are not likely to confuse them.

TABLE 4.1   Suggested Scope and Sequence of Phonic Elements

Level 1	Level 2	Level 3
Initial consonants: *s, m, f, h, b*	Vowel: long-*a* vowels	Vowels: *r*-vowel patterns
Initial consonants: *l, n, c* = /k/, *r, g* = /g/	Clusters: *cl, tr, fl, pl*	Clusters: *sc, scr, sch, squ*
Vowels: -*am*, -*at*, -*an* patterns	Vowels: long-*e* patterns	Vowels: other-vowel patterns
Initial consonants: *t, d, j, p, w*	Clusters: *sl, cr*	Clusters: *sl, cr*
Initial consonants and digraphs: *k, y, v, ch, sh, wh, th*	Vowels: long-*i* patterns	
Vowels: additional short-*a* patterns	Clusters: *br, sk*	
Initial consonants: *g* = /j/, *c* = /s/, *z, qu, x*	Vowels: long-*o* patterns	
Vowels: short-vowel patterns	Clusters: *sp, spl, sn, gr, fr, gl, str, sm*	
Clusters: *st, sl, sw*	Digraphs: *kn, ph, wr*	

When teaching initial consonants, use a combination of the analytic and synthetic approaches. Novice readers need to have the target sound emphasized by hearing it in isolation, which is what the synthetic approach does. And they need to hear it in the context of a real word, which is what the analytic approach does.

Presented below is a sample lesson for introducing the consonant correspondence *s* = /s/. The lesson starts with auditory perception to make sure students can perceive the sound of the element and proceeds to the visual level, where the children integrate sound and letter knowledge. The lesson assumes that the students can segment a word into its separate sounds, have a concept of beginning sounds, and realize that sounds are represented by letters. If possible, relate your presentation to a story, song, or rhyme that you have read aloud or share-read. This helps students relate the phonics they are learning to real reading.

■ SAMPLE LESSON 4.1: CONSONANT CORRESPONDENCE

Step 1: Auditory Perception.   In teaching the correspondence (letter–sound relationship) *s* = /s/, read a story such as *Six-Dinner Sid* (Moore, 1991) that contains a number of *s* words. Call students' attention to words in the book: *six, sick, said, Sid.* Stressing the initial sound as you say each word, ask students to tell what is the same about the words: *sssix, sssick, sssaid,* and *SSSid.* Help students to note that the words all begin with the same sound. Present the sound /s/ both in isolation and within the context of a word. Although saying the sound in isolation distorts it, struggling readers may have difficulty perceiving a sound in the context of a word. Explain that *six, sick, said,* and *Sid* begin with the sound /s/ as in *sun.* Ask the class if there are students whose first names begin with /s/. Help the class determine whether or not the names do actually begin with /s/ and write them on the board. Note that the names begin with an uppercase *s.* If students volunteer names such as *Cecil* or *Cicely* that begin with an /s/ sound but are spelled with a *C,* explain that the sound /s/ can sometimes be spelled with a *C.*

If students experience difficulty perceiving initial sounds, ask silly questions that focus on /s/. Holding up a toy saw, ask, "Is this a paw? Is this a law?" Lead students to see that *paw* and *law* begin with the wrong sound and must be changed to /s/ to make *saw.* Other silly questions might include the following: "Is this a lock? (holding up a picture of a sock). Is this a meal?" (holding up a picture of a seal).

Step 2: Letter–Sound Integration.   Write each of the *s* words from Step 1 on the board: *six, sick, said,* and *Sid.* Read each name and have students tell which letter each of the words begins with. Lead students to see that the letter *s* stands for the sound /s/ heard at the beginning of *six, sick, said,* and *Sid.* Compose a Consonant Chart. On this chart include a model word and a picture to illustrate the key word. A model word is one that would most likely be a part of the students' listening vocabulary and is easy to illustrate so that it can be accompanied by an illustration. An appropriate model word for *s* = /s/ is *sun.* If students forget the sound that a letter represents, the model word accompanied by its picture can be used as a reminder. Tell students that if they forget what sound *s* stands for, they can use the Consonant Chart to help them. A sample Consonant Chart is presented in Figure 4.1.

Step 3: Guided Practice.   Have students read signs or labels containing /s/ words: *salt, syrup, soap.* You might also conduct a shared reading of a big book that contains a number of words that begin with *s* and conduct a sorting exercise as explained in the Extension and Application section that follows, or create an

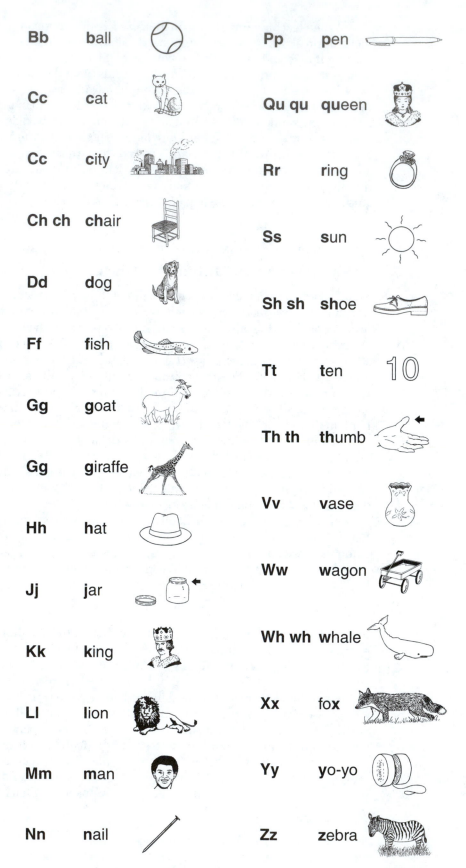

Bb	**b**all		**Pp**	**p**en	
Cc	**c**at		**Qu qu**	**qu**een	
Cc	**c**ity		**Rr**	**r**ing	
Ch ch	**ch**air		**Ss**	**s**un	
Dd	**d**og		**Sh sh**	**sh**oe	
Ff	**f**ish		**Tt**	**t**en	
Gg	**g**oat		**Th th**	**th**umb	
Gg	**g**iraffe		**Vv**	**v**ase	
Hh	**h**at		**Ww**	**w**agon	
Jj	**j**ar		**Wh wh**	**wh**ale	
Kk	**k**ing		**Xx**	fo**x**	
Ll	**l**ion		**Yy**	**y**o-yo	
Mm	**m**an		**Zz**	**z**ebra	
Nn	**n**ail				

FIGURE 4.1   Consonant Chart

From *Word Building Book A, with Predictable Stories,* by T. Gunning, 1997. New York: Phoenix Learning Resources. Reprinted by permission of Galvin Publications.

interactive story that contains *s* words. You might also share-read the following verse or another that contains a number of *s* words.

> **Sing, Sing**
>
> Sing, sing,
>   What shall I sing?
> The cat's run away
>   With the pudding string!

Step 4: Spelling and Writing.   Review or introduce the formation of capital and lowercase *s*. Present some simple words beginning with s, such as *see*. Students might create a pattern story about some things that they see: I see _____. Show students how to form the word *see* by adding *s* to *ee*. To introduce *ee* = /ē/, write *ee* on the board. Ask students to name the letters. Explain that the letters *ee* make the sound /ē/ as in *see* and *tree*. Ask students to tell what letter they would add to *ee* to make the word *see*. After the word *see* has been formed, have volunteers read it. Then write *I* in front of it. Ask students if they know the name of the letter. Explain that this is also the word *I*. Read the two words with students. Then cooperatively compose "I see" sentences that tell what the students see. To provide additional practice with *s* = /s/, you might encourage students to tell what they see that begins with /s/: I see Sue. I see a seven. I see socks. I see a sandwich. Using an interactive writing approach, begin composing a class alphabet book. Start with the *s* page. Encourage students to draw or paste pictures of items whose names begin with *s*. Help students label these items and encourage them to read the page.

Step 5: Application.   Students apply their skill by reading books that contain words that begin with *s*, or you might create experience stories that contain *s* words. Also encourage students to use *s* as they compose stories.

Additional Application and Reinforcement

1. Help students create an alphabet book. Show students how you want them to set up their books. One possibility is to distribute thirty sheets, one for each letter of the alphabet, and one for *ch, sh, th,* and *wh* (later you might have separate pages for *c* = /s/ and *g* = /j/). Each sheet is marked with the letters in uppercase and low-ercase form. Students might create covers for the books, which could then be sta-pled or stitched together. Once students have studied a letter, they can draw illustrations or paste pictures of things whose names begin with the sound repre-sented by that letter.

2. Conduct every-pupil response activities. In every-pupil response activities, students hold up cards to respond. That way all can respond at the same time. Say a series of words, some of which begin with the target letter. Have students hold up the letter card when words beginning with that letter are called out. If students know several correspondences, give them several letters (but not more than three or four) and have them hold up the letter that represents the beginning sound of the word being spoken. For example, you might say, "Which of these begins with the letter *s*? Seal, dog, sun." Students should hold up the *s* card when you say *seal* and *sun.*

3. Continue to share-read books with students. As you encounter *s* words, point them out and have students tell you what sound the words begin with. Continue to read and discuss alphabet books and environmental print. Also share-read rhymes that illustrate the correspondence.

4. Have students conduct a word search. Students search classroom walls and their books for words that begin with the correspondence being taught.

5. Have students create a word bank of words that they can read and words that they are learning to read. Have students locate and read words in their word bank that begin with the target letter.

6. If students continue to have difficulty grasping the concept of consonant correspondences, try the partial word technique. Holding up a picture of the sun, ask, "Is this the un?" Note that a sound is missing. Have students tell what the word should be and what sound is missing. Stress the fact that you need to add /s/ to /un/ to make *sun*. Write *un* on the board, explaining that this stands for /un/. Then add *s*, explaining as you do so that this letter stands for /s/. Then say the word, emphasizing /s/. Follow the same procedure with other *s* words: *saw, seal*. Avoid initial clusters, as in *snake*, since it is harder to isolate a single consonant sound in a cluster.

7. Create highly predictable stories in which students use their knowledge of initial consonants. This shows students the purpose of learning initial consonants and gives them a sense of what reading is, so that they feel like readers. As students read these highly predictable stories, encourage them to point to each word as they read it, so they match up print with what they are saying. Appendix B provides several highly predictable fold-and-read books designed to reinforce initial consonants. Two of the books use the "I see _____" pattern. In presenting the books, teach the words *I, see, a* and show students how to use picture clues and initial consonants to figure out the ending word in each pattern. Each ending word will begin with a recently presented consonant. Follow the same procedure with the "I like _____" predictable book. Read the books with your students and encourage them to read them with partners, with family members, and on their own.

◾ SORTING

Sorting is a highly effective way to reinforce letter–sound correspondences. After at least two correspondences have been introduced, students can sort them. When supplying correspondences for students to sort, choose ones that are distinctively different. For instance, students might sort *f* and *h* because they are formed in different parts of the mouth and the letters that represent them are very different from each other. Pairs such as *m* and *n* or *p* and *b* are not good candidates for sorting, especially for students in the beginning stage of learning letter–sound relationships. Create letter cards for the sounds to be sorted and assemble pictures that begin with the target sounds (illustrations for initial consonant sounds can be found at the end of this chapter). (To make the cards more durable, copy them onto card stock, which is available at most stationery stores. You might also laminate the cards.) Place each letter card at the head of a column, say the sound each represents, and then place under it an illustration of the sound's model word. For *f*, place an *Ff* card at the head of the column and say *f* stands for /f/, the sound that you hear at the beginning of *fish*. Place a picture of a fish under *f* and say, "*Fish* is the model word for /f/." Follow this same procedure for the correspondence *h* = /h/ as in Figure 4.2.

Pointing to a stack of cards containing objects whose names begin with /f/ or /h/, tell students, "We're going to sort these picture cards. If the name of the picture begins with /f/ as in *fish*, we're going to put it in the *fish* column. If the name of the picture begins with /h/ as in *hat*, we'll put it in the *hat* column." Holding up a picture of a four, ask, "What is this? What sound does it begin with? What column should we put it in?" Affirm or correct students' responses. "Yes, *four* begins with the sound /f/ that we hear at the beginning of *fffish*, so we put it in the *fish* column." Go through the rest of the cards in this fashion. Once all the cards have been categorized, have volunteers say the names of all the cards in a column and note that they all begin with /f/ or /h/. Encourage students to suggest other words that

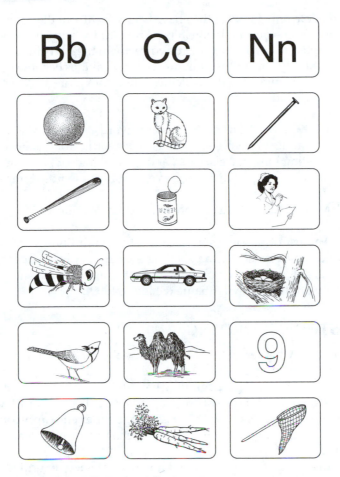

FIGURE 4.2   Consonant Sort

might fit into the columns. Also have them re-sort the pictures on their own to promote speed of response. You might also add a third item to be sorted. If students
seem to be using a picture card as a basis for sorting—they put *fan* under fish
because they both begin the same way—remove the picture cards as soon as they
have been sorted so that they are matching the cards to the letter: *fan* is placed
under the letter *f* because it begins with the sound represented by /f/ (Morris,
1999).

Three correspondences are the maximum that students should be asked to
sort. After students have mastered a group of three or four correspondences, you
might drop the best-known correspondence and add a new one, or simply introduce three new correspondences.

After students have become fairly proficient at sorting cards, introduce a
writing sort. In a writing sort, students write whole words or parts of them in
columns headed by the appropriate consonant sound. For instance, after sorting
words beginning with /m/, /s/, or /f/, students arrange their papers into three
columns and head the columns: *m, s,* and *f.* You then say a series of two or three
words for each sound. The words are in random order. Students write the words in
the appropriate column—*fish* in the /f/ column, for instance. As you say the
words, stress the beginning sound, and encourage students to say the words as
they write them so that they are better able to detect the words' sounds. Encourage
students to write as much of each of the words as they can, but focus on the initial
sounds and only correct errors in placing the words in the wrong column or errors
in writing the initial consonants. The basic principle is that students are held

responsible only for what they have been taught, but they should be encouraged to explore letter–sound relationships. After students learn vowel patterns, they will be expected to spell whole words correctly in their writing sorts.

A highly effective technique, sorting activities become more advanced as students' knowledge of phonics elements becomes more advanced. Some other possible sorts include:

- Digraphs and clusters: *s* versus *sh* words; *s* versus *sl* words, for instance.
- Rhyming patterns: *-at* versus *-am* words, for instance. Different ways of spelling long vowels: *ay, ai,* and *a-e* spellings of /a/ words.
- Nonrhyming words: short-*a* versus short-*i* words. Long-vowel versus short-vowel words.
- Multisyllabic words according to syllable pattern.

The list of possible sorts is almost without limit. Through sorting, students make discoveries about the spelling system. Because sorting is active and challenging, students also enjoy sorting. Best of all, research supports sorting as being a highly effective activity (Santa & Høien, 1999).

■ STUDENT WRITING

As noted in Chapter 3, students naturally explore the spelling–sound system when they are encouraged to write and use invented spelling. In the early stages, they attempt to represent the beginning sounds of words, so that *farm* is spelled *F;* later, they add ending consonants so that *farm* is spelled *FM* or *FRM.* Students' writing might be supplemented with the language experience approach in which students dictate stories or shared writing in which students and teacher collaborate in the writing of a story.

In a form of shared writing known as interactive writing, the students "share the pen" and do some of the actual writing of the selection. Interactive writing begins with the selection of a topic. As with the traditional experience story approach, students can write about a trip they have taken, a classroom pet, a story they have read, or a similar topic. With the teacher's help the students compose their message orally. Interactive writing provides extra practice in reading. After a word has been written interactively, the story is reread from the beginning. Words chosen for interactive writing are those that provide a basis for growth. The teacher writes words that are readily known by all and those that are so difficult that students would not be able to supply any parts. Students are invited to write word parts that they can handle if the teacher elongates them or if they are related to a student's name or another familiar word. The teacher "shares the pen" with all students, so that even those with the most limited grasp of writing have the opportunity to participate. As part of the scaffolding, the teacher also asks questions such as the following:

"Where do we begin writing?"
"How many words are there in our sentence?"
"Would you say the word slowly?"
"What sounds do you hear?"
"What sound do you hear in the beginning?"
"Can you write the letter that stands for that sound?"

After planting a tree, the class might compose the sentence, "We planted a tree today." The teacher repeats the message and might have the class clap out the words as she says them: "We—planted—a tree—today," if she wants to reinforce the concept of separate words. The teacher and the class then write the story. The teacher scaffolds the writing so that students contribute as much as they can. Emphasizing the word's sounds, the teacher says "we" and asks the class what sounds they hear. She notes that *we* begins like *William,* so she has William write the first letter. The story is written on chart paper. Meanwhile, the rest of the class might use white boards to attempt to represent the first sound in *w.* Using white boards gives each student the opportunity to participate. The teacher then asks the class what other sound they hear in *we.* When a volunteer responds /$\bar{e}$/, the teacher invites the volunteer to add it to *w.* Meanwhile, students add an *e* to the *w* on their white boards. The teacher points to *we* and the class reads it chorally. Since it has been several minutes since the target sentence was spoken, the teacher repeats it and reminds the class that now they are writing the word *planted.* Paul supplies *p* for *planted,* Lisa the *l,* Nan, the *an,* Tom, the *t,* the teacher, the *e,* and Brad adds the final *d.* Once again, the class reads chorally the part that has been written so far. Maria adds *a.* Again, the class reads chorally the part that has been written so far. Tracy supplies initial *t* for *tree.* Reginald supplies the *r.* Several students report hearing an /$\bar{e}$/ sound. James adds one *e,* and the teacher tells him to add a second *e.* She explains that the sound /$\bar{e}$/ is sometimes spelled with two *e's.* The teacher reads the sentence, pointing to each word as she does so. The class reads it chorally and individual volunteers then read it.

The scaffolding and explanations that the teacher offers are geared to the students' level of understanding. Skills and understandings that students are currently working on are emphasized. For students in the very early stages, the teacher might emphasize the concept of word and consonant sounds. Later, she might focus on short-vowel sounds or high-frequency words. Interactive stories are posted and students are encouraged to read them from time to time.

As a reference, all of the students' first names are listed in alphabetical order. An alphabet strip is also available in case students forget how to form a letter. As students learn high-frequency words such as *the,* these are listed on the class's Word Wall. As students grow in their knowledge of consonants, the teacher suggests that they say the word slowly and think of each sound and the letter used to spell it. In time they are asked to represent additional sounds in the word.

After an interactive story has been completed, it is displayed so that it can be share-read or read independently. In an activity known as "reading around the room," students read interactive and other experience stories that have been placed on the walls. A sample interactive story is shown in Figure 4.3. It is a retelling of Eric Carle's (1987) *Have You Seen My Cat?*

Here is sample dialog to show how interactive writing might be implemented. After reading Eric Carle's *Have You Seen My Cat?,* students decide that they would like to retell the story. After creating a title, they decide on the first sentence: "The boy lost his cat." To reinforce the concept of each word, the teacher has the class clap as she says the sentence: "The—boy—lost—his—cat." The class then begins writing the story.

FIGURE 4.3   Sample Interactive Story

The Lost Cat

The boy lost his cat.
He asked people, "Have you seen my cat?"
The people pointed to cats.
The cats were not the boy's cat.
At last the boy found his cat.
He was surprised.
His cat had kittens.

TEACHER: Who can write *the? The* is on our word wall.

TANYA: I can write *the.*

TEACHER (pointing to spot on chart paper):   Tanya, will you write *the* here? Class, you can write *the* on your white boards. Who can point to *the* on our word wall?

TEACHER (pointing to *the* that Tanya has written):   Very good, Tanya. Notice that *the* is written with a capital letter because it is the first word in a sentence. Check your white boards, boys and girls, to make sure that you have written *the* correctly. What word comes after *the?*

JAMES: *boy.*

TEACHER: How does *boy* begin? Who has a name that begins like *boy*?

BERNARD: I do.

TEACHER: How does your name begin?

BERNARD: With a *b*. My name begins with a *b*.

TEACHER (pointing to Bernard's name on the name chart):   Can you write a *b* here? (Judging that /oi/ is too advanced for the class, the teacher says) I will add the /oi/ sound to /b/. Now we have *boy.* Who can read what we have written so far?

GERMAINE: *The boy.*

TEACHER: Good, Germaine. What comes next?

NINA: *lost.*

TEACHER: Say *lost* slowly. *LLLost.* What sound do you hear?

MARIA: *lll.*

TEACHER: What letter makes a /l/, which is the sound that we hear at the beginning of *lion*? No one's name begins like lion. Let's look at out Consonant Chart. What letter makes the /l/ sound as in *lion*?

SANDRA: *l.*

TEACHER: Good, Sandra. *L* makes the /l/ sound that you hear at the beginning of *lost.* I'll add the letters that make the /os/ sounds (teacher adds *os*). What sound do you hear at the end of *losttt*? (getting no response) Whose name ends like *lost*? Does *Nat* end like *lost*?

NAT: Yes, it does.

TEACHER: Nat, will you add a *t* to *los*?

The teacher has a volunteer read what has been written so far. The class continues working on the story.

▨ USING CHILDREN'S BOOKS

Read alphabet and alliterative books to students and encourage them to read some of the simpler ones on their own. An excellent series of books for reinforcing initial consonant correspondences is Ray's Readers (Outside the Box Publishing Company). Each 8-page booklet provides practice with a single correspondence. *The Hungry Goat,* for instance, provides practice with *g* = /g/ by telling a story about a goofy goat that gobbles up gold, gifts, gowns, games, and gum. The books are available in both big book and regular formats. Listed below are a number of other alphabet and alliterative books.

Berenstain, S., & Berenstain, J. (1971). *The Berenstains' b book.* New York: Random House. Big brown bear, a blue bull, and a beautiful baboon undertake activities that begin with *b*.

Brown, R. (1994). *What rhymes with snake?* New York: Tambourine. Uses lift-the-flap to foster consonant substitution. For instance, lifting the picture of a hen, the reader finds a picture of a hen. Lifting the *h* from the word *hen,* the reader uncovers the word *pen.*

Dr. Seuss. (1973). *Dr. Seuss's ABC.* New York: Random House. Each letter is accompanied by a humorous alliterative story.

Dr. Seuss. (1979). *Oh say can you say.* New York: Random House. Presents a series of humorous tongue-twisters.

Eastman, P. D. (1974). *The alphabet book.* New York: Random House. Each letter is accompanied by alliterative phrases.

Elting, M., & Folsom, M. (1980). *Q is for duck.* Boston: Houghton Mifflin. Readers are invited to guess why *A is for Zoo, B is for Dog* (Animals live in the zoo, Dogs bark, etc.)

Hofbauer, M. P. (1993). *All the letters.* Bridgeport, CT: Green Bark Press. Letters of the alphabet are depicted with objects and labels, such as Dd: dinosaur, duck, dog.

Le Tord, B. (1981). *An alphabet of sounds.* New York: Scholastic. Each letter of the alphabet is illustrated with sounds spelled with that letter: B = buzz.

Modesitt, J. (1990). *The story of Z.* Saxonville, MA: Picture Book Studios. Z leaves the alphabet, so people must say things such as "ip your ipper."

Pallotta, J. (1987). *The bird alphabet book.* Watertown, MA: Charlesbridge. Each letter of the alphabet is represented by a bird. A brief description of the bird is provided.

Phillips, T. (1989). *Day care ABC.* Niles, IL: Whitman. The alphabet is presented through alliterative sentences telling about day-care experiences.

Potter, B. (1987). *Peter Rabbit's ABC.* Middlesex, England: Frederick Warne. Old-fashioned illustrations accompany a letter of the alphabet and a word that begins with that letter: *b* is for *butter.*

■ TECHNOLOGY

Use software, such as Dr. Peet's Talk/Writer (Edmark) or Write Out Loud (Don Johnston) that helps students discover letter–sound relationships. These word processing programs will say words that have been typed in. Simon Sounds It Out (Don Johnston), an award-winning piece of software, pronounces and helps students build words by combining initial consonants (onsets) and word patterns (rimes). Featuring an electronic tutor, it provides especially effective practice for Word Building. Because it pronounces and shows parts of words, it also helps develop phonemic awareness. A demo disk is available. Tenth Planet (Sunburst) includes sorting activities and the writing of songs and verses.

■ FUNCTIONAL READING

Encourage students to read labels, signs, and other real-world materials. Point out both visual and graphic clues that they might use. Food labels and other possible functional reading items are listed for most correspondences in the next section.

■ HOLISTIC APPLICATION

Whenever possible, present letter–sound relationships and other understandings about reading in a holistic, functional context. Along with alphabet books, use enlarged text to convey initial consonant correspondences and general concepts of print. As noted earlier, enlarged text may take the form of commercially produced big books, big books that you create yourself, poems or songs written on the chalkboard, or experience stories written on large sheets of paper or on the chalkboard. Because the text is enlarged, the class can follow along as you read a selection. As you share-read the text the first time, concentrate on having the students understand and enjoy it. During a second reading of the text, highlight a target initial consonant. For instance, note all the words that begin with *s*. Discuss the fact that the words begin with the same sound and the same letter. During subsequent readings, pause before the *s* words and invite students to read them. Give help as needed. If this task is too difficult for students—if they can't read the words—call attention to the *s* words as you read them.

Most important of all, surround students with reading materials and the tools of literacy. Set up reading and writing corners and listening centers. Place easy-to-read signs on the wall. Set the scene for engaging in a variety of literacy tasks.

RESOURCES FOR TEACHING CONSONANT CORRESPONDENCES

In this section, words that might be used to present consonant correspondences are listed. For the most part, these are words that can be illustrated. Drawings have been created for most of these words and can be found at the end of this chapter. Also listed are food labels and other possible functional reading items. Presented, too, are rhymes and songs that might be used to reinforce the target correspondence. At this point, the students' reading vocabulary is probably very limited, so share-read the rhymes with students. The correspondences are listed in the order in which they might be taught, but feel free to adapt the sequence to meet the specific needs of your class.

s = /s/ CORRESPONDENCE

See sample lesson.

m = /m/ CORRESPONDENCE

Correspondence words that can be illustrated: man, moon, mop, map, mouse
Rhyme:

The Three Little Kittens
Eliza Lee Follen

Three little kittens lost their mittens;
And they began to cry,
"Oh mother dear,
We very much fear
That we have lost our mittens."

"Lost your mittens!
You naughty kittens!
Then you shall have no pie!"
"Mee-ow, mee-ow, mee-ow."
"No, you shall have no pie."

Functional reading: milk, mustard, mayonnaise, muffins, macaroni

Sorting: Have students sort picture cards beginning with /m/ or /s/. Cards should be placed under the *m* or the *s* so that students make the association between the initial sound of the name of the card and the letter that spells that sound. Illustrations for cards can be found at the end of this chapter.

Writing: Review or introduce the formation of capital and lowercase *m*. Students might draw a picture of some things that they see that begin with *m*. Review the "I see _____" pattern that was previously introduced, and model the process of drawing pictures of things that begin with /m/ and writing an "I see _____" caption for them. Also introduce *a* so that students can write sentences such as "I see a man." Review the *s* page in the class alphabet book and add an *m* page.

■ *f* = /f/ CORRESPONDENCE

Correspondence words that can be illustrated: fish, four, five, fox

Rhyme:

> **Fuzzy Wuzzy**
>
> Fuzzy Wuzzy was a bear.
> Fuzzy Wuzzy had no hair.
> Fuzzy Wuzzy wasn't fuzzy,
> Was he?

Functional reading: frozen fish

Sorting: Have students sort picture cards beginning with /s/, /f/, or /m/.

Writing: Review or introduce the formation of capital and lowercase *f*. Review the *m* and *s* pages in the class alphabet book and add an *f* page. As a group, write an experience or interactive story about things that are fun.

■ *h* = /h/ CORRESPONDENCE

Correspondence words that can be illustrated: hat, ham, hand, hook, horn, horse, house

Rhyme:

> **Hickup, Hickup**
>
> Hickup, hickup, go away!
> Come again another day.
> Hickup, hickup, when I bake,
> I'll give to you a butter-cake.

Functional reading: canned ham

Sorting: Have students sort picture cards beginning with /h/, /f/, or /m/.

Writing: Review or introduce the formation of capital and lowercase *h*. Review the *f* and *m* pages in the class alphabet book and add an *h* page. As part of an interactive writing project, have students write about some things that they have.

■ *b* = /b/ CORRESPONDENCE

Correspondence words that can be illustrated: book, bell, bee, boat, bat, ball

Rhyme:

> **Baa, Baa, Black Sheep**
>
> Baa, baa, black sheep,
> Have you any wool?
> Yes, sir, yes, sir,
> Three bags full.
>
> One for the master,
> One for the dame,
> But none for the little boy
> Who cries in the lane.

Functional reading: baked beans, butter, bacon, beets, biscuits

Sorting: Have students sort picture cards that begin with /b/, /h/, or /m/.

Writing: Review or introduce the formation of capital and lowercase *b*. Students might draw a picture of some things that they see that begin with /b/.

Review the "I see _____" pattern and model the process of drawing pictures of something that begins with /b/ and writing an "I see _____" caption for it. Review the *h* and *f* pages in the class alphabet book and add a *b* page.

l = /l/ CORRESPONDENCE

Correspondence words that can be illustrated: lion, lamp, lock, lettuce, leopard, ladder

Rhyme:

Three Little Bugs

Three little bugs in a basket,
Hardly room for two.
One like Lee, one like Linda,
And one that looks like you.

Functional reading: lemonade, lima beans

Reading: Have students read the *I See a Lion* fold-and-read book which can be found in Appendix B. Review the phrase "I see," and model how you would use the initial consonant and illustration to read the last word in each pattern sentence.

Sorting: Have students sort picture cards beginning with /h/, /b/, or /l/.

Writing: Review or introduce the formation of capital and lowercase *l.* Review the *h* and *b* pages in the class alphabet book and add an *l* page. Introduce the word *like* and have students draw pictures or write about some things that they like.

n = /n/ CORRESPONDENCE

Correspondence words that can be illustrated: nine, nail, net, nickel, necklace

Rhyme:

It Ain't Going to Rain No More

It ain't going to rain no more, no more,
It ain't going to rain no more;
How in the heck can I wash my neck
If it ain't going to rain no more?

Functional reading: box of nails, box of noodles

Sorting: Have students sort picture cards beginning with /n/, /l/, or /b/.

Writing: Review formation of capital and lowercase *n.*

c = /k/ CORRESPONDENCE

Correspondence words that can be illustrated: can, cat, cup, car, comb

Functional reading: corn, carrots, cat food, cocoa, cake mix

Sorting: Have students sort picture cards beginning with /l/, *c* = /k/, or /n/.

Writing: Review or introduce the formation of capital and lowercase *n.* Review the *l* and *c* = /k/ pages in the class alphabet book and add an *n* page. Show students how to form the word *can.* First form the word *an.* Say the word *an,* stretching out the sounds as you do so. Have students tell what sounds they hear and then tell what letters spell those sounds. After *an* has been formed, have volunteers read it. Then have students tell what letter would need to be added to *an* to make the word *can.* After *can* has been formed, have volunteers read it. Also have a volunteer add *I* to form the phrase "I can." Have volunteers read the phrase. Then compose sentences telling about something that you can do. Use words that begin with correspondences that have already been introduced, so that students can tell what sound and what letter these words begin with as you write them on the board. Discuss with students some things that they can do. Write the words interactively and add them to the Word Wall. Invite students to create "I can" books in which they tell about some things that they can do.

r = /r/ CORRESPONDENCE

Correspondence words that can be illustrated: fish, four, five, fox

Rhyme:

Rain, Rain, Go Away

Rain, rain, go away,
Come again another day;
Little Robert wants to play.

Functional reading: raisins, raisin bran, rice

Sorting: Have students sort picture cards beginning with /r/, c = /k/, or /n/.

Writing: Review or introduce the formation of capital and lowercase *r*. Review c = /k/ and *n* pages in the alphabet book and add an *r* page.

g = /g/ CORRESPONDENCE

Correspondence words that can be illustrated: gum, goat, gorilla, girl, gate

Rhyme:

A-Hunting We Will Go

A-hunting we will go,
A-hunting we will go.
We'll catch a fox
And put him in a box.
And then we'll let him go.

Functional reading: gum

Sorting: Have students sort picture cards beginning with /g/, /r/, or c = /k/.

Writing: Review or introduce the formation of capital and lowercase *g*. Review *r* and c = /k/ pages in alphabet book and add a *g* = /g/ page.

t = /t/ CORRESPONDENCE

Correspondence words that can be illustrated: ten, tire, toe, tiger, table, tent, teeth

Functional reading: tea, toothpaste, tomatoes, tomato juice

Rhyme:

Little Tommy Tucker

Little Tommy Tucker
Sings for his supper.
What shall we give him?
White bread and butter.
How shall he cut it
Without a knife?

Sorting: Have students sort picture cards beginning with /t/, /g/, or /r/.

Writing: Review or introduce the formation of capital and lowercase *t*. Review the *g* and *r* pages in the class alphabet book and add a *t* page.

▨ *d* = /d/ CORRESPONDENCE

Correspondence words that can be illustrated: dog, desk, dish, deer, door, duck

Rhyme:

> **My Son John**
>
> Deedle, deedle, dumpling, my son John,
> Went to bed with his stockings on;
> One shoe off, and one shoe on,
> Deedle, deedle, dumpling, my son John.

Sorting: Have students sort picture cards beginning with /d/, /t/, or /g/.

Reading: Have students read the *I See a Turtle* fold-and-read book, which can be found in Appendix B. Review the phrase "I see," and model how you would use the initial consonant and illustration to read the last word in each pattern sentence.

Writing: Review or introduce the formation of capital and lowercase *d*. Review the *h* and *t* pages in the class alphabet book and add a *d* page. In interactive style, create booklets in which drawings of animals are accompanied by captions that tell what the animal is: For instance, drawing of a deer can be accompanied by the caption, "I am a deer."

Functional reading: donuts, hot dogs

▨ *j* = /j/ CORRESPONDENCE

Correspondence words that can be illustrated: jar, jeep, jet, jeans

Rhyme:

> **Jack, Be Nimble**
>
> Jack, be nimble
> Jack, be quick,
> Jack, jump over the candlestick.
>
> Jump it lively,
> Jump it quick,
> But don't knock over
> The candlestick.

Functional reading: jam, jelly, tomato juice

Sorting: Have students sort picture cards beginning with /j/, /t/, or /d/.

Writing: Review or introduce the formation of capital and lowercase *j*. Review the *t* and *d* pages in the class alphabet book and add a *j* page.

▨ *p* = /p/ CORRESPONDENCE

Correspondence words that can be illustrated: pen, pie, pencil, pillow, piano, purse

Rhyme:

> **Pease Porridge**
>
> Pease porridge hot,
> Pease porridge cold,
> Pease porridge in the pot,
> Nine days old.

Functional reading: can of peas, can of pears

Sorting: Have students sort picture cards beginning with /p/, /j/, or /d/.

Writing: Review or introduce the formation of capital and lowercase *p.* Review the *j* and *d* pages in the class alphabet book and add a *p* page.

▪ *w* = /w/ CORRESPONDENCE

Correspondence words that can be illustrated: wagon, window, wig, well, web, wallet

Rhyme:

Fuzzy Wuzzy

Fuzzy Wuzzy was a bear.
Fuzzy Wuzzy had no hair.
Fuzzy Wuzzy wasn't fuzzy,
Was he?

Functional reading: Replicas of Walk and Don't Walk signs, wax beans

Sorting: Have students sort picture cards beginning with /w/, /p/, or /j/.

Writing: Review or introduce the formation of capital and lowercase *w.* Review the *p* and *j* pages of the class alphabet book and add a *w* page.

▪ *k* = /k/ CORRESPONDENCE

Correspondence words that can be illustrated: key, king, kite, kangaroo

Rhyme:

Polly, Put the Kettle on

Polly, put the kettle on,
Polly, put the kettle on,
Polly, put the kettle on,
And let's drink tea.

Functional reading: ketchup

Sorting: Have students sort picture cards beginning with /k/, /w/, or /p/.

Writing: Review or introduce the formation of capital and lowercase *k.* Review the *w* and *p* pages of the class alphabet book and add a *k* page. Show students how the word *like* is formed. Have them draw pictures and write stories about things they like to do.

▪ *y* = /y/ CORRESPONDENCE

Correspondence words that can be illustrated: Yo-Yo, yarn, yogurt, yawn

Clouds
Christina Rossetti

White sheep, white sheep,
On a blue hill,
When the wind stops
You all stand still.
When the wind blows
You walk away slow.
White sheep, white sheep,
Where do you go?

Functional reading: yogurt

Sorting: Have students sort picture cards beginning with /w/, /k/, or /y/.

Reading: Review the phrase "I like _____" and introduce the fold-and-read book *I like kangaroos,* which can be found in Appendix B.

Writing: Review or introduce the formation of capital and lowercase *y.* Review the *w* and *k* pages in the class alphabet book and add a *y* page.

▨ *c* = /s/ CORRESPONDENCE

Correspondence words that can be illustrated: circle, cent, city

Functional reading: apple cider

Sorting: Have students sort picture cards beginning with /y/, /k/, or *c* = /s/.

Writing: Review or introduce the formation of capital and lowercase *c* = /s/. Review the *y* and *k* pages in the class alphabet book and add a *c* = /s/ page.

Note: When presenting *c* = /s/, teach the variability principle. Tell students that *c* can stand for the sound /k/ as in *can* or the sound /s/ as in *cent.* Tell them to try the /k/ pronunciation first; if that doesn't work, try the /s/ pronunciation.

▨ *g* = /j/ CORRESPONDENCE

Correspondence words that can be illustrated: giraffe, giant, gym

Functional reading: ginger ale, ginger snaps

Sorting: Have students sort picture cards beginning with /y/, *c* = /s/, or *g* = /j/.

Writing: Review or introduce the formation of capital and lowercase *g* = /j/. Review the *y* and *c* = /s/ pages in the class alphabet book and add a *g* = /j/ page.

Note: When presenting *g* = /j/, teach the variability principle. Tell students that *g* can stand for the sound /g/ as in *girl* or the sound /j/ as in *giraffe.* Tell them to try the /g/ pronunciation first; if that doesn't work, try the /j/ pronunciation.

▨ *v* = /v/ CORRESPONDENCE

Correspondence words that can be illustrated: vase, van, violin, vest, vet

Functional reading: vegetables, vanilla ice cream

Sorting: Have students sort picture cards beginning with /v/, *c* = /s/, or *g* = /j/.

Writing: Review or introduce the formation of capital and lowercase *v.* Review the *g* = /j/ and *c* = /s/ pages in the class alphabet book and add a *v* page.

▨ *z* = /z/ CORRESPONDENCE

Correspondence words that can be illustrated: zebra, zoo, zipper

Rhyme:

The Zigzag Boy and Girl
I know a little zigzag boy
Who goes this way and that.
He never knows just where he put
His coat, or shoes, or hat.

I know a little zigzag girl
Who flutters here and there.
She never knows just where to find
Her brush to fix her hair.

If you are not a zigzag child
You'll have no cause to say,
That you forgot, for you will know
Where things are put away.

Functional reading: zucchini

Sorting: Have students sort picture cards beginning with g = /j/, /v/, or /z/.

Writing: Review or introduce the formation of capital and lowercase z. Review the g = /j/ and v pages in the class alphabet book and add a z page. In interactive style, create booklets in which students draw pictures of zoo animals and write captions telling what each animal is and where it is: "I am a tiger. I am in the zoo."

qu = /kw/ CORRESPONDENCE

Correspondence words that can be illustrated: queen

Rhyme:

Five Little Ducks

Five little ducks went out one day,
Over the hills and far away.
One little duck went,
Quack, quack, quack.
Four little ducks came swimming back.

Four little ducks went out one day,
Over the hills and far away.
One little duck went,
"Quack, quack, quack."
Three little ducks came swimming back.

Three little ducks went out one day,
Over the hills and far away.
One little duck went,
"Quack, quack, quack."
Two little ducks came swimming back.

Two little ducks went out one day,
Over the hills and far away.
One little duck went,
"Quack, quack, quack."
One little duck came swimming back.

x = /z/, *x* = /ks/ CORRESPONDENCES

Correspondence words that can be illustrated: xylophone, x-ray, box

The letter x rarely appears as an initial consonant, but it should be introduced for the sake of completeness.

CONSONANT DIGRAPHS

Consonant digraphs (*di* = "two," *graphs* = "letter") are correspondences in which single consonant sounds are represented by two letters, such as *ch* in *church* and *sh* in *ship*. Because they represent just one sound, digraphs are taught in the same way as single consonant–letter correspondences are. However, because digraphs are spelled with two letters, students find them somewhat more difficult to learn.

▨ *sh* = /sh/ CORRESPONDENCE

Correspondence words: sheep, shirt, shell, shark, shovel

Rhyme:

I'm a Little Teapot

I'm a little teapot, short and stout:
Here is my handle and here is my spout.
When I get all steamed up, I just shout:
"Just tip me over and pour me out!"

Functional reading: shaving cream, shrimp

Reading: Rohman, C. (1996). *Sherman shoots.* Thousand Oaks, CA: Outside the Box. Sherman shoots pictures with his camera. One of Ray's Readers.

Sorting: Have students sort picture cards beginning with *qu* = /kw/, /s/, or /sh/.

Writing: Review or introduce the formation of capital and lowercase *sh*. Review the *qu* = /kw/ and *z* pages in the class alphabet book and add an *sh* = /sh/ page.

▨ *ch* = /ch/ CORRESPONDENCE

Correspondence words: chair, cheese, chain, chipmunk, church

Rhyme:

Let's Be Merry
Christina Rossetti

Mother shake the cherry-tree,
    Susan catch a cherry;
Oh how funny that will be,
    Let's be merry!

One for brother, one for sister,
    Two for mother more,
Six for father, hot and tired,
    Knocking at the door.

Functional reading: cheese, Cheerios, chocolate chip cookies

Reading: Rohman, C. (1996). *Charles.* Thousand Oaks, CA: Outside the Box. Portrays Charles at school. One of Ray's Readers.

Sorting: Have students sort cards beginning with /ch/, /sh/, or *c* = /s/.

Writing: Review capital and lowercase *ch*. Review the *qu* = /k/ and *sh* = /sh/ pages in the class alphabet book and add a *ch* = /ch/ page.

▨ *th* = /th/ CORRESPONDENCE

Correspondence words: thumb, thermos, thirteen, thorn

Reading: Rohman, C. (1996). *Theodore.* Thousand Oaks, CA: Outside the Box. Portrays Theodore the rabbit. One of Ray's Readers.

Sorting: Have students sort picture cards beginning with /ch/, /sh/, or /th/.

Writing: Review or introduce the formation of capital and lowercase *th*. Review the *sh* = /sh/ and *ch* = /ch/ pages in the class alphabet book and add a *th* = /th/ page.

▨ *wh* = /hw/ CORRESPONDENCE

Correspondence words: whale, wheel, whistle, whip

Rhyme:

Whistle, Daughter

Whistle, daughter, whistle; whistle, daughter dear.
I cannot whistle, mommy; I cannot whistle clear.
Whistle, daughter, whistle; whistle for a pound.
I cannot whistle, mommy; I cannot make a sound.

Sorting: Have students sort picture cards beginning with /sh/, /th/, or /wh/.

Writing: Review or introduce the formation of capital and lowercase *wh*. Review the *sh* = /sh/ and *th* = /th/ pages in the class alphabet book and add a *wh* = /wh/ page.

Note: When presenting *ch* = /ch/, *sh* = /sh/, *th* = /th/, and *wh* = /hw/ stress that the two letters make just one sound.

▨ ADVANCED CONSONANT DIGRAPHS

▨ *kn* = /n/

Correspondence words: knee, know, knot, knock

Rhyme:

The Zigzag Boy and Girl

I know a little zigzag boy
Who goes this way and that.
He never knows just where he put
His coat, or shoes or hat.

I know a little zigzag girl
Who flutters here and there.
She never knows just where to find
Her brush to fix her hair.

If you are not a zigzag child
You'll have no cause to say,
That you forgot, for you will know
Where things are put away.

▨ *ph* = /f/

Correspondence words: phone, phonics, photograph

▨ *wr* = /r/

Correspondence words: wrap, wring, wrist, write, wrong, wrote

■ CONSONANT CLUSTERS

Although consonants, consonant clusters, and vowel patterns are presented separately, their introduction should be integrated. Clusters, which are sometimes known as blends, are combinations of consonants, as in *spot* or *straw*. Clusters represent two (/s/ + /t/) or more (/s/ + /t/ + /r/) sounds clustered or blended together. They are difficult for novice readers and spellers and should be taught directly and systematically. When teaching clusters, build on the knowledge of initial consonants that students already possess. If possible, show how words with clusters build on known words. For instance, when presenting *stop*, show how it is related to *top*. When presenting *stay*, show how it is related to *say*. When presenting *stand*, show how it can be related to *sand*. Teach the simplest *s* clusters first. They occur with high frequency and are easier to discriminate than *l* or *r* clusters. A listing of major consonant clusters appears in Table 4.2.

■ CONSONANT CLUSTER TEACHING LESSON

Step 1: Building Clusters by Adding an Initial Consonant.   Write the following words on the chalkboard: *nail, nap*. Have a volunteer read *nail*. Ask students to tell what letter needs to be added to *nail* to make *snail*. After *snail* has been formed, have students read it. Have students read *nap* and tell what letter needs to be added to *nap* to make the word *snap*. After *snap* has been formed, have students read it. Then have students read both *snap* and *snail*.

Step 2: Building Clusters by Adding a Second Consonant.   Write *sack* and *sake* on the board. Have a volunteer read *sack*. Ask students to tell what letter needs to be added to the *s* in *sack* to make *snack*. After *snack* has been formed, have a volunteer read *sake* (as in "for safety's sake"). Ask students to tell what letter needs to be added to *s* to make the word *snake*. After *snake* has been formed, have students read it. Then have students read both *snack* and *snake*.

Step 3: Letter–Sound Integration.   Have students read all four *sn* words: *snail*, *snap, snack,* and *snake*. Lead them to see that some words begin with two consonant sounds and that these are known as clusters. Explain that *sn* spells the cluster that appears in *snake* (*snake* is the model word for the cluster *sn*). Post the model word *snake* on a Cluster Chart. Point out *snake* in the Cluster Chart. Remind students to use the chart if they forget the sound that *sn* stands for.

TABLE 4.2   Consonant Clusters

L clusters

bl (**bl**anket), *cl* (**cl**oud), *fl* (**fl**ower), *gl* (**gl**ass), *pl* (**pl**ane), *sl* (**sl**ed)

R clusters

br (**br**ead), *cr* (**cr**ab), *dr* (**dr**um), *fr* (**fr**og), *gr* (**gr**apes), *pr* (**pr**etzel), *tr* (**tr**ee)

S clusters

sc (**sc**arecrow), *sch* (**sch**ool), *scr* (**scr**eam), *shr* (**shr**ink), *sk* (**sk**unk), *sl* (**sl**ed), *sm* (**sm**ile), *sn* (**sn**ake), *sp* (**sp**oon), *spl* (**spl**ash), *spr* (**spr**ing), *st* (**st**ar), *str* (**str**ing), *squ* (**squ**irrel), *sw* (**sw**ing)

Other clusters

tw (**tw**elve), *qu* (**qu**een)

Step 4: Guided Practice.   Share read a rhyme, song, or other short piece that contains *sn* words.

Step 5: Application.   Have students read stories and real-world materials that contain *sn* words. They might read *Hooray for Snail* (Stadler, 1985), for instance. Students might also write stories that contain *sn* words. Select additional practice and application exercises from the reinforcement activities listed below.

■ REINFORCEMENT ACTIVITIES

1. To help students distinguish between single consonants and clusters, have them sort stacks of word or picture cards containing single consonants or clusters. For instance, have students sort *s* and *st* words. Because students might have difficulty discriminating between the sound of /s/ and the sound of /st/, begin with picture sorts so the students can focus on sounds. Students might sort the following picture cards: sun, saw, sandwich, socks, six, seal, stapler, stamp, star, stick, stop sign, and store (see illustrations of words beginning with consonants and clusters at the end of this chapter). Pointing to a stack of cards containing objects whose names begin with /s/ or /st/, tell students, "We're going to sort these picture cards. If the name of the picture begins with /s/ as in *sun,* we're going to put it in the sun column. If the name of the picture begins with /st/ as in *star,* we'll put it in the star column. Holding up a picture of a stick, ask, "What is this? What sound does it begin with? What column should we put it in?" Affirm or correct students' responses. "Yes, *stick* begins with the sound /st/ that we hear in the beginning of *stick,* so we put it in the *star* column." Go through the rest of the cards in this fashion. Once all the cards have been categorized, have volunteers say the names of all the cards in a column and note that they all begin with /s/ or /st/. Encourage students to suggest other words that might fit into the columns. Also have them re-sort the pictures on their own to promote speed of response. You might then have them sort /s/ and /sp/ pictures and words and then /s/, /sp/, and /st/ pictures and words.

2. Use real-world materials to reinforce clusters. When introducing *sp,* for example, have students read food labels for spaghetti and spinach and such brand names as Spam and Spic and Span.

3. Have students create words by adding newly learned clusters to previously presented word patterns. After being introduced to *st,* for instance, students might add it to short-vowel patterns that they have been taught: *-and, -ill, -ick,* and *-ing.*

4. To further emphasize the difference between words beginning with a single consonant and those beginning with a cluster, have students spell words containing these elements. For words beginning with *s* or *st,* they might spell the words *sick, stick, sing, sting, sand, stand, sore, store, sad, stop, sack, stack.* To make the task easier, you might set up two columns, one for *s* words and one for *st* words.

5. Secret word, secret message, and other word games described in the next chapter can also be used to provide practice with clusters.

■ BOOKS THAT REINFORCE CLUSTERS

The best reinforcement is for students to meet clusters in their reading. Clusters occur naturally in most books, so it is simply a matter of looking over the texts and deciding which clusters you wish to emphasize. However, the following books have a high proportion of clusters or present clusters in such a way as to lend themselves to instruction or reinforcement.

Axworthy, A. (1993). *Along came Toto.* Cambridge, MA: Candlewick Press. Reinforces several major clusters.

Ehlert, L. (1990). *Fish eyes, A book you can count on.* New York: Harcourt. Reinforces several major clusters.

Emberley, Ed. (1992). *Go away, Big Green Monster.* Boston: Little, Brown. Reinforces *s* clusters.

Janovitz, M. (1994). *Look out, bird!* New York: North-South. Reinforces a variety of clusters.

Kline, S. (1985). *Don't touch.* Niles, IL: Whitman. Reinforces *fl* cluster.

McMillan, B. (1984). *Kitten can.* New York: Lothrop, Lee & Shepard. Reinforces several clusters.

Miller, J. (1988). *Farm noises.* New York: Simon & Schuster. Reinforces a variety of clusters.

Milstein, L. (1995). *Coconut mon.* New York: Tambourine. Coconut man sells his goods by calling out that his coconuts are "crrr-unchy," "crrr-isp," thus emphasizing sounds of clusters.

O'Brien, J. (1995). *Sam and Spot, A silly story.* Boca Raton, FL: Cool Kids. Good alliterative read-aloud that emphasizes *s* clusters.

Rohman, C. (1996). *Grumpy Grizzly.* Live Oaks, CA: Outside the Box. Grumpy Grizzly growls at grapes and grass and other items beginning with *gr.* Reinforces *gr* cluster.

Rohman, C. (1996). *Stories.* Live Oaks, CA: Outside the Box. Reinforces *st* cluster.

Rohman, C. (1996). *Tricksters.* Live Oaks, CA: Outside the Box. Reinforces *tr* cluster.

Serfozo, M. (1993). *Joe Joe.* New York: Macmillan. Reinforces a variety of clusters.

RESOURCES FOR TEACHING CONSONANT CLUSTERS

In this section, words that might be used to present consonant clusters are presented. Also listed are food labels and other possible functional reading items. Listed, too, are rhymes and songs that might be used to reinforce the target cluster. Clusters should not be introduced until after most single consonants, digraphs, and a number of short-vowel patterns have been taught. The cluster correspondences are listed in the order in which they might be presented, but feel free to adapt the sequence to meet the specific needs of your class. For instance, if students are about to read a story about how sneakers are made, then introduce the *sn* cluster.

st = /st/ CORRESPONDENCE

Cluster words: star, stand, stay, step, stick, still, stone, stop, stood, store, story

Rhyme:

The Little Bird

Once I saw a little bird
    Come hop, hop, hop;
So I cried, "Little bird,
    Will you stop, stop, stop?"

I was going to the window
    To say, "How do you do?"
But he shook his little tail,
    And far away he flew.

Functional reading: stop sign

str = /str/ CORRESPONDENCE

Cluster words: street, string, strange, stream, straw, strike

Rhyme:

> **Sing, Sing**
>
> Sing, sing,
> > What shall I sing?
> The cat's run away
> > With the pudding string!
>
> Do, do,
> > What shall I do?
> The cat's run away with the pudding, too.

Functional reading: strawberry ice cream label, street sign

sp = /sp/ CORRESPONDENCE

Cluster words: space, speak, speed, spell, spend, spider, spin, spoke, spoon, spot, sports

Rhyme:

> **I'm a Little Teapot**
>
> I'm a little teapot, short and stout:
> Here is my handle and here is my spout.
> When I get all steamed up, I just shout:
> "Just tip me over and pour me out!"

Functional reading: spinach, spaghetti

spl = /spl/ CORRESPONDENCE

Cluster words: splash, split

sn = /sn/ CORRESPONDENCE

Cluster words: snail, snack, snake, snap, sneakers, sneeze, snip, snow

Rhyme:

> **The Little Turtle**
> *Vachel Lindsay*
>
> There was a little turtle.
> He lived in a box.
> He swam in a puddle.
> He climbed on the rocks.
>
> He snapped at a mosquito.
> He snapped at a flea.
> He snapped at a minnow.
> And he snapped at me.
>
> He caught the mosquito.
> He caught the flea.
> He caught the minnow.
> But he didn't catch me.

▨ *br* = /br/ CORRESPONDENCE

Cluster words: brush, bread, break, brick, bright, bridge, bring, brother

Rhyme:

The Mocking Bird

Hush, little baby, don't say a word,
Papa's going to buy you a mocking bird.
If the mocking bird won't sing,
Papa's going to buy you a diamond ring.

If the diamond ring turns to brass,
Papa's going to buy you a looking-glass.

If the looking-glass gets broke,
Papa's going to buy you a billy goat.

If that billy goat runs away,
Papa's going to buy you another today.

Functional reading: bread, brown rice

▨ *gr* = /gr/ CORRESPONDENCE

Cluster words: grapes, grass, gray, great, green, ground, group, grow

Rhyme:

Go and Tell Aunt Nancy

Go and tell Aunt Nancy,
Go and tell Aunt Nancy,
Go and tell Aunt Nancy,
    The old gray goose is dead.

The one that she was saving,
The one that she was saving,
The one that she was saving,
    To make a feather bed.

She died on Friday,
She died on Friday,
She died on Friday,
    Behind the old barn shed.

She left nine little goslings,
She left nine little goslings,
She left nine little goslings,
    To scratch for their own bread.

Functional reading: green beans, grape juice, grapefruit

▨ *tr* = /tr/ CORRESPONDENCE

Cluster words: trap, train, tree, truck, trunk

Rhyme:

Twinkle, Twinkle, Little Bat!
Lewis Carroll

Twinkle, twinkle, little bat!
How I wonder what you're at!
Up above the world you fly,
Like a tea-tray in the sky.
Twinkle, twinkle—

▨ *bl* = /bl/ CORRESPONDENCE

Cluster words: black, blame, blank, blind, blood, blow, blue

Functional reading: blueberry muffins box

▨ *cl* = /kl/ CORRESPONDENCE

Cluster words: class, clam, clay, clap, claw, click, climb, clock, close, cloth, clothes, cloud, clown

Rhyme:

> **The Mulberry Bush**
>
> Here we go round the mulberry bush,
>   the mulberry bush,
>   the mulberry bush,
> Here we go round the mulberry bush,
> On a cold and frosty morning.
>
> This is the way we clap our hands,
>   clap our hands,
>   clap our hands,
> This is the way we clap our hands,
> On a cold and frosty morning.

Functional reading: clam label

▨ *fl* = /fl/ CORRESPONDENCE

Cluster words: flag, flame, flap, flock, flat, flea, flour, flower, float, floor, flew, fly

Functional reading: corn flakes, flour

▨ *pl* = /pl/ CORRESPONDENCE

Cluster words: plate, place, plan, plane, plant, play, please, plug, plus

Rhyme:

> **The Little Plant**
> *Kate L. Brown*
>
> In the heart of a seed
>   Buried deep, so deep,
> A dear little plant
>   Lay fast asleep.
>
> "Wake!" said the sunshine
>   "And creep to the light,"
> "Wake!" said the voice
>   Of the raindrops bright.
>
> The little plant heard,
>   And it rose to see
> What the wonderful
>   Outside world might be.

Functional reading: plums

▨ *sl* = /sl/ CORRESPONDENCE

Cluster words: slap, slid, slide, sled, sleep, sleeve, slip, slipper, slow

▨ *sw* = /sw/ CORRESPONDENCE

Cluster words: swam, swan, swamp, swim, sweater, swing, switch, sweep

Rhyme:

Swim, Swan, Swim

Swan swam over the sea,
   Swim, swan, swim!
Swan swam back again,
   Well swum, swan!

Functional reading: sweet corn, sweet peas

▨ *sm* = /sm/ CORRESPONDENCE

Cluster words: small, smart, smash, smile, smell, smoke, smooth

▨ sk = /sk CORRESPONDENCE

Cluster words: skate, ski, skin, skirt, skunk, sky

▨ *fr* = /fr/ CORRESPONDENCE

Cluster words: free, fresh, Friday, friend, frog, front, from, frozen, fruit, fry

Rhyme:

Swing, Swing
William Allingham

   Swing, swing,
   Sing, sing,
Here! my throne and I am a king!
   Swing, sing,
   Swing, sing,
Farewell, earth, for I'm on the wing.

   Low, high,
   Here I fly,
Like a bird through sunny sky;
   Free, free,
   Over the lea,
Over the mountain, over the sea!

   Soon, soon,
   Afternoon,
Over the sunset, over the moon;
   Far, far,
   Over all bar,
Sweeping on from star to star!

   No, no,
   Low, low.
Sweeping daisies with my toe.
   Slow, slow,
   To and fro,
Slow—
      slow—
         slow—
            slow.

Functional reading: French fries, fruit cup, Friday

▓ *pr* = /pr/ **CORRESPONDENCE**

Cluster words: pray, pretty, price, prince, print, prize, problem, probably, promise

Functional reading: pretzels, prunes

▓ *cr* = /cr/ **CORRESPONDENCE**

Cluster words: crab, crack, crash, crawl, crayon, cream, crocodile, crow, crowd, crown, cry

Rhyme:

> **If You Should Meet a Crocodile**
>
> If you should meet a crocodile,
> Don't take a stick and poke him;
> Ignore the welcome in his smile,
> Be careful not to stroke him.
> For as he sleeps upon the Nile,
> He thinner gets and thinner;
> And whenever you meet a crocodile,
> He's ready for his dinner.

Functional reading: crackers, cranberry sauce, cream

▓ *gl* = /gl/ **CORRESPONDENCE**

Cluster words: glass, glad, glance, globe, glove, glow, glue

Functional reading: glue

▓ *dr* = /dr/ **CORRESPONDENCE**

Cluster words: dragon, draw, drum, dream, dress, drink, drip, drive, dry

Functional reading: French dressing

▓ *sc* = /sk/, *sch* = /sk/ **CORRESPONDENCES**

Cluster words: scale, scar, scare, scarecrow, scoop, score, scout; school

Rhyme:

> **Mary's Lamb**
> *Sara Josepha Hale*
>
> Mary had a little lamb,
> Its fleece was white as snow,
> And everywhere that Mary went
> The lamb was sure to go.
> It followed her to school one day—
> That was against the rule;
> It made the children laugh and play
> To see a lamb at school.

▓ *scr* = /skr/ **CORRESPONDENCE**

Cluster words: scrap, scrape, scratch, scream, scribble, scrub

Rhyme:

> **Ice Cream Rhyme**
>
> I scream, you scream,
> We all scream for ice cream.

■ *squ* = /skw/ CORRESPONDENCE

Cluster words: square, squirrel, squeak, squeeze, squawk

Rhyme:

Mr. Nobody

Tis he who always tears our books,
    Who leaves the door ajar,
He pulls the buttons from our shirts,
    And scatters pins afar.
That squeaking door will always squeak,
    For don't you see,
We leave the oiling to be done
    By Mr. Nobody.

The fingermarks upon the door
    By none of us are made,
We never leave the blinds unclosed,
    To let the curtains fade.
The ink we never spill; the boots
    That lying round you see
Are not our boots—they all belong
    To Mr. Nobody.

Functional reading: squash

■ *tw* = /tw/ CORRESPONDENCE

Cluster words: twelve, twice, twin, twenty, twig, twist, twinkle

Functional reading: Twinkies

Rhyme:

Twinkle, Twinkle, Little Star

Twinkle, twinkle, little star,
How I wonder what you are!
Up above the world so high,
Like a diamond in the sky.

Beginning Consonant Illustrations

Beginning Consonant Illustrations

Beginning Consonant Illustrations

Beginning Consonant Illustrations

Beginning Consonant Illustrations

Beginning Consonant Illustrations

Beginning Consonant Illustrations

Beginning Consonant Illustrations

Beginning Consonant and Consonant Digraph Illustrations

Consonant Digraph Illustrations

Consonant Cluster Illustrations

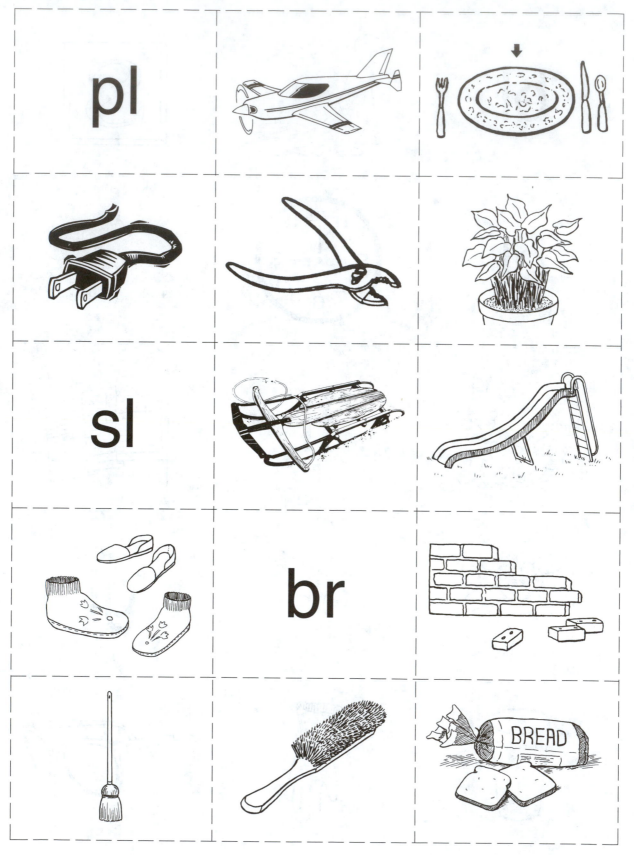

pl

sl

br

Consonant Cluster Illustrations

Consonant Cluster Illustrations

Consonant Cluster Illustrations

sc sch

sk

sm

sn

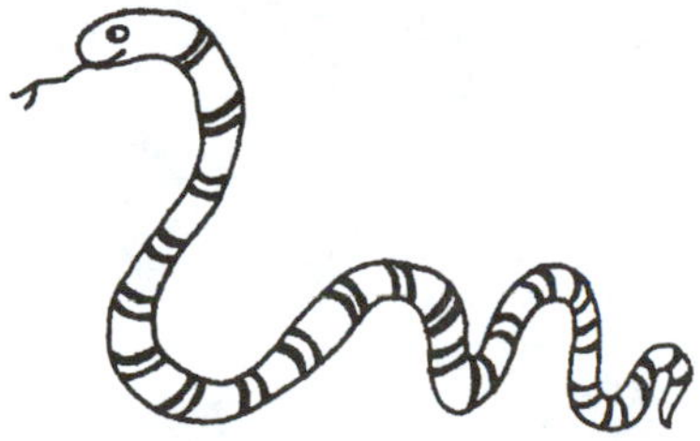

Consonant Cluster Illustrations

sp spr

squ

st str

Consonant Cluster Illustrations

sw

tw

12   20

Consonant Cluster Illustrations

■ Chapter 5

TEACHING VOWEL PATTERNS

As noted earlier, the approach recommended by this text combines elements of analytic, synthetic, and pattern methods. Known as Word Building, this approach starts with the easiest-to-learn, most readily perceived element in a pattern and involves students in building whole words. Thus, provided with an *o,* students build the words *no, so,* and *go.* Provided with *at,* they build the words *cat, rat, sat,* and *hat.* Rimes or patterns are generally easier to learn than individual sounds. The program also presents multisyllabic patterns. A scope and sequence was presented in Table 4.1. This scope and sequence is flexible and should be adapted to suit your situation.

By showing how phonic elements are used to construct words, students get a more concrete understanding of the alphabetic spelling system. They are then shown how to use this knowledge to decode unfamiliar words independently. When faced with a word that is unfamiliar, students use the strategy of seeking a pronounceable word part and then using that pronounceable word part as the basis for reconstructing the word. A student who is unable to pronounce the printed word *plant* might use the pronounceable word part *an* to reconstruct the word, saying "an," "ant," "plant" or the student might use the rime *ant* as the pronounceable word part and say "ant, plant." If the pronounceable word-part strategy does not work, the student might then try an analogy strategy. Unable to find a pronounceable word part in the unknown word *blank,* the student might compare it to the known word *thank* and work out the pronunciation through analogy. The overall sense of the selection and the immediate context in which the unfamiliar word appears are woven into the pronounceable word-part and analogy strategies. Students check to make sure the word they have constructed is a real one and fits the sense of the selection in which it appears. Context, including picture clues, is also used when neither the pronounceable word-part nor the analogy strategy works.

The patterns can be presented to students of any age: young novice readers, older disabled readers, or even adults learning to read English. However, many of the activities is this guide are geared for younger students. There are few mature materials written on a beginning reading level. Because of the scarcity of appropriate materials, you might want to use a language experience approach with older students, as explained in Chapter 3.

Sample lessons are presented below but should be adapted to fit the needs of your students and your personal approach to teaching basic phonics skills. The lesson assumes that students can name most of the letters of the alphabet and know at least ten initial consonant correspondences.

■ SHORT-VOWEL PATTERN LESSON

Procedures for introducing patterns that end in a consonant are slightly different from those that end in a vowel. The vowel and the consonant that comes after it are presented as a unit. Vowels that appear alone or at the end of a word or syllable (*no, no-tice*) are generally long. However, those that are followed by a consonant are usually short (*bat, bat-ter*). Therefore, students should get used to associating vowel–consonant or consonant–vowel–consonant patterns with short vowels.

Step 1: Phonemic Awareness and Building the Rime.   Read a selection, such as *Green Eggs and Ham* (Dr. Seuss, 1988) or a rhyme in which there are a number of *-am* words. Call the students' attention to the pattern words in the selection: *ham, am, Sam.* Stressing the rhyming element as you say each word, ask students to tell what is the same about the words. Lead students to see that they all have an /am/ sound as in *ham.* Ask the students to listen carefully so they can tell how many sounds the word *am* has. Articulate it slowly, stretching out the sounds as you do so: *aaamm.* Tell the students to say the word *am* and stretch out the sounds as they do so. Discuss how many sounds the word *am* has. Then tell students that you are going to spell the word *am.* Ask students to tell what letter should be used to spell the sound /a/ in *am.* Write *a,* commenting as you do so that it makes an /a/ sound. Have students tell what sound they hear at the end of *am.* Ask them what letter is needed to spell /m/. Add *m,* saying /m/ as you do so. Explain that now you have the word *am.* Run your hand under each letter as you say its sound. Have several students read *am.*

Step 2: Adding the Onset.   Explain to students that you can use *am* to make other words. (Write a second *am* under the first one.) Ask students: What do I need to add to *am* to make the word *hhhham?* As you add *h* to *am,* carefully enunciate the *h* and the *am* and then the whole word. Have several students read the word. Then have students read *am* and *ham.* Then write *am* underneath *ham.* Ask the students: What do I need to add to *am* to make the name *SSSSam?* As you add *S* to *am,* carefully enunciate the *S* and the *am* and then the whole word. Have several students read the word. Then have students read *am, ham,* and *Sam.* Form *Pam* and *jam* in this same way and have all the *am* words read. Lead students to see what is the same about the words—that they all end in *am.* Ask the students if they know of any other words that rhyme with *ham.* If so, write these on the board and discuss them.

Step 3: Adding the Rime.   To make sure that students have a thorough grasp of both key parts of the word—the onset, which is the initial consonant or cluster, and the rime, which is the vowel and an ending consonant or cluster—present the onset or initial consonant and have students supply the rime or vowel–consonant element. Writing *h* on the board, have students tell what sound it stands for. Then ask them to tell what you should add to /h/ to make the word *ham.* After adding *-am* to *h,* say the word in parts, /h/—/a/—/m/, and then as a whole. Point to *h* and say /h/, point to *a* and say /a/, point to *m* and say /m/. Running your hand under the whole word, say "hhhaaammm—ham." Form *Sam, Pam,* and *jam* in this way. After all the words have been formed, have students read them.

Step 4: Providing Mixed Practice.   Realizing that they are learning words that all end in the same way, students may focus on the initial letter and fail to take careful note of the rest of the word, the rime, when asked to read a list of pattern words. After presenting a pattern, mix in words from previously presented patterns and have these read. For instance, after presenting the *-at* pattern, present a list of mixed *-at* and *-am* words: *hat, ham, sat, Sam, jam, cat, Pam, pat.* Besides being a good review, this trains students to use all the word's letters in their decoding processes. Otherwise, students might say the first word in a series of pattern words and then just use the initial consonant to say the rest. If students fail to use all the letters when reading on their own, they may misread *Pam* for *Pat, ham* for *hat,* etc. Reading mixed patterns fosters accurate reading.

Step 5: Introducing the Model Word.   Choose one of the pattern words to be a model word. Select a word that has a high frequency, is easy, and—if possible—can be depicted. For the *-am* pattern, you might choose *ham,* which is easily illustrated. Create a model words chart for your class. An illustrated chart of model words for short-vowel patterns is presented in Figure 5.1.

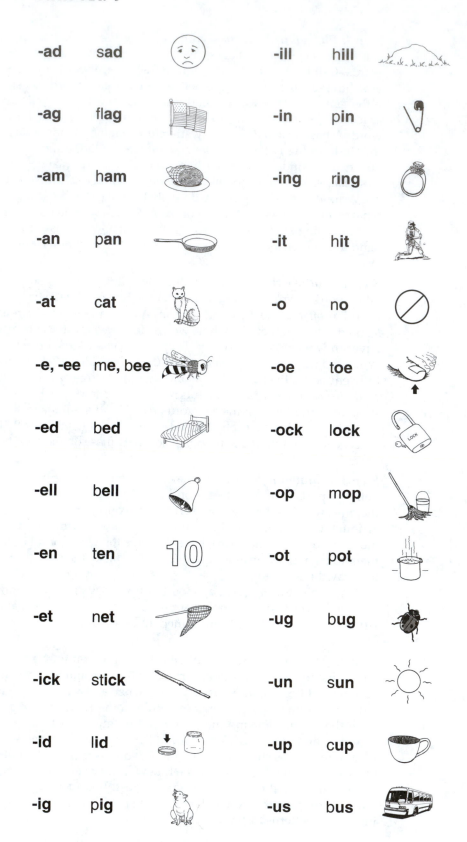

-ad	sad		-ill	hill	
-ag	flag		-in	pin	
-am	ham		-ing	ring	
-an	pan		-it	hit	
-at	cat		-o	no	
-e, -ee	me, bee		-oe	toe	
-ed	bed		-ock	lock	
-ell	bell		-op	mop	
-en	ten		-ot	pot	
-et	net		-ug	bug	
-ick	stick		-un	sun	
-id	lid		-up	cup	
-ig	pig		-us	bus	

FIGURE 5.1   Model Words

From *Word Building A, with Predictable Stories,* by T. Gunning, 1997. New York: Phoenix Learning
Resources. Reprinted by permission of Galvin Publications.

After a pattern has been introduced, add its model word to the chart. If students forget the pattern, they can refer to the model words chart. Point out the model word *ham* and explain that it has a picture that shows the word. Tell students that if they forget how to say the model word, the picture will help them. If students encounter difficulty with -*am* words, help them to look for a part of the word they can say (*am*) and, if that doesn't work, to use the model word *ham* as an analogy word to help them decipher the unknown word. Also encourage the use of context.

Step 6: Guided Practice. As a group activity, have students suggest sentences containing -*am* words. Write the sentences on the board and have students read them. Give help as necessary. Share-read a book, rhyme, or song that contains a number of -*am* words. Also use functional reading materials to provide practice with the pattern. Holding up a jar of jam, ask the class to tell which word on the jar says *jam*. Do the same with a ham label.

You can also compose a brief experience story using *am*. Say to your students: "I can use *am* to write something about myself. I can write, I am Mr. Thomas. I am a teacher. I am a man." (As you write each word, stretch out the word's sounds.)

Sorting activities also provide excellent reinforcement. After being introduced to the -*am* pattern, students might be asked to sort a group of words composed of -*am* words and other known words into two piles: those that rhyme with *ham* and those that don't. Later, after being introduced to several short-*a* patterns, they might sort words according to whether they fall into the -*at*, -*an*, or -*am* pattern. Sorting helps students to note differences in patterns and to generate their own conclusions about how the patterns are spelled. A sample sort is shown in Figure 5.2. After students have been introduced to several patterns, try a spelling sort. In a spelling sort, the students write in the appropriate column words dictated by the teacher. Columns can be created by folding a piece of paper lengthwise into three equal parts. A heading is created for each column. It might be -*am*, -*an*, and -*at*. The teacher then dictates words containing these elements and students write them in the appropriate column. After each word is dictated, the teacher checks to see that the word has been put in the correct column. A sample spelling sort is presented in Figure 5.3.

Step 7: Application. Many phonics programs are heavy on instruction and practice and light on application, with countless hours being spent on workbook pages. Actually, what students need most is the opportunity to apply skills to real

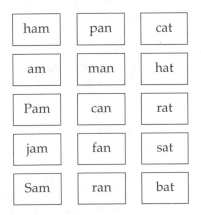

FIGURE 5.2 Word Pattern Sort

-am	-an	-at
am	pan	cat
ham	man	sat
jam	can	at
	ran	that

FIGURE 5.3   Spelling Sort

reading. Have students apply their knowledge of the *-am* pattern by reading selections that contain *am* words. If possible share-read *Green Eggs and Ham* with students. Also have them read the "I am a _____" fold-and-read book in Appendix B. Show students how to fold their booklets and then conduct a text-walk. In a text-walk, you go through a book page by page and help students with any words, phrases, or concepts that might be difficult for them. In preparation for reading the "I am a tiger booklet," make sure that students can identify all the animals. Also show students how to use their knowledge of the *-am* pattern and the illustrations and initial consonants to read the booklet. For instance, for the sentence, "I am a fox," ask students to look at the picture and tell what word beginning with /f/ would make sense. Some students might think that the picture shows a wolf or a dog. Help them to see that the word couldn't be *dog* or *wolf* because it begins with an *f*. Also, lead them to see that *lamb* contains the familiar word part *am* and can be used to help them read the word.

Step 8: Spelling: am, jam.   Learning to spell new pattern words is excellent reinforcement. For the most part, pattern words have been chosen that students will most likely use in their writing. In this lesson, only two pattern words are used. In other lessons, up to five words will be chosen for the spelling lesson. To introduce the spelling lesson, explain to students that they will be learning how to spell words that use the pattern just presented. To introduce the words, give a pretest. Dictate the words and have students attempt to spell them. Say each word, use the word in a sentence, and then say each word: "am. I am a teacher. am. jam. I like jam on my toast. jam." Have students say the word, enunciating it carefully before writing it. This will help them focus on the word's sounds. After the pretest, write the correct spellings on the board, and have students check their attempts, making any corrections necessary. They should focus their studying on words that were difficult for them.

Step 9: Writing.   Students compose an illustrated "I am" piece, telling about themselves. They might write a piece similar to the following: "I am Sam. I am a boy. I am 7." Encourage the use of invented spelling. However, students are expected to spell pattern words correctly.

■ ADDITIONAL REINFORCEMENT ACTIVITIES

Little Books.   An inexpensive way to obtain easy-to-read books is to create your own little books. The simplest type of little book can be made by folding one or two sheets of 8½ by 11 paper. These books can be teacher-created or they can be composed by students, with your help. The books can simply contain words or they can be illustrated with student or teacher drawings, photos, or magazine illustrations, or, if you have access to a desktop publishing system, clip art. Little books can be helpful devices for reinforcing *-at, -am,* and *-an,* and other basic patterns. Some patterns that might make effective little books include:

The cat _____.	I play _____.
I can _____.	I help _____.
I am _____.	I saw _____.
I like _____.	Yesterday, I _____.
I see _____.	Saturday, I will _____.

You might also create caption books devoted to a topic: numbers, colors, seasons, pets, dogs, cats, birds, farm animals, cars, trucks, toys, or similar topics. Several sample caption books, which were created using a desktop publishing system, can be found in Appendix B.

Modified Concentration.   In traditional concentration, pairs of cards are shuffled and placed face down on a table or desk. The first player turns over a card and then tries to guess where its match might be. If the player turns over its match, she removes it and places the pair in front of her. The player then continues to play until she fails to make a match. Then the next player attempts to make a match. In modified concentration, the cards are composed of pairs of rhyming words. Students make a match by locating the rhyming partner of the word turned over, as shown in Figure 5.4. When a player turns over a card, she must read it. She then must find its rhyming partner and read it also. Concentration requires keeping the rime in mind as you search for its partner. It fosters focusing on the rime that the two words share (Morris, 1999). Illustrations that can be used to make short-vowel pattern cards can be found at the end of the chapter. The cards can be used for concentration, bingo, sorting, or other activities.

Modified Bingo.   Modified bingo, which is a sorting activity in a gamelike format, may be played with just three or four columns instead of five. Rather than being a letter, the heading for each column is a pattern word, as shown in Figure 5.5. (A blank bingo card that may be duplicated and used with students is presented in Figure 5.6). A row must be filled with words in the same pattern or with wild cards. Cards are placed in the center of the table and players take turns choosing cards. After selecting a card, the player reads it and looks to see if he can place it on one of the squares. After placing a card, he reads the column heading word and all the words that have been placed in the column. This provides added practice reading pattern words (Morris, 1999). Bingo cards can be created on a variety of levels. An early set might contain only short-*a* patterns. A later set might contain a short-*a,* short-*e,* short-*i,* and short-*o* patterns. A more advanced set might reinforce long-vowel or other-vowel patterns.

Additional Writing.   Have students start composing "All about Me" books in which, after the *-am* pattern has been introduced, they complete the sentence, "I am _____." After the *-an* pattern has been presented, they can tell things that they

FIGURE 5.4   Matching Cards

Word Bingo			
hat	pot	hit	pet
cat	hot	sit	wet
	not		get
	pot		
	got		

FIGURE 5.5   Sample Bingo Card

Word Bingo			

FIGURE 5.6   Sample Bingo Card

can do. Later, they can tell about their families, favorite foods, best-liked activities, and dislikes. At this stage of their development, youngsters should be encouraged to use invented spelling for words they wish to write but don't know how to spell. However, they should be held to the correct spelling of words that have been introduced to them. If students are reluctant to attempt invented spelling, tell them to write as best they can. Show them examples of invented spellings. As an alternative, you might have students dictate their stories to you or another adult, who could write the stories down and help the students read them.

■ LONG-VOWEL PATTERN LESSON

When teaching long vowels that come at the end of the word, the presentation is simpler because many of the words have just two sounds, and the vowel says its own name.

Step 1: Auditory Perception.   Read a selection, such as *Feed Me* (Hooks, 1992) or *Put Me in the Zoo* (Lopshire, 1960) in which there are a number of long-*e* words. Call students' attention to long-*e* words from the book: *me, see, we, he.* Stressing the vowel sound as you say each word, ask students to tell what is the same about the words: *meee, seee, weee,* and *heee.* Lead students to see that they all have an /ē/ sound as in *bee.*

Step 2: Adding the Onset (Consonant).   Write the letter *e* on the board and ask for a volunteer to identify it. Explain to students that the letter *e* says its own name: /ē/. Tell students that you want to form some words. Ask them to tell what letter needs to be placed in front of *e* to make the word *me.* If no one is able to respond correctly, tell the class that the letter *m,* when put in front of *e,* spells *me.* Have volunteers read the word. Directly under the word *me,* write another *e.* Have students tell what sound *e* makes and what letter should be placed in front of *e* to make the word *he.* Have students read *he* and tell how *he* is different from *me* and then read both words. Introduce *we* and *she* in the same way. Then have students read all the words.

Step 3: Adding the Rime (Vowel Pattern).   To make sure that students have a thorough grasp of both key parts of the word—the onset, which is the initial consonant, and the rime, which is the vowel pattern or phonogram—present the consonants and have students add the vowels. Writing *m* on the chalkboard, have students say the sound it stands for. Then ask them to tell you what to add to *m* to make *me.* After adding *e* to *m,* say the word sound by sound and then as a whole. Pointing to *m,* say /m/; pointing to *e,* say /ē/. Running your hand under the whole word, say *me* (saying consonant sounds in isolation distorts them, but it helps youngsters, especially those who are having difficulty detecting individual sounds in words, make the necessary connections between letters and sounds). Present *he, we,* and *she* in the same way and then have students read all the words.

Normally only one pattern is presented at a time, but because the -*ee* pattern is so similar to the -*e* pattern, introduce it and have the words *see* and *bee* formed. Write *ee* on the board and ask students to tell what sound *ee* makes. Then ask students to tell you what letter to add to *ee* to make the word *see.* Form the word *bee* in the same way. Then, writing *s* on the chalkboard, have students say the sound it stands for. Ask students to tell you what to add to *s* to make *see.* After adding *ee* to *s,* say the word sound by sound and then as a whole. Write *b* on the board and have the word *bee* formed in the same way. Explain to students that if it has two *e*'s, the word *bee* is the name of the bee that flies, stings, and makes honey.

Step 4: Providing Mixed Practice.   Realizing that they are learning words that all end in the same way, students may focus on the initial letter and fail to take careful note of the rest of the word, the rime. After presenting a pattern, mix in words from previously presented patterns and have these read. For instance, if students have already learned the *-o* pattern, you might have them read the following words: *bee, no, he, go, we, see, so.* Besides being a good review, this trains students to use all the word's letters in their decoding processes. Otherwise, students may say the first word in a series of pattern words and then just use the initial consonant to say the rest. If students fail to use all the letters when reading on their own, they may misread words. This procedure provides students practice in processing both the onset and the rime and also reviews previously presented patterns.

Step 5: Introducing the Model Word.   A model word is an easy, high-frequency word used to provide an example of a particular pattern. In most instances, model words can be illustrated, so if a student forgets how to say a model word he can use the drawing of it as a memory aid. Since the model word is often the easiest word in the pattern, it can be used as an analogy or basis of comparison when a student encounters a pattern word that he doesn't recognize. The student works out the pronunciation of the unknown word by comparing it to the model word. Sample model words for easy long-vowel and short-vowel patterns are presented in Figure 5.1. (Note that there is no drawing for the *-e* pattern because there is no *-e* pattern word that can be depicted unambiguously. However, students might use the drawing of the bee to help them remember the pronunciation of both *bee* and *me,* which is the model word for the *-e* pattern.) Add the pattern to your model words chart.

When students encounter difficulty with *-e* words, encourage them to look for parts of the word that they can pronounce and use those parts to reconstruct the word. If that doesn't work, refer them to the chart and help them figure out the unknown word by comparing it with the model word *me.* Also encourage the use of context.

Step 6: Guided Practice.   As a group, have students compose orally a sentence containing the new words. Write these on the chalkboard. Read the sentence to students, but pause before the new words and have students read them. Have students copy each of the words onto a 3" by 5" card, mix these up, and reassemble them into a sentence. In addition to building word recognition, this activity also fosters awareness of sentence elements and builds sentence comprehension. Explain the activity to students and discuss steps they might take to put the words in the right order: read all the words in the sentence, look for the word that is capitalized because that will be the first word, and change the order of the words until the sentence makes sense. If students find some of the words in the sentence troublesome, encourage them to use pronounceable word parts, analogies, and contextual strategies to help them read words that pose problems. Students might also engage in a sorting activity or share-read a rhyme, song, or riddle. It will also be helpful if patterns are reinforced during spelling, social studies, science, music, or art activities.

Step 7: Application.   Although the suggested activities provide students with varied practice with the *-e* pattern, it is essential that they apply this knowledge. This may take the form of writing original stories, dictating group or individual experience stories, and, most important, reading appropriate children's books such as the ones listed below. To apply a correspondence just taught, choose a selection that contains a number of words that fit the target pattern. Walk students through the selection. Discuss the title and illustrations, clarify unfamiliar concepts, point out and read to them difficult words (they should follow along with you in their books). Place particular emphasis on words that follow the pattern you just introduced. Note a sentence or caption that contains a pattern word and ask them to find the pattern word and point it out to you. If the sentence or caption is not too difficult, have them read it as well. Some good application books are:

Carle, E. (1983). *Have you seen my cat?* New York: Scholastic.
Martin, B. (1983). *Brown bear, brown bear, what do you see?* New York: Holt.

Step 8: Spelling (Optional).   Explain to students that they will be learning how to spell words that use the patterns just leaned. To introduce the words, give a pretest. Dictate the words and have students attempt to spell them. Say each word, use the word in a sentence, and then say each word: "He. I think he is ten years old. He." Have students say a word, enunciating it carefully, before writing it. This will help them focus on the word's sounds. After the pretest, write the correct spellings on the board, and have students check their attempts, making any corrections necessary. They should focus their studying on words that were difficult for them. For the *-e, -ee* patterns, present the words *he, me, we, she, see,* and any other words that you feel are important for students to learn. Emphasize words that students are most likely to need in their writing.

Step 9: Writing.   Students write about three things that they like to do in their free time.

USING A SOUND-BY-SOUND APPROACH

Building words by adding onsets to rimes is an efficient, effective approach to teaching phonics. However, at the earliest stages of learning to read, some students may have difficulty dealing with combinations of sounds. For this reason, Word Building presents rimes as units (*at, eep*) and as individual elements (*a-t, ee-p*). However, some students may still have difficulty with rimes. For these students, modify the approach by placing greater emphasis on the individual sounds in words. Later, as they begin to see patterns in words, place more emphasis on rimes.

IMPLEMENTING STRATEGIES

The implementation of strategies is the heart of Word Building. It should pervade all reinforcement and application activities, for this step shows students how to use newly learned patterns to decode words. In this step students are shown how to use two key decoding strategies: pronounceable word parts and analogy. To show students how to use the pronounceable word part strategy, write a series of pattern words on the board that were not presented in the lesson. For instance, after presenting the *-e, -ee* patterns, you might write the following on the board: *Lee, seem.* Urge students to find the letters that make the /ē/ sound. Then help them use this pronounceable part to reconstruct the whole word. Explain to students that whenever they come across a word that they can't read, they should look to see if there are any parts of the word they can pronounce. Then tell them that if that doesn't work—if they can't find a part that they can say—they should see if the word is like *bee* or another model word that they know. Also discuss the use of picture and context clues.

As students encounter difficult words, use a "pause, prompt, praise" approach (Tunmer & Chapman, 1999). At first, say nothing and, if this is during a group activity, do not allow other students to chime in. Give the student the opportunity to work out the word on his own. If the student is not able to decode the word, provide a prompt. Unless the word has an irregular spelling or contains elements that have not been taught, provide a pronounceable word part prompt. Ask: "Is there any part of that word that you can say?" If the student does not respond, provide additional assistance. For instance, if a student who has been taught the -*ee* pattern has difficulty with a word such as *seem* and is unable to note any known parts in the word, you might cover up all but the middle *ee* and have her say what sound *ee* makes. Uncovering the *s*, have her pronounce *see* and then, uncovering the final *m*, lead her to pronounce *seem*. If the child is unable to pronounce the *ee* in *seem*, use an analogy strategy. Using the model word *bee*, have her compare *seem* with *bee* (cover the *m* in *seem* if necessary, so that she can read *see* and then *seem*).

Some students may be slow detecting patterns in words, such as the -*an* in *man* or the -*in* in *pin*. For these students the pronounceable word part might be the initial consonant, or they may need to say each sound of the word individually. If this is the case, encourage them to do so. In time, perhaps as they approach the word pattern stage, they should be able to detect patterns in words.

If the student is unable to use a pronounceable word part or analogy strategy or if the word does not lend itself to a sounding-out strategy, prompt the use of context. Urge the student to skip the word and read to the end of the sentence. Ask: "What word would make sense here?" Even when a sounding-out strategy is used, context should be used as a cross-check. After a student has used the pronounceable word part or analogy strategy, prompt to see if the word is a real word and fits the sense of the sentence.

If the student is unable to decode the word, even with the help of prompts, use a starter prompt. A starter prompt supplies the word but does so in the form of a question, so that the student has some input and is asked to think about what the word might be. For instance, if the difficult word is *stand*, you might ask: "Does it look like *stand*?" or "Would *stand* fit here?"

The main goal of reading instruction is for students to read for meaning. After they have decoded a word, students should make sure that it is a real word. They might ask themselves, "Is this a real word? Does it sound right?" They should also make sure that the word they have decoded fits the context. They might ask themselves, "Does this fit? Does this make sense?" In fact, whenever students read, they should be monitoring to make sure that what they are reading makes sense. If students read a passage and the passage doesn't make sense because of a misreading error and they don't notice it, prompt them to check their reading. Ask: "Does that make sense? Does that sound right?"

Ultimately, you want students to be able to select appropriate strategies to use when encountering difficult words. As they grow in their ability to analyze words, occasionally have them decide which strategy they might use to decode an unfamiliar word. Ask: "What might you do to figure that word out?" In addition to nudging them toward independence in the application of strategies, the prompt supplies you with useful information about the student's use of decoding strategies.

After a student has applied a strategy, praise the student's efforts. The praise should be very specific: "I like the way you used that pronounceable word part to figure that word out." Or "I like the way you reread the sentence when you noticed that it didn't make sense." Affirming the students' efforts rewards them and also highlights the use of the particular strategy that they applied. Students may have applied a strategy without realizing its value. Affirming it strengthens their knowledge of the strategy and the likelihood that they will use it in the future.

After students have successfully decoded a difficult word on their own, ask them how they figured out that hard word. Make a note of their response. Their response can shed light on their use of word analysis strategies. As part of your ongoing assessment of students' use of strategies, observe students as they grapple with difficult words. If possible, administer the Student Decoding Interview, which is presented in Table 5.1.

TABLE 5.1   Student Decoding Interview

Name _____   Date _____

Grade _____   Age _____

1. What is the hardest thing for you to do in reading?

2. What do you do when you come to a hard word?

3. What makes it hard to figure out words?

4. If someone asked you how to figure out a hard word, what would you tell that person?

5. How do you try to figure out hard words?

Observations while student is reading:

As student is figuring out a hard word, make notes of his attempts.

After student has figured out a hard word, ask: How did you figure out that word?

Make a note of students' attempts to decode a difficult word. Are they using context or sounding-out strategies? Are they analyzing the word sound by sound, or by chunks? A listing of strategies and prompts is presented in Table 5.2.

Give students as much guidance as they need, but gradually lead them to the point where they can decode independently. Listed below are steps that students might take when confronting a word that is unfamiliar in print.

◼ STEPS FOR FIGURING OUT HARD WORDS

1. See if there is any part of the word that I can say. (If I can't say any part of the word, go to step 4.)
2. Say the part of the word I know. Then say the rest of the word. (If I can't say the rest of the word, go to step 4.)
3. Ask: "Is the word I said a real word? Does it make sense in the story?" (If not, try again or go to step 4.)

TABLE 5.2   Word Analysis Prompts

Strategy	When Used	Prompt
Pronounceable word part	Unknown word contains a part student can say: *am* or *amp* in *champ*	Can you say any part of that word?
Analogy	Unknown word is like a word student knows: unknown word *grain* is like known word *rain.*	Is this word like any word that you know?
Sound by sound	Student is unable to chunk word. Works out word sound by sound: /s/-/p/-/e/-/l/: spell.	Can you say the first sound, the next sound, the next sound?
Context	Student is unable to use phonics clues, but the text provides usable context clues.	What would make sense here? Read to the end of the sentence and see what word would fit.
Monitoring	Student checks to see if the word pronounced is a real word and fits the context of the selection (actually, students should monitor for meaning whenever they read)	Is that a real word? Does that make sense? Does that sound right?
Affirmation	Teacher wishes to reinforce the student's correct use of a strategy	I like the way you used a part of the word that you knew to help you say the whole word.
Assessment	Teacher wants to see what strategies the student is using	How did you figure out that word?
Starter	Student is unable to use any of the strategies to decode an unknown word	Could the word be _____?

4. Is the word like any word I know? Is it like one of the model words? (If not, go to step 6.)
5. Say the word. Is it a real word? Does it make sense in the story? (If not, try again, or go to step 6.)
6. Say "blank" for the word. Read to the end of the sentence. Ask myself: "What word would make sense here?"

At times, your guidance may need to be more highly directive. For instance, if a student who has been taught the *-at* pattern has difficulty with a word such as *drat* and is unable to identify any known parts in the word, you might cover up all but the *at* and have her say what sound *at* makes. Uncovering the *r*, have her pronounce *rat*, and then, uncovering the *d*, lead her to pronounce *drat*. If the child is unable to pronounce the *at* in *drat*, you might use an analogy strategy. Using the model word *cat*, have her compare *drat* with *cat* (cover the *d* in *drat* if necessary so that she can read *rat* and then *drat*).

Some students may be slow detecting patterns in words, such as the *at* in *cat* or the *et* in *pet*. For these students the pronounceable word part might be the initial consonant, or they may need to say each sound of the word individually. If this is the case, encourage them to do so. In time, perhaps as they approach the word pattern stage, they should be able to detect patterns in words. Give students as much guidance as they need, but lead them gradually to the point where they can decode independently.

HIGH-PAYOFF REINFORCEMENT ACTIVITIES

There are dozens of ways to reinforce patterns. Some of the most highly effective are described in the following.

MAKE-AND-BREAK TECHNIQUE FOR INTRODUCING OR REVIEWING PATTERNS

A technique known as make-and-break is an excellent on-the-spot device for reinforcing Word Building (Iverson & Tunmer, 1993). Selecting a word such as *man*, the teacher forms it with magnetic or cut-up letters, says the word, and requests that the student say it. The teacher then scrambles the letters and asks the student to recreate the word and say it. Once the student is able to do this without hesitation, the teacher forms other words using the rime. Substituting *v* for *m*, the teacher says that the word is now *van*. The student says the word. The letter *v* is removed, and the teacher explains that the word now says *an*. The student is asked to make the word *van* and read it. This process is repeated with *pan* and *tan*. Make-and-break works especially well when students need an on-the-spot review of a pattern or fail to note all the sounds or letters in words.

WORD WALL

One way to emphasize essential or troublesome printed words is to post them on the wall. There they are readily reviewed. They also serve as a handy reference for students who are trying to decode or spell them. Newly learned pattern words can be posted on the wall, as can high-frequency words such as *what, one,* and *is.* Words should be arranged in alphabetical order so they can be located readily. Pattern words should be arranged by the first letter in the rime rather than the initial consonant. Thus, all -*ag* words appear together and before all -*at* words. Because their vowel spellings may be irregular, high-frequency words should be placed in order by initial letter. To keep the two systems straight, put them on different walls. To help students further differentiate among words, you might use a variety of colors. Short-vowel words might be red. Long-vowel words might be blue. Irregular high-frequency words might be yellow. You might also group some words by category—animals, colors, numbers, for example. A sample word wall is shown in Figure 5.7.

Review the wall words periodically. To review -*at* words, you might have students read all the words that rhyme with *cat.* Or students might read all the number or color words. Students might also be asked to locate opposites. Shown *cold,* they should find *hot.*

Students might also create personal word walls. These might contain words that are personally important to the students or words that the student needs in his reading or writing. A grid for a personal word wall is presented in Figure 5.8.

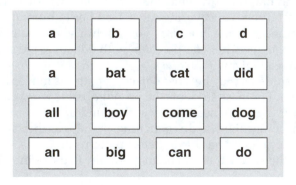

FIGURE 5.7   Word Wall

My Word Wall							
a	b	c	d	e	f	g	h
i	j	k	l	m	n	o	p
qu	r	s	t	u	v	w	xyz

FIGURE 5.8 A Personal Word Wall

■ SECRET WORD

Choose a familiar pattern word and write it down on a slip of paper, but don't tell the students what the word is (Cunningham & Allington, 1999). Select a word that will provide a review or extension of a pattern or other element. Tell students that the word is a secret and that you are going to give them a series of clues and see who can guess the word using the fewest number of clues. Ask students to number their papers 1 through 5. Give a series of five clues to the identity of the word. After each clue, students should write down their guess. Possible clues for the secret word *trunk* include:

1. The secret word is in the *-unk* pattern.
2. It has five letters.
3. It can be used to pick up things.
4. It belongs to an animal.
5. For its nose, the elephant has a long _____.

After supplying the five clues, show the secret word (*trunk*) and discuss students' responses. See who guessed the secret word first. If the word is one that appears in a story students are about to read, have them find it in the selection.

■ MAKING WORDS

"Making Words" is a group activity in which students put letters together to create words. Beginning with two-letter words and extending to five-letter or even longer words, students form as many as a dozen words (Cunningham & Cunningham, l992). The last word that the students construct contains all the letters that they were given. Here's how it works. Students are given cut-up or magnetic letters *a-s-n-t-d* and are asked to do the following:

1. Use two letters to make *an*.
2. Add a letter to make *ant*.
3. Take away a letter to make *an*.
4. Add a letter to make *tan*.
5. Change a letter to make *pan*.
6. Add a letter and change a letter to make *sand*.
7. Now break up your word and see what word you can make with all the letters (*stand*).

■ SECRET MESSAGES

Secret messages give students the opportunity to manipulate phonic elements and should be especially helpful for providing practice with onsets and rimes (Education Department of Western Australia, 1994). Secret messages are formed by adding or deleting parts of words and can be geared to virtually any decoding skill at any level of difficulty. At the easiest levels students can manipulate beginning and ending consonants. At more advanced levels they may manipulate vowels, syllables, prefixes, suffixes, and even roots. Once students become proficient at solving secret messages, they can be challenged to create their own.

Secret messages should be composed in such a way that new elements being substituted for old elements have the same sound as the old elements. For instance, taking the *r* from *raid* and substituting *p* so as to make *paid* is acceptable. But substituting *pl* for *r* in raid is not, because the *aid* in *plaid* is not pronounced in the same way as the *aid* in *paid*. Although they are a gamelike activity, secret messages should also meet specific instructional objectives. The first sample secret message is designed to reinforce the -*at* pattern. For your convenience, a secret message has been created for each phonics unit and appears in the Word Pattern Resources section.

Secret Message.   Write the words on the lines and read the secret message.

1. Take the **H** from **hats** and put **C** in its place. __ __ __ __
2. Take the **t** from **to** and put **d** in its place. __ __
3. Take the **h** from **hot** and put **n** in its place. __ __ __
4. Take the **b** from **bike** and put **l** in its place. __ __ __ __
5. Take the **b** from **bats** and put **r** in its place. __ __ __ __

_____ _____ _____ _____ _____ .

■ SORTING

As noted throughout the text, sorting is a highly effective technique and should be used regularly. In addition to actively involving students, sorting helps students discover underlying relationships among words. For instance, students may be able to read *net, set, wet,* and *let* but may not realize that these words all fit a pattern until they sort them. Vowel patterns can be sorted in a number of ways. Short vowels can be contrasted with long vowels and can also be contrasted with each other. Vowels can be sorted according to sound or according to sound and spelling. Long *a*, for instance, could be sorted according to its *ai* (*nail*), *ay* (*hay*), and *a-e* (*gate*), spellings as in Figure 5.9. If you are using a pattern approach, as is recommended in this text, vowels can be sorted according to patterns so that -*an* and -*ad* and other short-vowel patterns are contrasted with each other and with long-vowel patterns.

If students are having difficulty discriminating between the sounds of the -*at* and -*an* patterns, have them sort pictures depicting -*at* and -*an* words: *bat, hat, cat, pan, man, van, can, fan.* Using cat and man as the model pictures, have students place rhyming cards under them. Once students are adept at sound sorting, have them sort the patterns according to sound and spelling. Again, using the pictures of the cat and man as models, have students place -*at* words under the picture of the cat and -*an* words under the illustration of the pan.

Students can work individually, in pairs, or in small groups. After a sort has been completed, have students read the words in each category and note what is

FIGURE 5.9   Long-Vowel Sort

the same about the sound and spelling of the words in each category. If students are slow or hesitant, discuss any questions they might have and ask them to sort again. After students have completed a sort under your guidance, have them sort the items a second time for additional practice. If students are simply sorting the words according to their spellings and not noting the sounds of the words, try blind sorts. In a blind sort, the teacher or a student calls out a word, and the student points to the model word it would fall under. For instance, the teacher would call out "bat" and the student would point to the model word *cat*.

To make sorts more challenging, you can create an "other" or "question" category. These are for items that don't seem to fit elsewhere. Sorts can also be open. In an open sort, categories are not specified, so students create their own. Illustrations for sorting patterns can be found at the end of the chapter.

▨ CUT-UP SENTENCES

After a pattern or series of high-frequency words has been presented, create or have students compose a sentence that incorporates some of the words that have been taught. Write the word on a strip of tagboard. Have students read the sentence. Then give it to them in cut-up form and have them reassemble it. Sentences can be reassembled by students working alone or in pairs. Keep cut-up sentences in envelopes.

▨ READING RHYMES

Reading rhymes is especially good for reinforcing patterns. Because they contain rhyming lines and a distinctive rhythm, verses, poems, and songs are easy and fun to read. They lend themselves to being read over and over again. Because of their rhyme and rhythm, they also promote accuracy of reading.

▨ FLIP BOOKS

Rimes, such as *at* or *oat*, are printed on a piece of card stock. A space is left for placement of the onset. Onsets—initial consonants and clusters—are also printed on pieces of card stock. The cards are placed on rings so that the onsets fit directly in front of the rimes. Words are formed when the student moves an onset so that it lines up with the rime, as shown in Figure 5.10. By moving the onsets the students form and read a variety of words. The booklets are usually about 4 inches wide and 2 inches tall but can be larger if you plan to use them with large groups.

FIGURE 5.10   Flip Book

▇ USING WORD ANALYSIS REFERENCES

At all stages of word analysis development, students should have references that they can use to help them read and spell unfamiliar words (Pinnell & Fountas, 1998). These references may include picture dictionaries, real dictionaries (for older students), illustrated charts of model words, lists of pattern and other words, word walls, a chart listing the steps for decoding a difficult word, and a talking word processor, such as *Dr. Peet's Talk Writer* (Edmark) or *Writing Out Loud* (Don Johnston), or a talking electronic dictionary, such as those manufactured by Franklin Electronics, so that students could type in an unknown word and hear it pronounced.

▇ COMMERCIAL MATERIALS

The best way to reinforce phonics skills and strategies is to use the teaching techniques already presented, including shared reading; language experience stories and especially interactive writing; student-generated writing and spelling; the high-payoff techniques described earlier; and lots and lots of group and individual reading. Reading children's books on the appropriate level of difficulty is especially effective. Specific titles are suggested throughout this text. In addition, there are kits of books designed to foster word analysis skills. These kits can be classified as being sight-word texts or decodable texts.

▇ SIGHT-WORD TEXTS

Sight texts are also know as predictable or pattern books. They are generally brief books that are heavily illustrated. Students use predictable and repeated words and phrases and picture clues to help them read the books. One problem with some of these books is that they are so predictable and so heavily illustrated that students memorize them or simply use the pictures to "read" them. This, of course, deprives them of the opportunity to apply newly acquired skills. One way of getting around that problem is to have students cover the illustrations as they read the book a second time, or use the predictable book technique, which is discussed in Chapter 6. Some suggested series are:

Joy Readers (Dominie Press). Series of eighty minibooks that progress in difficulty from beginning first-grade level to end of first-grade level.
Literacy 2000 (Rigby). Includes hundreds of books ranging from beginning reading through grade 3.
Little Celebrations (Celebration Press). Sets of thirty-six minibooks arranged in levels from beginning reading to about third grade.
Little Red Readers (Sundance). Series of eighty 8- to 16-page minibooks that progress in difficulty from beginning first-grade level to end of first-grade level.
Reading Corners (Dominie Press). Series of thirty-eight 8- to 32-page minibooks that progress in difficulty from beginning first-grade level to second grade.
Seedling Books (Seedling). Series of sixty 8- to 16-page booklets that range from early first-grade to end of first-grade level.
Story Box (The Wright Group). Booklets range from beginning reading to about third grade.
Sunshine Series (The Wright Group). Features more than a hundred titles ranging in difficulty from beginning reading to third grade.

Word Books (Phoenix Learning Resources). Series of fifty books that range from those that include just ten different high-frequency words to those that include sixty different sight words.

Additional listings of books for beginning readers can be found in the following sources:

Fountas, I. C., and Pinnell, G. S. (1999). *Matching books to readers: Using leveled books in guided reading. K–3.* Portsmouth, NH: Heinemann.
Gunning, T. G. (1998). *Best books for beginning readers.* Boston: Allyn & Bacon.
Gunning, T. G. (2000). *Best books for building literacy for elementary school children.* Boston: Allyn & Bacon.

■ DECODABLE TEXTS

Decodable texts look much like sight-word texts. Both types are brief and heavily illustrated. However, decodable texts were written to provide practice with a specific phonic element—short-*a* or short-*e* words, for instance. As a result, depending on the skill of the author, the books may seem contrived and artificial. Some of the story words may not even be in the students' listening vocabularies, but were included simply because they incorporated the pattern being taught. Because the language of decodable texts may be somewhat artificial, these books may actually be more difficult to read. Use of artificial language also makes it more difficult to make use of context clues. However, some decodable texts are well done and can be used effectively. It is suggested that you judge each title for yourself.

A First Book (Barron's). Series of five 16-page books that provide practice with short vowels.
Let's Read Together Books (Kane Press). Series of five 32-page books that focus on short vowels.
Real Kids Readers (Millbrook Press). Series of 32-page books that use color photos of real kids.
Start to Read Book (School Zone). Series of 16-page books on three levels.

In addition to sets of trade books designed to reinforce phonics, the following sets of decodable readers are available from educational publishers:

Hello Reader! Phonics Fun (Sundance). Series of twelve books that provide practice with consonants, consonant clusters, digraphs, rimes, and short and long vowels.
Phonics Readers (Sundance). Series of fifty-one minibooks written at six different levels.
Phonics Storybooks (Hampton-Brown). Reinforces consonants, consonant clusters, vowel patterns, and endings.
Ready Readers. (Modern Curriculum Press). Series of 200 minibooks progressing from early first to third grade.

■ SOFTWARE

Because of speech capability and interactive features, phonics software has the potential to provide excellent practice. The best phonics software titles present phonics in a functional way that motivates students. Simon Sounds It Out (Don

Johnston), an award-winning program, pronounces and helps students build words by combining initial consonants (onsets) and word patterns (rimes). Featuring an electronic tutor, it provides especially effective practice for Word Building. Since it pronounces and shows parts of words, it also helps develop phonemic awareness. A demo disk is available. Tenth Planet (Sunburst) provides a variety of practice activities including sorting and composing rhymes and songs.

■ VOWEL PATTERN RESOURCES

This Vowel Pattern Resources section provides possibilities for teaching and reinforcing each of the vowel patterns. Included are some or all of the following: a listing of pattern and mixed practice words with possible model words being starred, scrambled sentences, spelling words, books, songs, sorting activities, riddles, rhymes, and real-world signs or labels that reinforce the element. A number of secret word and making word activities are also presented, along with writing topics related to the phonic element.

Patterns are presented in approximate order of difficulty and frequency. The most frequently occurring and easiest-to-learn patterns are introduced first. Short-vowel patterns are introduced first, followed by long-vowel, *r*-vowel, and other-vowel patterns. The first short-vowel pattern is *am,* because the *m* is a continuant and makes the pattern especially easy to perceive. In addition, students can use the word *am* to write brief stories about themselves. The *-at* pattern is introduced next because it also has a high frequency and *at* and *am* are easy to distinguish from each other. Once a second pattern is introduced, the two patterns are contrasted with each other through sorting and other activities. The third pattern to be introduced is *an* because it, too, has a high utility. The *-an* pattern is contrasted through sorting with *am* and *at*. Sorting is one way of reviewing previously presented patterns. Sort no more than three patterns at a time. When students encounter a fourth pattern, sort the fourth pattern with the second and third patterns.

■ SHORT-VOWEL PATTERNS

Short-a Patterns

-am *Pattern*   See sample lesson in this chapter.

> *Pattern words:* am, ham,* jam, Sam
>
> *Mixed practice:* am, an, ham, hat, Sam, sat
>
> *Scrambled sentence:* I am Sam.
>
> *Shared reading:* Dr. Seuss (1988). *Green eggs and ham.* New York: Random House.
>
> *Functional reading:* jar of jam and can of ham labels
>
> *Reading:* *I am a tiger* fold-and-read book.
>
> *Spelling:* am, jam
>
> *Writing:* Students compose an illustrated "I am" piece telling about themselves: I am Sam. I am a boy. I am 7.

-at *Pattern*

> *Pattern words:* at, bat, cat,* fat, hat, mat, pat, rat, sat
>
> *Mixed practice:* bee, bat, he, hat, me, mat, she, sat
>
> *Scrambled sentence:* I see a fat cat.

Reading:

> Cameron, A. (1994). *The cat sat on the mat.* Boston: Houghton.
>
> Carle, E. (1973). *Have you seen my cat?* New York: Scholastic.
>
> Wildsmith, B. (1986). *Cat on a mat.* New York: Oxford.
>
> *One cat sat on the mat* fold-and-read book.
>
> *Text Walk:* Discuss where cats like to sit and what might make them run. As you preview the book have students point to *mat, ran,* and *after,* which are potentially hard words.

Rhyme:

> **Jack Hall**
>
> Jack Hall,
> He is so small,
> A rat could eat him,
> Hat and all.

Sorting: bat, cat, hat, rat, sat, am, ham, jam, Pam

Spelling: cat, sat, at, that

Writing: Students draw a picture of a favorite, unusual, or interesting cat and write a caption to go along with the drawing.

-an *Pattern*

Pattern words: an, can, man, pan,* ran, van

Mixed practice: an, at, can, cat, man, mat, pan, pat

Scrambled sentence: The man has a van.

Reading: Create a pattern book that shows what the main character can do: I can run, I can jump, I can read, I can sing, What can you do?

> *I am a cat* fold-and-read book.
>
> *Text Walk:* Discuss things that students can do. As you preview the book with them, discuss how they might use word patterns, beginning letters, and pictures to help them read the story. Have them point to *run, frog, jump, fish, swim, rabbit,* and *hop,* which are potentially hard words.

Rhyme:

> **Higher than a House**
>
> Higher than a house,
> Higher than a tree,
> Oh! Whatever can that be?

Sorting: Students sort a mixed group of *-at* and *-an* pictures such as cat, hat, can, man, bat, van, rat, and later, *-at* and *-an* words.

Riddle: I am a he. I am not a she. My name rhymes with *van.* What am I? (a man)

Spelling: can, man, an, ran

Writing: Students compose an illustrated booklet telling about things they can do.

-ad *Pattern*

Pattern words: bad, dad, had, mad, sad*

Mixed practice: bad, bat, had, hat, mad, mat, sat, sad

Scrambled sentence: I had a bad cat.

Reading: Antee, N. (1984). *The good bad cat.* Grand Haven, MI: School Zone.

    Matt is sad fold-and-read book.

    Text Walk: As you preview the book, call attention to *has, with, after,* and *yells,* which are potentially hard words.

Song:

Old MacDonald

Old MacDonald had a farm, E-I-E-I-O.
And on this farm he had some sheep, E-I-E-I-O.
With a baa-baa here and a baa-baa there,
Here a baa, there a baa, eve-ry-where a baa-baa,
Old MacDonald had a farm, E-I-E-I-O.

Sorting: bad, had, mad, sad, sat, hat, cat, rat, Sam, jam, am, ham

Riddle: I have a little boy. And I have a little girl. But I am not a mom. I rhyme with *sad.* What am I? (a dad)

Spelling: had, bad, mad, sad

Writing: Students write about things that make them mad.

-ag *Pattern*

Pattern words: bag, flag,* rag, tag, wag

Mixed practice: bad, bat, rag, rat

Scrambled sentence: A happy dog wags its tail.

Sorting: bag, flag, wag, tag, bad, had, sad, dad, mad

Riddle: I can be a game or a thing that you put your name on. What am I? (tag)

Spelling: bag, flag

Writing: Students make up a flag for themselves. The flag shows two or three important things about the student. It might show what students like to do, their favorite colors, and their favorite animals or possessions.

-ap *Pattern*

Pattern words: cap, map,* nap, tap, snap, trap

Mixed practice: bad, bat, rag, rat, sat, snap

Scrambled sentence: The cat naps on my cap.

Reading: Coxe, M. (1996). *Cat traps.* New York: Random House.

Sorting: cap, map, nap, tap, trap, bag, flag, tag, wag

Making words: Distribute the letters: *a, n, p, s*

1. Use two letters to make *an.*
2. Add a letter to make *pan.*
3. Keeping the same letters, make the word *nap.*
4. Using the letters *a, p, s,* make the word *sap,* like the *sap* that flows in a tree.
5. Using all the letters, make a word. (*snap* or *pans*)

Spelling: map, snap

Writing: Students draw and label a map of their neighborhood.

-ack *Pattern*

    Pattern words: back, pack, tack,* black, snack, track

    Mixed practice: back, black, bad, pat, pack, sat, snack

    Scrambled sentence: I have a snack in my back pack.

    Sorting: back, pack, black, snack, track, cap, map, nap, tap, trap

    Rhyme riddle: What do you call a back pack that has lots of things to eat? (snack pack)

    Spelling: back, black, pack

    Writing: Students make a list of items that they carry in their back packs or might carry if they had back packs.

Short-a Unit Review.   On the chalkboard or an overhead, write the short-*a* vowel pattern words presented in this unit. Mix the patterns so students are not simply using the first word as a clue to the other words in that column. Words listed in the sorting exercise can be used for this purpose. If students are not able to read 90 percent of the words, continue to review them until they are able to do so.

    Sorting (words should be sorted by rhyming sound): Have students sort the following words: cat, sad, flag, ham, pan,* tack,* hat, mad, can, bag, back, jam, ran, wag, dad, rat, am, sat, had, tag, Sam, Pam, tan, bat, pack, bad, track, rag, van

    Secret message: Write the words on the lines and read the secret message.

      1. Take the **P** off **Pack** and put in **J.** __ __ __ __
      2. Take the **s** off **sand.** __ __ __
      3. Take the **S** off **Sam** and put in **P.** __ __ __
      4. Take the **b** off **bike** and put in **l.** __ __ __ __
      5. Take the **h** off **ham** and put in **j.** __ __ __

      _____ _____ _____ _____ _____.

Short-e Patterns

-ed *Pattern*

    Pattern words: bed,* fed, led, red, sled

    Mixed practice: bed, bad, rat, red, fed, fat

    Scrambled sentence: Ted has a red sled.

    Reading: Create a pattern book that tells what things can be red: Red, What can be red? A sled can be red. Color the sled red. A bed can be red. Color the bed red. A hat can be red. Color the hat red. A van can be red. Color the van red. A flag can be red. A flag can be red, white, and blue. Color the flag red, white, and blue.

    Shared reading: One of Norman Bridwell's Big Red Dog books.

    Rhyme:

      Bedtime

      Down with the lambs
        Up with the lark,
      Run to bed, children,
        Before it gets dark.

    Sorting: back, pack, tack, black, snack, track, bed, fed, led, red, sled

Rhyme riddle: What do you call a bright place to sleep? (red bed)

Spelling: bed, red

Writing: Students draw and label objects that are red.

-ell *Pattern*

Pattern words: bell, fell, sell, tell, well, yell, shell, smell, spell

Mixed practice: bell, bed, fat, fell, sell, sad

Scrambled sentence: The man sells bells.

Song:

The Farmer in the Dell

The farm-er in the dell,
The farm-er in the dell,
Heigh-ho the der-ry-o,
The farm-er in the dell.

The farm-er takes a wife.
The farm-er takes a wife.
Heigh-ho the der-ry-o,
The farm-er takes a wife.

Rhyme:

Out

Out goes the rat,
Out goes the cat,
Out goes the lady
With the big green hat.
Y, O, U spells you;
O, U, T spells out!

Sorting: bed, fed, led, red, sled, bell,* fell, sell, tell, well, yell, shell, smell,

Spelling: tell, well, yell

Writing: Students write about bells that they hear: school bells, doorbells, church bells, etc.

-en *Pattern*   (In some areas the *e* in *-en* has a short-*i* pronunciation, so that *ten* sounds like *tin*. Adjust your teaching to fit the dialect spoken in your area.)

Pattern words: ten, hen, men, pen, when, well

Mixed practice: hen, hat, ten, tell, men, met, pen, pet, when, wet

Scrambled sentence: Ten hens are in a pen.

Reading: Gregorich, B. (1984). *Nine men chase a hen.* Grand Haven, MI: School Zone.

Ten hens are in a pen fold-and-read book.

Text-walk: As you walk through the story with students, discuss the meaning of *pen* and have them point to the potentially hard words: *out, shut,* and *gate.*

Rhyme:

Little Blue Ben

Little Blue Ben, who lives in the glen,
Keeps a blue cat and one blue hen,
Which lays of blue eggs a score and ten;
Where shall I find the little Blue Ben?

Song:

Roll Over

Ten men in the bed, and the lit-tle one said,
"Roll o-ver! Roll o-ver!"
They all rolled o-ver
And one fell out.

Nine men in the bed, and the lit-tle one said,
"Roll o-ver! Roll o-ver!"
They all rolled o-ver
And one fell out
(Continue until there is just one left).

One man in the bed, and the lit-tle one said,
"Alone at last!"

Sorting: ten, hen, men, pen, when, bed, fed, led, red, sled, bell, fell, sell, tell, well, yell, shell, smell

Rhyme riddle: Where do hens live? (hen pen)

Spelling: ten, men, when

Writing: Students list ten things that they like to do.

-et *Pattern*

Pattern words: get, let, met, net,* pet, set, wet, yet

Mixed practice: hen, get, ten, net, men, met, pen, pet, when, wet

Scrambled sentence: Did your pet get wet?

Reading: Create a pattern book that shows what kinds of animals can be pets: *Pets,* A cat can be a pet. A dog can be a pet. A bird can be a pet. A fish can be a pet. A horse can be a pet. A pig can be a pet. A goat can be a pet. What kind of pet do you like?

Reading: Snow, P. (1984). *A pet for Pat.* Chicago: Children's Press.

A puppy can be a pet fold-and-read book.

Text-walk: Discuss what kinds of animals can be pets. As you walk through the book with students, have them point out *horse, goat,* and *pig,* which are potentially hard words.

Sorting: get, let, met, net, pet, set, wet, yet, fell, sell, tell, well, yell

Rhyme riddle: What do you call a vet who helps cats and dogs? (a pet vet)

Spelling: get, let, pet, set, wet, yet

Writing: Students write about their pets or a pet that they might like to have.

-end *Pattern*

Pattern words: end, bend, lend, send, spend

Mixed practice: bet, bend, let, lend, set, send, spend

Scrambled sentence: Do not spend the pennies.

Sorting: end, bend, lend, send, spend, ten, hen, men, pen, when

Riddle: I am part of a story. I can be happy, or I can be sad. But I am always last. What am I? (the end)

Making words: Distribute the letters: *d, e, n, p, s*

1. Use three letters to make *pen.*
2. Add a letter to make *pens.*

3. Use three letters to make the word *end*.
4. Add a letter to make the word *send*.
5. Using all the letters, make a word (*spend*).

Spelling: end, send, bend

Writing: Students write a piece telling how they might spend ten dollars.

-ent *Pattern*

Pattern words: cent, lent, sent, spent, tent,* went

Mixed practice: let, lent, send, sent, tend, tent,* when, went

Scrambled sentence: We went to our tent.

Reading: Create a pattern book that shows how money was spent: *How I spent my money*, I went to the zoo. I spent 50 cents. I went to the candy store. I spent 60 cents. I went to the ice cream store. I spent 60 cents. I spent all my money.

Rhyme:

The Bear Went over the Mountain

The bear went over the mountain,
The bear went over the mountain,
The bear went over the mountain,
To see what he could see.

Rhyme riddle: What would you call a tent that cost only a penny? (cent tent)

Sorting: cent, lent, sent, tent, went, end, bend, lend, send, spend, spent

Spelling: cent, went, sent

Writing: Students write about a place they went to that was fun or interesting.

-est *Pattern*

Pattern words: best, nest,* rest, pest, test

Mixed practice: bend, best, net, nest, pet, pest, ten, test

Scrambled sentence: Which bird makes the best nest?

Rhymes:

Turn to the East

Turn to the east,
And turn to the west,
And turn to the one that you love best.

Good, Better, Best

Good, better, best,
Never let it rest,
Till your good is better
And your better best.

Sorting: best, nest, rest, pest, test, cent, lent, sent, tent, went

Rhyme riddle: What would you call a bird's nest that is better than the rest? (best nest)

Spelling: best, nest, rest

Writing: Students compose a booklet or write a piece about the things they like best: best books, foods, games, etc.

Short-e Unit Review.   On the chalkboard or an overhead, write the short-*e* vowel pattern words presented in this unit. Mix the patterns so students are not simply using the first word as a clue to the other words in that column. Words listed in the sorting exercise can be used for this purpose. If students are not able to read 90 percent of the words, continue to review them until they are able to do so.

Sorting (words should be sorted by rhyming sound): tent, bed, ten, bell, net, get, pen, well, pet, tell, men, went, hen, cent, sled, red, wet, then, well, vet, yell, fed

Secret message: Write the words on the lines and read the secret message.

1. Take **P** from **Pets** and add **V.** __ __ __ __
2. Take **s** from **helps.** __ __ __ __
3. Take **s** from **set** and put in **p.** Then add **s.** __ __ __ __
4. Take **n** from **net** and put in **g.** __ __ __
5. Take **b** from **bell** and add **w.** __ __ __ __

_____ _____ _____ _____ _____.

Short-**i** Patterns

-it *Pattern*

Pattern words: it, bit, fit, hit,* sit, little

Mixed practice: it, at, bit, bat, hit, hat, sit, sat

Scrambled sentence: Does this mitt fit?

Reading: Create a pattern book that shows what can be little: *Little,* A kitten can be little. A puppy can be little. A bug can be little. A bird can be little. A fish can be little. Can a horse be little? Yes, a horse can be little. This horse is as little as a dog. (Miniature horses are just fifteen inches tall.)

Shared singing:

If You're Happy and You Know It

If you're hap-py and you know it,
Clap your hands.
If you're hap-py and you know it,
Clap your hands.
If you're hap-py and you know it,
And you really want to show it,
If you're hap-py and you know it,
Clap your hands.

Sorting: it, bit, fit, hit, sit, little, bet, let, met, net, pet

Riddle: If the ball is hit, I catch it. My name rhymes with *hit,* but there are two *t*'s at the end of my name. What am I? (a mitt)

Spelling: it, sit, little

Writing: Students write about places where they like to sit.

-in *Pattern*

Pattern words: in, pin,* tin, win, chin, skin, thin

Mixed practice: it, in, pin, pan, tin, ten, thin, wet, win

Scrambled sentence: Did you win that pin?

Song:

Go In and Out the Window

Go in and out the win-dow,
Go in and out the win-dow,
Go in and out the win-dow,
As we have done be-fore.

Reading: Wolcott, P. (1975). *My shadow and I*. Reading, MA: Addison-Wesley.

Sorting: in, pin, tin, win, chin, skin, thin

Rhyme riddle: What do you call a pin that is not fat? (a thin pin)

Spelling: in, win, skin

Writing: Have students make a list of fun things that they can do when they have to stay in the house.

-ill *Pattern*

Pattern words: bill, fill, hill,* will, spill, still

Mixed practice: bill, bit, fill, fit, hill, hit, set, still

Scrambled sentence: Jack and Jill went up the hill.

Rhymes:

Jack and Jill

Jack and Jill went up the hill,
To fetch a pail of water;
Jack fell down and broke his crown,
And Jill came tumbling after.

There Was an Old Woman

There was an old woman
Who lived under a hill.
And if she's not gone
She lives there still.

There Were Two Blackbirds

There were two blackbirds
Sat upon a hill,
The one named Jack,
The other named Jill;
Fly away Jack,
Fly away Jill,
Come again Jack,
Come again Jill.

Sorting: bill, fill, hill, will, spill, still, in, pin, tin, win, thin

Making words: Distribute the letters: *i, p, l, l, s*

1. Use three letters to make *ill,* as in I am ill.
2. Add a letter to make *sill,* as in window sill.
3. Change a letter to make the word *pill.*
4. Use three letters to make the word *lip.*
5. Change a letter to make the word *sip,* as in I will sip my soda.
6. Add a letter to make the word *slip.*
7. Using all the letters, make a word. (*spill*)

Spelling: will, hill

Writing: Students write about something that they will do today.

Riddle: What goes up and comes down but stays in the same place? (a hill)

-id *Pattern*

Pattern words: did, hid, kid, lid,* rid, slid

Mixed practice: lid, led, rid, red, hid, slid, sled

Scrambled sentence: Did you get rid of the old tin cans?

Reading: Wang, M. L. (1989). *The ant and the dove.* Chicago: Children's Press.

Shared singing:

Did You Ever See a Lassie?

Did you ever see a lassie, a lassie, a lassie,
Did you ever see a lassie go this way and that?
Go this way and that way and this way and that way,
Did you ever see a lassie go this way and that?

Sorting: did, hid, kid, lid, rid, slid, in, pin, tin, win, thin

Spelling: did, hid, kid

Writing: Students draw a picture and write a story about something they did that was fun.

Rhyme riddle: What do you call a hat for a little girl or boy? (kid lid)

-ig *Pattern*

Pattern words: big, wig, dig, pig*

Mixed practice: big, bill, pig, pill, wig, will

Scrambled sentence: The big pigs are in the pen.

Shared reading: Three Little Pigs.

Reading: Compose a pattern book. One possibility is: *Pigs,* Pigs can be big. Pigs live in pens. Pigs can dig. Pigs can dig for food.

Sorting: big, wig, dig, pig, did, hid, kid, lid, bill, fill, hill, will, spill, still

Rhyme riddle: What do you call a large hog? (big pig)

Spelling: big, pig, dig

Writing: Students write about some things they would like to do when they get big.

-ing *Pattern*

Pattern words: king, ring,* sing, wing, bring, spring, thing

Mixed practice: rat, ring, sat, sing, tin, thing, when, wing, sing, spring

Scrambled sentence: The king can sing.

Rhyme:

Happy Thought
Robert Louis Stevenson

The world is so full of a number of things,
I'm sure we should all be as happy as kings.

Reading: Greydanus, R. (1968). *Let's get a pet.* Mahwah, NJ: Troll.

A bird can be little fold-and-read book.

Text-walk: Discuss the smallest bird—the bee hummingbird—and the biggest bird—the ostrich. As you preview the book with students, have them point to *bird, little, but, bigger, fly,* and *legs,* which are potentially hard words.

Sorting: king, ring, sing, wing, bring, big, wig, dig, pig

Making words: Distribute the letters: *g, i, n, p, r, s.*

1. Use four letters to make the word *sing.*
2. Change a letter to make *ring.*
3. Change a letter to make the word *ping,* as in Ping-Pong.
4. Using all the letters, make a word. (*spring*)

Riddle: A bell can do this. And you can put this on. It rhymes with *sing.* What is it? (a ring)

Spelling: ring, sing, thing, bring

Writing: Students write a piece telling what they would do if they were a king or a queen.

-ip *Pattern*

Pattern words: lip, tip, drip, ship,* skip, slip, trip

Mixed practice: tip, tap, trip, sat, ship, sled, slip

Scrambled sentence: Did you take a trip on a ship?

Reading: Share-read a version of *The Three Billy Goats Gruff* that ends with the lines: "Trip, trap, trip. This tale's told out."

Sorting: lip, tip, drip, ship, skip, slip, trip, king, ring, sing, wing, bring

Riddle: You need two of these to kiss. (lips)

Spelling: ship, trip, slip

Writing: Students write about a trip they might like to take on a ship.

-ick *Pattern*

Pattern words: chick, kick, lick, pick, sick, stick,* trick

Mixed practice: lick, let, pick, pet, sick, set, tap, trick

Scrambled sentence: I will pick up the stick.

Rhyme:

> **Jack Be Nimble**
>
> Jack be nimble,
> Jack be quick.
> Jack jump over the candlestick.
>
> Jump it lively,
> Jump it quick,
> But don't knock over
> The candlestick.

Song:

> **A Tisket, A Tasket**
>
> A tis-ket, a tas-ket, a green and yel-low bas-ket,
> I wrote a let-ter to my love,
> And on the way, I lost it,
> I lost it, I lost,
> And on the way I lost it.
> A little boy picked it up and put it in his pock-et.

Sorting: kick, lick, pick, sick, stick, trick, lip, tip, drip, ship, skip

Rhyme ridddle: What do you call a hen that is not well? (sick chick)

Making words: Distribute the letters: *c, i, k, s, t.*

1. Use three letters to make the word *sit.*
2. Change a letter to make the word *kit.*
3. Use four letters to make the word *sick.*
4. Change a letter to make the word *tick.*
5. Using all the letters, make a word. (*stick*)

Spelling: pick, sick, trick

Writing: Have students make a list of things that make them feel sick.

-ish *Pattern*

Pattern words: dish, fish,* wish

Mixed practice: dish, den, fish, fit, wish, we

Scrambled sentence: Did you wish for a fish?

Rhyme:

> **Star Light, Star Bright**
>
> Star light, star bright,
> First star I see tonight,
> I wish I may, I wish I might
> Have the wish I wish tonight.

Reading: Cox, M. (1997). *Big egg.* New York: Random.

Sorting: dish, fish, wish, kick, lick, pick, sick, stick, trick

Riddle: I can be in the sea, or I can be on a dish. I rhyme with *wish.* What am I? (fish)

Spelling: dish, fish, wish

Writing: Students write about some things they might wish for. Compose a class booklet of student wishes and place it in the class library.

Short-i Unit Review: On the chalkboard or an overhead, write the short-*i* vowel pattern words presented in this unit. Mix the patterns so students are not simply using the first word as a clue to the other words in that column. Words listed in the sorting exercise can be used for this purpose. If students are not able to read 90 percent of the words, continue to review with them until they are able to do so.

Sorting (words should be sorted by rhyming sound): stick, pig, hill, ring, pin, will, dig, tin, king, pick, big, fill, win, thing, wig, sing, trick, in, bill, kick, thin, Jill, wing.

Secret message: Write the words on the lines and read the secret message.

1. Take **D** off **Dig** and put on **B.** __ __ __
2. Add **s** to **bird.** __ __ __ __ __
3. Take **m** from **man** and put on **c.** __ __ __ __
4. Keep **have** as it is. __ __ __ __ __
5. Add **tle** to **lit.** __ __ __ __ __ __
6. Take **th** from **things** and put in **w.** __ __ __ __ __ __.

_____   _____   _____   _____   _____   _____.

Short-o Patterns

-op *Pattern*

Pattern words: hop, mop,* pop, top, shop

Mixed practice: hop, hid, mop, map, pop, pill, top, tin

Scrambled sentence: Can pop hop?

Rhyme:

Hippity Hop to the Barber Shop

Hippity hop to the barber shop,
To get a stick of candy,
One for you and one for me,
And one for sister Mandy.

Reading: Foster, A., & Erickson, B. (1991). *A mop for pop.* New York: Barron.

Shared reading: Geisel, T. S. (Dr. Seuss). (1963). *Hop on pop.* New York: Random House.

Sorting: hop, mop, pop, top, shop, dish, fish, wish

Spelling: hop, top, shop

Writing: Students write about some animals that like to hop.

-ot *Pattern*

Pattern words: dot, hot, lot, not, pot,* spot

Mixed practice: hot, hop, mop, not, pot, pop, dot, got

Scrambled sentence: The pot is not hot.

Rhyme:

Hot Cross Buns!

Hot cross buns!
Hot cross buns!
One a penny, two a penny,
Hot cross buns!

If you have no daughters,
Give them to your sons;
One a penny, two a penny,
Hot cross buns!

Reading: McKissack, P. C. (1983). *Who is who?* Chicago: Children's Press.

A kangaroo can hop fold-and-read book.

Text-walk: Discuss animals that can hop. As you walk students through the story, have them point to *kangaroo, rabbit,* and *this.*

Sorting: dot, hot, lot, not, pot,* spot, hop, mop,* pop, top, shop

Making Words: Distribute the letters: *o, p, s, t*

1. Use three letters to make the word *pot.*
2. Use the same three letters to make the word *top.*
3. Add a letter to make the word *stop.*
4. Using all the letters, make a word. (*spot*)

Rhyme riddle: What do you call a very warm place? (hot spot)

Spelling: lot, hot, not, spot

Writing: Students write about things they like to do on a hot day.

-ock *Pattern*

Pattern words: lock, rock, sock, block, clock

Mixed practice: lock, lot, clock, sat, sock, red, rock

Scrambled sentence: We will lock up the gold rocks.

Rhyme:

Hickory, Dickory, Dock

Hickory, dickory, dock,
The mouse ran up the clock.
The clock struck one,
The mouse ran down!
Hickory, dickory, dock.

Sorting: lock, rock, sock, block, clock, dot, hot, lot, not, pot, spot

Riddle: How can you make time fly? (throw a clock high in the sky)

Spelling: block, clock

Writing: Students tell what they are doing at certain times of the day: 9 o'clock (morning), 12 o'clock (noon), 3 o'clock (afternoon), 6 o'clock (evening), 12 o'clock (midnight).

Short-o Unit Review.   On the chalkboard or an overhead, write the short-*o* vowel pattern words presented in this unit. Mix the patterns so students are not simply using the first word as a clue to the other words in that column. Words listed in the sorting exercise can be used for this purpose. If students are not able to read 90 percent of the words, continue to review them until they are able to do so.

Sorting (words should be sorted by rhyming sound): lock, mop, pot, hop, clock, top, hot, rock, not, stop, got, drop, sock, spot, lot, pop, block

Secret message: Write the words on the lines and read the secret message.

1. Add **s** to **Elephant.** __ __ __ __ __ __ __ __
2. Take **r** away from **ran** and put in **c.** __ __ __
3. Take **h** away from **hot** and put in **n.** __ __ __
4. Take **t** away from **top** and put in **h.** __ __ __

    _____ _____ _____ _____.

Short-u Patterns

-ug *Pattern*

Pattern words: bug,* dug, hug, mug, rug

Mixed practice: bug, bag, dug, den, hug, hen, mug, man, rug, ran

Scrambled sentence: A bug ran on the rug.

Rhyme:

Three Little Bugs

Three little bugs in a basket,
Hardly room for two.
One like Mary, one like Tom,
And one that looks like you.

Reading: McKissack, P., & McKissack, F. (1988). *Bugs!* Danbury, CT: Children's Press.

Sorting: bug, dug, hug, mug, rug, dot, hot, lot, not, pot, spot

Riddle: Bugs run on me. Cats and dogs run on me. And you run on me. I rhyme with hug. What am I? (a rug)

Spelling: bug, rug, hug

Writing: Students draw a picture of a bug and then write a story about the bug.

-un *Pattern*

Pattern words: fun, gun, run, sun*

Mixed practice: fun, fat, gun, got, run, ran, sat, sun

Scrambled sentence: We had fun in the sun.

Reading: Hawkins, C., & Hawkins, J. (1988). *Zug the bug.* New York: Putnam.

Rhyme:

Hot Cross Buns!

Hot cross buns!
Hot cross buns!
One a penny, two a penny,
Hot cross buns!

If you have no daughters,
Give them to your sons;
One a penny, two a penny,
Hot cross buns!

Sorting: fun, gun, run, sun, bug, dug, hug, mug, rug

Riddle: I get up before you get up. And I get up before hens and pigs get up. I am not a son. But I sound just like *son.* What am I? (the sun)

Spelling: fun, run, sun

Writing: Students draw a picture of something that is fun to do and write a story about it.

-ut *Pattern*

Pattern words: but, cut, nut,* shut

Mixed practice: bat, but, cut, cat, nut, not, shot, shut

Scrambled sentence: He has a cut on his hand.

Sorting: but, cut, nut, shut, fun, gun, run, sun

Rhyme riddle: What do you call a cut that has closed up? (shut cut)

Spelling: but, cut, shut

Writing: Students write a sentence that uses the word *but.*

-up *Pattern*

Pattern words: up, cup,* pup

Mixed practice: us, up, cup, cap, pup, pet

Scrambled sentence: Do not pick up the pup.

Song:

Lazy Mary

La-zy Mar-y, will you get up,
Will you get up, will you get up?
La-zy Mar-y, will you get up,
Will you get up to-day?

Oh, no, moth-er, I won't get up,
I won't get up, I won't get up.
Oh, no, moth-er, I won't get up,
I won't get up to-day.

Reading: Hawkins, C., & Hawkins, J. (1988). *Zug the bug.* New York: Putnam.

Functional reading: pudding cup

Shared reading: Dr. Seuss. (1974). *Great day for up.* New York: Random House.

Sorting: up, cup, pup, but, cut, nut, shut, fun, gun, run, sun

Rhyme riddle: What do you call a puppy that is not down? (an up pup)

Spelling: up, cup, puppy

Writing: Students draw a picture of a puppy that they now have, had in the past, or might like to have. Then they write a story about the puppy.

-ub *Pattern*

Pattern words: cub, rub, tub*

Mixed practice: cub, cut, ran, rub, tub, ten

Scrambled sentence: A cub is in the bath tub.

Rhyme:

Rub-a-Dub-Dub

Rub-a-dub-dub,
Three men in a tub,
And who do you think they be?
The butcher, the baker,
The candlestick maker.

Sorting: cub, rub, tub, up, cup, pup, shut, fun, gun, run, sun

Spelling: cub, rub, tub

Rhyme riddle: What do you call a bath tub for baby bears? (cub tub)

-ump *Pattern*

Pattern words: bump, dump, jump,* lump

Mixed practice: bump, but, den, dump, jet, jump, let, lump

Scrambled sentence: Can you jump over the bump?

Rhyme:

Jack, Be Nimble

Jack, be nimble,
Jack, be quick.
Jack, jump over the candlestick.

Jump it lively,
Jump it quick,
But don't knock over
The candlestick.

Reading: Compose a pattern book. One possibility is: *I can,* I can run. I can jump. I can jump over a lump. I can jump over a bump. Can you jump?

How many fold-and-read book.

Text-walk: Discuss how many bugs are on the first page. Have students point to the words *how many.* Invite them to read the booklet and write their answers on the lines.

Sorting: bump, dump, jump, lump, cub, rub, tub, bug, dug, hug, mug, rug

Spelling: bump, jump, dump

-unk *Pattern*

Pattern words: bunk, junk, skunk,* trunk

Mixed practice: bunk, but, jump, junk, skunk, sun, trunk, tent

Scrambled sentence: A skunk hid in the trunk.

Sorting: bunk, junk, skunk, trunk, bump, dump, jump, lump

Rhyme riddle: What do you call a trunk that is full of old broken things? (junk trunk)

Making Words: Distribute the letters: *k, n, r, t, s, u*

1. Use two letters to make the word *run.*
2. Change a letter to make *sun.*
3. Add a letter to make the word *sunk.*
4. Using all the letters, make a word. (trunks)

Riddle: I cannot walk or run, but I can take you places. I rhyme with *us.* What am I? (a bus)

Spelling: junk, skunk, trunk

Writing: Students make a list of things they might pack in a trunk if they were taking a long trip.

-us(s), -ust, -uck *Patterns*

Pattern words: bus,* us; dust,* just, must; duck, luck, truck*

Mixed practice: bus, but, luck, fun, fuss, us, up, just, luck, must, truck

Scrambled sentence: The bus is taking us up the hill.

Readings:

> Capucilli, A. S. (1996). *Biscuit.* New York: HarperCollins.
>
> Lewison, W. C. (1992). *"Buzz," said the bee.* New York: Scholastic.
>
> *What is red?* fold-and-read book.
>
> *Text-walk:* Discuss things that are red and things that are yellow. As you preview the book with students, help them see the *yell* in *yellow.* Also help them use phonics and context to read *black stripes.*

Sorting: bus, fuss, us, bunk, luck, junk, just, skunk, trunk, duck, but, cut, must, nut, shut, truck

Spelling: us, bus, must, just, truck

Writing: Students write a piece about a bus trip they have taken or might like to take.

*Short-*u *Unit Review.* On the chalkboard or an overhead, write the short-*u* vowel pattern words presented in this unit. Mix the patterns so students are not simply using the first word as a clue to the other words in that column. Words listed in the sorting exercise can be used for this purpose. If students are not able to read 90 percent of the words, continue to review them until they are able to do so.

Sorting (words should be sorted by rhyming sound): bug, sun, cup, bus, skunk, fun, rug, us, dug, fuss, run, trunk, gun, junk, up, tug, bunk, pup.

Secret message: Write the words on the lines and read the secret message.

1. Take **n** away from **An.** __
2. Put **p** before **up** and add **py.** __ __ __ __ __
3. Take **b** away from **bikes** and put in **l.** __ __ __ __ __
4. Take **d** away from **do** and put in **t.** __ __
5. Take **f** away from **fun** and put in **r.** __ __ __

_____ _____ _____ _____ _____ .

■ LONG-VOWEL PATTERNS

Long-a Patterns

-ake Pattern

Pattern words: bake, cake,* lake, take, wake, shake, snake

Mixed practice: back, bake, cake, cat, let, lake, win, wake, snack, snake

Scrambled sentence: We will bake a cake.

Reading: Robart, R. (1986). *The cake that Mack ate.* Boston: Little, Brown.

Functional reading: cake mix, baked beans

Rhyme:

Pat-a-Cake

Pat-a-cake, pat-a-cake, baker's man,
Bake me a cake just as fast as you can.
Pat it and stick it, and mark it with a B.
Put it in the oven for baby and me.

Sorting: bake, cake, lake, take, wake, shake, snake, back, tack, pack, Jack

Riddle: I have no legs, so I cannot run. But I can go fast on land or in water. I rhyme with *cake*. What am I? (a snake)

Spelling: cake, take, wake, lake, shake, snake

Writing: Students draw a picture and write about something they would like to make.

-ame Pattern

Pattern words: came, game,* same, tame, name

Mixed practice: came, cake, Sam, same, tame, take

Scrambled sentence: What is the name of that game?

Reading: Oppenheim, J. (1990). *Wake up, baby!* New York: Bantam.

Shared singing:

Bingo

There was a farm-er who had a dog.
And Bing-o was his name-o.
B-I-N-G-O, B-I-N-G-O, B-I-N-G-O,
And Bing-o was his name-o.

Reading: Hall, K. (1995). *A bad, bad day.* New York: Scholastic.

Sorting: came, game, same, tame, name, bake, cake, lake, take, wake, shake, snake

Riddle: You write me on your paper, but other boys and girls write their own. I rhyme with *game*. What am I? (name)

Spelling: came, name, same, game

Writing: Students write about games they like to play.

-ate, -ait Patterns

Pattern words: ate, date, gate,* hate, late, plate, skate; wait

Mixed practice: at, ate, den, date, hate, hat, lake, late, pat, plate

Scrambled sentence: I hate to be late.

Rhyme:

Garden Gate
Two, four, six, eight.
Meet me at the garden gate.
If I'm late, do not wait.
Two, four, six, eight.

Sorting: ate, date, gate, hate, late, plate, skate, came, game, same, tame, name, bake, cake, lake, take, wake, shake, snake

Riddle: I can swing back and forth, but I cannot swing up and down. I rhyme with *late*. What am I? (a gate)

Spelling: ate, date, late, hate, wait

Writing: Students draw a picture and write about a plate containing the foods they like best.

-ave *Pattern*

Pattern words: cave, gave, save, wave,* brave

Mixed practice: cake, cave, gate, gave, save, sat, wake, wave, bake, brave

Scrambled sentence: We gave Dave a cake for being brave.

Sorting: cave, gave, save, wave, brave, ate, date, gate, hate, late, plate, skate

Riddle: Flags do this. And boys and girls do it when they want to say, "Hi" or "Good-bye." It rhymes with *brave*. What is it? (wave)

Writing: Students write about a time when they or someone they know was brave.

Spelling: gave, save, wave, brave

-ade, -aid *Patterns*

Pattern Words: made,* wade, grade, shade, paid*

Mixed practice: gate, gave, made, wade, wave, late, brave

Scrambled sentence: The second grade made puppets.

Sorting: made, wade, grade, shade, paid, cave, gave, save, wave, brave

Riddle: Trees make this. But they only make it when the sun is out. It rhymes with *made*. (shade)

Spelling: made, grade, paid

Writing: Have students draw a picture of and/or write about something they made or something that someone they know made. Model the assignment for students by drawing a picture of a time when you made something and then writing about the picture.

-ace *Pattern*

Pattern words: face, race,* place

Mixed practice: face, fast, rat, race, paid, place

Scrambled sentence: She came in first place in the race.

Sorting: face, race, place, made, wade, grade, shade, paid

Riddle: I have eyes to see, a nose to smell, and a mouth for talking. I rhyme with *race*. What am I? (a face)

Spelling: face, race, place

Writing: Have students draw a picture of and/or write about the place where they live. Model the assignment for students by drawing a picture of the place where you live and then writing about the picture.

-age *Pattern*

Pattern words: age, page, cage,* stage

Mixed practice: page, place, rain, race, cage, face

Scrambled sentence: This page shows three cats in a cage.

Sorting: age, page, cage, stage, face, race, place, cake, lake, take, wake, shake, snake

Riddle: I have words but I cannot say anything. I am in a book. I rhyme with *cage.* What am I? (a page)

Spelling: age, page, cage

Writing: Have students bring in photos or draw pictures of themselves at various ages and write captions for the photos. The captions should include ages. Model the assignment for students.

-ale, -ail *Patterns*

Pattern words: whale,* nail,* mail, sail, tail, trail

Mixed practice: whale, page, tail, face, mail, race, sail

Scrambled sentence: The big whale has a big tail.

Rhymes:

If You Ever

If you ever ever ever ever,
If you ever ever ever ever meet a whale,
You must never never never never never,
You must never never never never never touch its tail,
For if you ever ever ever ever ever,
For if you ever ever ever ever ever touch its tail,
You will never never never never never,
You will never never never never never meet another whale.

I've Got a Dog

I've got a dog as thin as a rail,
He's got fleas all over his tail;
Every time his tail goes flop,
The fleas on the bottom all hop to the top.

Song:

I Saw Three Ships

I saw three ships come sail-ing by,
A sail-ing by, A sail-ing by,
I saw three ships come sail-ing by,
On New Year's Day, in the morn-ing.

Reading: Stadler, J. (1985). *Snail saves the day.* New York: Thomas Y. Crowell.

Sorting: whale, nail, mail, sail, tail, trail, age, page, cage, stage, face, race, place

Making words: Distribute the letters: *a, i, l, r, s, t*

1. Use four letters to make the word *sail.*
2. Change a letter to make the word *tail.*
3. Change a letter to make the word *rail.*
4. Using all the letters, make a word. (*trails*)

Rhyme riddle: What is a story about a whale called? (a whale tale)

Spelling: whale, tail, sail, mail

Writing: Students draw a picture of a place to which they would like to sail and then write a story that tells about the picture.

-ain, -ane *Patterns*

Pattern words: rain, train,* pain, chain; cane, Jane, plane*

Mixed practice: train, tail, chain, cane, pain, pail, rain, whale

Scrambled sentence: A plane is faster than a train.

Rhyme:

Rain, Rain

Rain, rain, go away,
Come again another day;
Little Robert wants to play.

Sorting: rain, train, pain, chain; cane, Jane, plane, whale, nail, mail, sail, tail, trail

Riddle: I fly high in the sky, but I am not a bird. I rhyme with *rain*. What am I? (a plane)

Spelling: rain, train, plane

Writing: Students write about a train or plane trip they have taken or would like to take. To help students prepare for this assignment, discuss some train or plane trips that they have taken or might like to take.

-ay *Pattern*

Pattern words: hay,* day, may, say, stay, gray, play

Mixed practice: may, mail, play, whale, way, stay, sail, trail, nail, gray

Scrambled sentence: Play a game with me.

Rhyme:

Bees

If bees stay at home,
Rain will soon come.
If they fly away,
Fine will be the day.

Sorting: hay, day, may, say, stay, gray, play, rain, train, pain, chain; cane, Jane, plane

Rhyme riddle: What do you call a day when you have a lot fun? (play day)

Spelling: day, may, say, stay, play

Writing: Students draw pictures of games they can play and then write captions for the pictures.

Long-a Unit Review.   On the chalkboard or an overhead, write the long-*a* pattern words presented in this unit. Mix the patterns so students are not simply using the first word as a clue to the other words in that column. Words listed in the sorting exercise can be used for this purpose. If students are not able to read 90 percent of the words, continue to review them until they are able to do so.

Sorting (words should be sorted by rhyming sound): bake, way, plane, whale, wade, chain, rain, wait, save, day, age, face, plate, gate, train, wave, came, made, hay, lake, ate, game, pain, gray, brave, sail, date, stage, race, cake, nail, pain, shade, wake, same, grade, shake, page, place, cane, snake, mail, name, skate, tail, tame, paid, gave, stay

Secret message: Write the words on the lines and read the secret message.

1. Take **n** away from **An.** __
2. Put **g** before **ray.** __ __ __ __
3. Take away **eel** from **wheel** and put in **ale.** Then add **'s.** __ __ __ __ __ __ __
4. Take **m** away from **mail** and put in **t.** __ __ __ __ __
5. Take **b** away from **books** and put in **l.** __ __ __ __ __ __
6. Take **n** away from **an.** __
7. Take **t** away from **tail** and add **s.** __ __ __ __ __

_____ _____ _____ _____ _____ _____ _____ .

Long-e Patterns

-e, -ee, -ea, -ey Patterns

> *Pattern words:* he, me, she, bee,* see, free, three, tree; sea, peas, tea;* key
>
> *Mixed practice:* bee, brave, see, save, trap, tree, three
>
> *Scrambled sentence:* The bees are in the tree.
>
> *Reading:* Vinje, M. (1992). *I don't like peas.* Grand Haven, MI: School Zone.
>
> *Functional reading:* frozen peas, boxes of tea bags
>
> *Rhymes:*

> #### A Sailor Went to Sea
>
> A sailor went to sea
> To see what he could see,
> And all that he could see,
> Was the sea, sea, sea.

> #### Rain
> *Robert Louis Stevenson*
>
> The rain is raining all around,
> It falls on field and tree,
> It rains on the umbrellas here,
> And on the ships at sea.

> #### Lock and Key
>
> "I am a gold lock."
> "I am a gold key."
> "I am a silver lock."
> "I am a silver key."
> "I am a brass lock."
> "I am a brass key."
> "I am a lead lock."
> "I am a lead key."
> "I am a don lock."
> "I am a don key."

> *Sorting:* bee, see, free, three, tree, hay, day, may, say, stay, gray, play
>
> *Riddle:* I sound just like *tea,* but I am not something to drink and I am not spelled *t-e-a.* I hold up a football or a golf ball. What am I? (a tee)
>
> *Spelling:* he, me, she, see, free, tree, three
>
> *Writing:* Have students make a list of the three things that they like to do most in their free time.

-eep Pattern

> *Pattern words:* jeep, deep, beep, keep, sleep, sheep*
>
> *Mixed practice:* bee, beep, see, sleep, she, sheep

Scrambled sentence: Sheep sleep at night.

Reading: Gregorick, B. (1984). *Beep, beep.* Grand Haven, MI: School Zone.

Rhyme:

Little Bo-Peep

Little Bo-Peep has lost her sheep,
    And can't tell where to find them;
Leave them alone, and they'll come home,
    And bring their tails behind them.

Rhyme riddle: What kind of a sleep do fish who are at the bottom of the sea have? (deep sleep)

Sorting: jeep, deep, beep, keep, sleep, sheep, bee, see, free, three, tree

Spelling: keep, sleep, jeep, sheep

Writing: Have students tell what they would keep if they had to leave their homes and they could keep only three things. Encourage them to explain their choices.

-een, -ean *Patterns*

Pattern words: queen,* green, seen; bean,* lean, mean, clean

Mixed practice: bean, beep, sleep, seen, sheep

Scrambled sentence: Have you seen the can of beans?

Reading: Simon, S. (1985). *Benny's baby brother.* Grand Haven, MI: School Zone.

Rhymes:

Rain

Rain on the green grass,
And rain on the tree,
Rain on the house-top,
But not on me.

Jack Sprat

Jack Sprat could eat no fat,
His wife could eat no lean.
And between them both, you see,
They licked the platter clean.

Functional reading: green beans, baked beans

Sorting: queen, green, seen; bean, lean, mean, clean, jeep, deep, beep, keep, sleep, sheep

Riddle: I sound like a name. But I am something that you put on. I rhyme with *beans.* What am I? (jeans)

Spelling: green, seen, mean, clean

Writing: Students make a list of things that they like that are green, or make a "What Is Green?" booklet in which they tell about things that are green.

-eet, eat *Patterns*

Pattern words: feet,* meet, sweet, street; seat,* eat, beat, heat, meat, neat

Mixed practice: bean, beat, seen, seat, keep, meat, mean

Scrambled sentence: Did you eat the meat?

Reading:

Tripp, V. (1987). *Baby koala finds a home.* Chicago: Children's Press.

Ziefert, H. (1995). *The little red hen.* New York: Puffin.

Writing: Students write about some sweet foods that they like.

Rhyme:

Little Hot Dog

My father owns the butcher shop
My mother cuts the meat,
And I'm the little hot dog
That runs around the street.

Song:

She'll Be Comin' 'Round the Mountain

She'll be com-in' 'round the moun-tain when she comes,
She'll be com-in' 'round the moun-tain when she comes,
She'll be com-in' 'round the moun-tain,
She'll be com-in' 'round the moun-tain,
She'll be com-in' 'round the moun-tain when she comes.

She'll be driv-in' six white hor-ses when she comes,
She'll be driv-in' six white hor-ses when she comes,
She'll be driv-in' six white hor-ses,
She'll be driv-in' six white hor-ses,
She'll be driv-in' six white hor-ses when she comes.

Oh, we'll all go out to meet her when she comes,
Yes, we'll all go out to meet her when she comes,
Oh, we'll all go out to meet her,
Yes, we'll all go out to meet her,
We will all go out to meet her when she comes.

Sorting: feet, meet, sweet; seat, beat, heat, meat, neat, queen, green, seen

Making words: Distribute the letters: *a, e, m, t*

1. Use two letters to make the word *me.*
2. Add a letter to make the word *met.*
3. Change a letter to make the word *mat.*
4. Using all the letters, make a word. (*meat*)

Riddle: I rhyme with *sweet*. And I am something to eat. What am I? (meat)

Spelling: feet, meet, sweet, heat

Writing: Students make a list of things they like that are sweet.

-eal, -eel *Patterns*

Pattern words: seal,* meal, real, steal; wheel,* feel, heel, peel

Mixed practice: feel, feet, heel, heat, meet, meal, seal, seat

Scrambled sentence: I saw a real seal.

Song:

Wheels on the Bus

The wheels on the bus
Go round and round,
Round and round,
Round and round.
The wheels on the bus
Go round and round,
All over town.

Sorting: seal, meal, real, steal; wheel, feel, heel, peel, feet, meet, sweet; seat, beat, heat, meat, neat

Rhyme riddle: What do you call fish that are given to a seal to eat? (seal meal)

Spelling: feel, meal, real

Writing: Students write about things that make them feel happy. Model the process of selecting and developing a topic by talking about some of the things that make you feel happy.

-ead, -eed *Patterns*

Pattern words: read, bead,* lead (v); seed,* feed, need, weed

Mixed practice: real, read, wheel, weed, feel, feet, seed, seal

Scrambled sentence: Feed the seeds to the birds.

Sorting: read, bead, lead (v); seed, feed, need, weed, seal, meal, real, steal; wheel, feel, heel, peel

Rhyme riddle: Where do weeds come from? (weed seeds)

Spelling: read, need, feed

Writing: Have students talk and then write about the kinds of books they like to read. You might also want to create a bulletin board featuring the drawings and written pieces about students' favorite books.

-eam *Pattern*

Pattern words: team, cream, dream,* scream, stream

Mixed practice: team, tame, cake, cream, dream, drag, seem, scream, stream

Functional reading: ice cream

Rhyme:

> #### Ice Cream Rhyme
>
> I scream, you scream,
> We all scream for ice cream.

Song:

> #### Row the Boat
>
> Row, row, row your boat
> Gently down the stream,
> Merrily, merrily, merrily, merrily,
> Life is but a dream.

Sorting: team, cream, dream, scream, stream, read, bead, lead (v); seed, feed, need, weed

Making words: Distribute the letters: *a, e, m, r, s, t*

1. Use two letters to make the word *me.*
2. Use three letters to make the word *tea.*
3. Add a letter to make the word *team.*
4. Add a letter to make the word *steam.*
5. Use four letters to make the word *meat.*
6. Using all the letters, make a word. (*stream*)

Rhyme riddle: What do you call it when you yell during a dream? (dream scream)

Spelling: dream, cream, stream

Writing: Have students talk and write about their dreams for the future.

Long-e Unit Review.   On the chalkboard or an overhead, write the long-*e* words presented in this unit. Mix the patterns so students are not simply using the first word as a clue to the other words in that column. Words listed in the sorting exercise can be used for this purpose. If students are not able to read 90 percent of the words, continue to review them until they are able to do so.

Sorting (words should be sorted by rhyming sound): bee, steam, feet, deep, team, street, read, seal, meal, queen, bead, neat, meat, real, see, free, jeep, meet, green, seen, three, scream, wheel, need, heel, bean, mean, clean, peel, keep, tree, beep, seat, cream, beat, heat, steal, sheep, sleep, see, keep, feed

Secret message: Write the words on the lines and read the secret message.

1. Change the **w** in **Wish** to **F**. __ __ __ __
2. Change the **t** in **steep** to l. __ __ __ __ __
3. Change the **j** in **jeep** to **d**. __ __ __ __
4. Take the **f** from **fin**. __ __
5. Keep **the** just as it is. __ __ __
6. Change the **t** in **tea** to **s**. __ __ __

_____ _____ _____ _____ _____ _____ .

Long-i Patterns

-ie, -igh Patterns

    Pattern words: pie, lie, tie,* die; high,* sigh

    Mixed practice: pie, tea, see, sigh, he, high

    Scrambled sentence: We ate the pie.

    Shared reading:

> **Little Jack Horner**
>
> Little Jack Horner
> Sat in a corner,
> Eating his Christmas pie;
> He put in his thumb,
> And pulled out a plum,
> And said, "What a good boy am I!"

    Functional reading: pie

    Sorting: pie, lie, tie, die; high, sigh, team, cream, dream, scream, stream

    Riddle: I am round and am good to eat. I rhyme with *tie.* What am I? (a pie)

    Spelling: pie, lie, high

    Writing: Students draw a picture of a pie that they like and write a piece that tells about it.

-ight Pattern

    Pattern words: night,* fight, light, might, right, sight, tight

    Mixed practice: tie, tight, light, lie, sigh, sight

    Scrambled sentence: I see a bright light.

    Readings:

        Shebar, S. (1979). *Night monsters.* Provo, UT: Aro Publishing.

        Ziefert, H. (1984). *Sleepy dog.* New York: Random.

Rhymes:

Fright and Bright

Poor Cat Fright
Ran off with all her might
Because the dog was after her—
Poor Cat Fright!

Poor Dog Bright
Ran off with all his might
Because the cat was after him—
Poor Dog Bright!

Star Light, Star Bright

Star light, star bright,
First star I see tonight,
I wish I may, I wish I might
Have the wish I wish tonight.

Sorting: night, fight, light, might, right, sight, tight, pie, lie, tie, die; high

Rhyme riddle: What do you call something that is easy to see and rhymes with *night?* (bright sight)

Spelling: night, light, might, right

Writing: Students make a list of things they like to do at night.

-ike *Pattern*

Pattern words: bike,* hike, like, Mike, strike

Mixed practice: bike, bake, hike, hate, like, late, strike, slip

Scrambled sentence: I like my bike.

Rhyme:

Three Little Bugs

Three little bugs in a basket,
Hardly room for two.
One like Mary, one like Tom,
And one that looks like you.

Reading: Greydanus, R. (1980). *Mike's new bike.* Mahwah, NJ: Troll.

Sorting: bike, hike, like, Mike, strike, night, fight, light, might, right, sight, tight, pie, lie, tie, die; high, sigh

Rhyme riddle: What do you call a long trip on a bike? (bike hike)

Spelling: bike, like, hike

Writing: Students make a list of things they like to do.

-ide *Pattern*

Pattern words: ride,* hide, side, slide, wide

Mixed practice: hide, hike, ride, rake, side, sight, wide, wake

Scrambled sentence: Do not ride side by side.

Rhyme:

Little Old Man

A little old man came riding by.
Said I, "Old man, your horse will die."
Said he, "If he dies, I'll tan his skin.
And if he lives, I'll ride him again."

Song:

The Bear Went over the Mountain

The bear went over the mountain,
The bear went over the mountain,
The bear went over the mountain,
To see what he could see.
And all that he could see,
And all that he could see was
The other side of the mountain,
The other side of the mountain,
The other side of the mountain,
Was all that he could see.

Reading: Ziefert, H. (1987). *Jason's bus ride.* New York: Puffin.

Making words: Distribute the letters: *d, e, i, l, s*

1. Use three letters to make the word *lie.*
2. Change a letter to make *lid.*
3. Add a letter to make the word *slid.*
4. Use four letters to make the word *side.*
5. Using all the letters, make a word. (*slide*)

Sorting: ride, hide, side, slide, wide, night, fight, light, might, right, sight, tight

Rhyme riddle: What do you call a slide that a whale might use? (a wide slide)

Spelling: hide, ride, side, wide

Writing: Students make a list of things they like to ride.

-ime, -yme *Patterns*

Pattern words: time, dime,* lime; rhyme*

Mixed practice: dime, den, time, Tim, like, lime

Scrambled sentence: Mike paid five dimes for a lime.

Functional reading: lime Jello or other labels that contain the word *lime*

Sorting: time, dime, lime, rhyme, ride, hide, side, slide, wide

Riddle: Some people say that I fly, but I have no wings. I go by every day, but no one sees me. I rhyme with *dime.* What am I? (time)

Spelling: time, dime, lime

Writing: Students draw a picture about the time of day they like best and then write a piece about their pictures. To stimulate students' writing, model the assignment by drawing a picture of your favorite time of day and writing a short piece about it.

-ine *Pattern*

Pattern words: nine,* line, mine, pine, vine, shine

Mixed practice: line, lime, main, mine, pain, pine, vine, van, shop, shine

Scrambled sentence: We got in line at nine.

Reading: Allen, J. (1987). *My first job.* Provo, UT: Aro Publishing.

Sorting: nine, line, mine, pine, vine, shine, ride, hide, side, slide, wide, night, fight, light, might, right, sight, tight

Rhymes:

One, Two, Three, Four, Five

One, two, three, four, five,
Once I caught a fish alive.
Six, seven, eight, nine, ten,
Then I let it go again.

Come on In

Come on in,
The water's fine.
I'll give you
Till I count nine.
If you're not
In by then,
Guess I'll have to
Count to ten.

Riddle: I have no hands or feet, but I can climb up a tree or a wall. My name rhymes with *nine*. What am I? (a vine)

Spelling: nine, line, mine, shine

Writing: Students list the nine best times in their lives, or nine things they like best.

-ice *Pattern*

Pattern words: mice,* ice, nice, rice, twice

Mixed practice: mice, mine, nine, nice, rice, rain, twice

Scrambled sentence: Mice like rice.

Rhyme:

What Are Little Boys Made of?

What are little boys made of?
    Frogs and snails
    And puppy dogs' tails.
That's what little boys are made of.

What are little girls made of?
    Sugar and spice
    And all things nice.
That's what little girls are made of.

Reading: Hoff, S. (1988). *Mrs. Brice's mice.* New York: HarperCollins.

Functional reading: labels containing the word *rice*: uncooked rice, rice pudding, rice cakes, Rice Krispies

Sorting: mice, ice, nice, rice, twice, nine, line, mine, pine, vine, shine

Riddle: I am a word. I have *ice* in me. I mean "two times." What word am I? (twice)

Spelling: ice, nice, rice, twice

Writing: Students make a list of things they think are nice.

-ile, -ife *Patterns*

Pattern words: mile, pile, smile,* while; life, wife, knife*

Mixed practice: mice, mile, pill, pile, slide, smile, wide, while

Scrambled sentence: He smiles while he is singing.

Rhymes:

Three Blind Mice

Three blind mice, see how they run!
They all ran after the farmer's wife,
Who cut off their tails with the carving knife.
Did you ever see such a sight in your life,
As three blind mice?

Little Tommy Tucker

Little Tommy Tucker
    Sings for his supper.
What shall we give him?
    White bread and butter.
How shall he cut it
    Without a knife?
How shall he be married
    Without a wife?

Functional reading: replica of a traffic sign containing the word *miles*

Sorting: mile, pile, smile, while, life, wife, knife, mice, ice, nice, rice, twice

Riddle: I have a *mile* in me, but I am not long. When you see me, you can tell that someone is happy. What word am I? (smile)

Spelling: mile, smile, while, life

Writing: Encourage students to make a list of things that make them smile. Model the process of developing a topic by talking about some of the things that make you smile.

-ite *Pattern*

Pattern words: bite, kite,* quite, white

Mixed practice: bite, bright, night, kite, quit, quite, white, while

Scrambled sentence: The moon was quite bright.

Rhyme:

One, Two, Three, Four, Five

One, two, three, four, five
Once I caught a fish alive,
Six, seven, eight, nine, ten,
Then I let it go again.
Why did you let it go?
Because it bit my finger so.
Which finger did it bite?
The little finger on the right.

Sorting: bite, kite, quite, white, mile, pile, smile, nice, rice, twice

Rhyme riddle: I am not a bird or a plane, but I can fly high in the sky. I rhyme with *white*. What am I? (kite)

Spelling: bite, quite, white

Writing: Students make a list of things that are white: clouds, snow, sheep.

-y *Pattern*

Pattern words: cry,* by, my, fly, dry, sky, why

Mixed practice: mile, my, sky, smile, wide, why, while

Scrambled sentence: Jets fly in the sky.

Rhymes:

I Asked My Mother for Fifteen Cents

I asked my mother for fifteen cents
To see the elephant jump the fence,
He jumped so high that he touched the sky
And never came back 'till the Fourth of July.

There Were Two Blackbirds

There were two blackbirds
Sat upon a hill,
One was named Jack,
The other was named Jill;
Fly away Jack,
Fly away Jill,
Come again Jack,
Come again Jill.

Sorting: cry, by, my, fly, dry, sky, why, mile, pile, smile, while

Rhyme riddle: What do you call a sky that has no rain? (dry sky)

Spelling: my, cry, sky, why, fly

Writing: Students draw a picture of a bird flying high in the sky and write a piece about their drawing.

Long-i Unit Review. On the chalkboard or an overhead, write the long-*i* words presented in this unit. Mix the patterns so students are not simply using the first word as a clue to the other words in that column. Words listed in the sorting exercise can be used for this purpose. If students are not able to read at least 90 percent of the words, continue to review them until they are able to do so.

Sorting (words should be sorted by rhyming sound): pie, hide, rice, night, rhyme, nine, bite, why, fight, slide, kite, smile, cry, lie, mile, wife, line, nice, knife, why, time, tie, ice, die, dime, lime, right, high, ride, light, sigh, my, strike, sight, like, while, wide, might, pine, bike, shine, white, twice, life, sky

Secret message: Write the words on the lines and read the secret message.

1. Add **B** to **right.** __ __ __ __ __ __
2. Add **s** to **miles.** __ __ __ __ __ __
3. Change the **t** in **tight** to l. __ __ __ __ __ __
4. Take the **c** from **cup.** __ __
5. Add **s** to **face.** __ __ __ __ __ __

_____ _____ _____ _____ _____.

Long-o Patterns

-o, -oe Patterns

Pattern words: go, no,* so; Joe, toe

Mixed practice: he, Joe, me, go, we, so, see, no, she, toe

Scrambled sentence: I see Joe.

Shared reading: Issacesen, B., & Holland, M. (1986). *No, no, Joan!* St. Petersburg, FL: Willowwisp Press.

Spelling: no, go, so

Riddle: What do you call when you have a bad toe? (a toe truck)

Writing: Students tell about things they like to go to see: I like to go to see _____.

-ow *Pattern*

Pattern words: crow,* row, low, grow, show, slow, know

Mixed practice: crow, cry, low, lie, row, rye, show, shy, slow, sly

Scrambled sentence: Row the boat slowly.

Readings:

Cobb, A. (1996). *Wheels*. New York: Random House.

Greene, C. (l982). *Snow Joe*. Chicago: Children's Press.

O'Connor, J. (l986). *The teeny tiny woman*. New York: Random House. (Especially appropriate for older students).

Rhymes:

One for the Money

One for the money,
Two for the show,
Three to make ready,
And four to go.

Clouds
Christina Rossetti

White sheep, white sheep,
On a blue hill,
When the wind stops
You all stand still.
When the wind blows
You walk away slow.
White sheep, white sheep,
Where do you go?

Song:

If You're Happy and You Know It

If you're hap-py and you know it,
    Clap your hands.
If you're hap-py and you know it,
    Clap your hands.
If you're hap-py and you know it,
    And you really want to show it,
If you're hap-py and you know it,
    Clap your hands.

Sorting: crow, row, low, grow, show, slow, know, bite, kite, quite, white

Rhyme riddle: What do you call it when you row, but you do not row fast? (slow row)

Spelling: low, grow, show, slow, know

Writing: Students write about some things that they know now but didn't know before the school year began. Discuss things that they know and model writing on the topic.

-oat, -ote *Patterns*

Pattern words: goat,* boat, coat, float; note,* wrote

Mixed practice: crow, coat, goat, grow, float, boat, belt, no, note, wrote

Scrambled sentence: A goat jumped into the boat.

Reading: Milos, Rita. (l989). *The hungry billy goat*. Chicago: Children's Press.

Song:

The Mocking Bird

Hush, little baby, don't say a word,
Papa's going to buy you a mocking bird.
If the mocking bird won't sing,
Papa's going to buy you a diamond ring.

If the diamond ring turns to brass,
Papa's going to buy you a looking-glass.
If the looking-glass gets broke,
Papa's going to buy you a billy-goat.

If that billy-goat runs away,
Papa's going to buy you another today.

Sorting: goat, boat, coat, float; note, wrote, crow, row, low, grow, show, slow, know

Making words: Distribute the letters: *h, o, r, t, w*

1. Use three letters to make the word *row.*
2. Change a letter to make the word *tow.*
3. Using all the letters, make a word. (*throw*)

Rhyme riddle: What do you call a ship that has a lot of goats? (goat boat)

Spelling: goat, boat, coat, note, wrote

Writing: Students write about a trip they have taken or a boat trip they might like to take.

-oad *Pattern*

Pattern words: toad, load, road*

Mixed practice: low, load, tow, toad, row, road

Scrambled sentence: There is a toad in the road.

Song:

I've Been Working on the Railroad

I've been work-ing on the rail-road
All the live-long day,
I've been work-ing on the rail-road
Just to pass the time a-way.
Don't you hear the whis-tle blowing?
Rise up so early in the morn.
Don't you hear the cap-tain shout-ing,
"Di-nah, blow your horn"?
Di-nah, won't you blow,
Di-nah, won't you blow,
Di-nah, won't you blow your horn?
Di-nah, won't you blow,
Di-nah, won't you blow,
Di-nah, won't you blow your horn?

Some-one's in the kitch-en with Di-nah,
Some-one's in the kitch-en, I know,
Someone's in the kitch-en with Di-nah,
Strum-ming on the old ban-jo, and sing-ing:
Fee-fi-fidd-lee-i-o, Fee-fi-fidd-lee-i-o,
Fee-fi-fidd-lee-i-o, Strum-ming on the old ban-jo.

Reading: Schade, S., & Buller, J. (1992). *Toad on the road.* New York: Random House.

Sorting: toad, load, road, goat, boat, coat, float; note, wrote

Rhyme riddle: What do you call a road that toads use? (toad road)

Spelling: toad, load, road

Writing: Students draw a picture or a map showing the road on which they live. They then write a piece that tells about the picture or map.

-ole, -oll *Patterns*

Pattern words: mole,* hole, pole, stole; roll,* toll

Mixed practice: roll, road, hole, hot, pole, mole, meet

Scrambled sentence: The ball rolled into the hole.

Song:

Merrily We Roll Along

Mer-ri-ly we roll a-long, roll a-long, roll a-long,
Mer-ri-ly we roll a-long, o-ver the deep blue sea.

Reading:

Armstrong, J. (1996). *The snowball.* New York: Random.

Gregorich, B. (1991). *Nicole digs a hole.* Grand Haven, MI: School Zone.

Functional reading: labels for rolls

Sorting: mole, hole, pole, stole; roll, toll; toad, load, road, goat, boat, coat, float; note, wrote

Riddle: This word means "all of it" but it has a *hole* in it. It rhymes with mole. What is it? (*whole*)

Spelling: hole, pole, roll

Writing: Discuss moles and have students write a sentence that tells about moles.

-old *Pattern*

Pattern words: old, gold,* cold, fold, hold, sold, told

Mixed practice: hold, hole, so, sold, go, gold, toe, told

Scrambled sentence: She told us an old story.

Rhyme:

Old King Cole

Old King Cole
Was a merry old soul,
And a merry old soul was he.
He called for his pipe,
And he called for his bowl,
And he called for his fiddlers three.

Reading: Ziefert, H. (1988). *Strike four!* New York: Penguin.

Functional reading: replica of a "Sold" sign

Sorting: old, gold, cold, fold, hold, sold, told; mole, hole, pole, stole; roll, toll; toad, load, road

Riddle: I am yellow and rhyme with *sold.* I am use to make rings. What am I? (gold)

Spelling: old, gold, cold, fold, hold, sold, told

Writing: Students draw a picture of themselves and then write a sentence telling how old they are.

-oak, -oke *Patterns*

Pattern words: oak,* soak; woke, joke, broke, spoke, smoke*

Mixed practice: poke, sold, soak, cold, choke, bold, broke

Scrambled sentence: Soak the dirt around the oak tree.

Rhyme:

Owl

A wise old owl lived in an oak,
The more he saw, the less he spoke.
The less he spoke, the more he heard.
Why can't we all be like that wise old bird?

Sorting: oak, soak; woke, joke, broke, spoke, smoke, old, gold, cold, fold, hold, sold, told

Rhyme riddle: What do you call a funny story about an oak tree? (oak joke)

Spelling: woke, joke, broke, spoke

Writing: Students write a favorite joke or riddle they have heard or read, or make one up.

-ose *Pattern*

Pattern words: hose, nose,* rose, chose, close, those

Mixed practice: hose, hole, nose, note, those, throw

Scrambled sentence: She chose a red rose.

Rhyme:

Little Girl, Little Girl, Where Have You Been?

Little girl, little girl, where have you been?
Gathering roses to give to the Queen.
Little girl, little girl, what gave she you?
She gave me a diamond as big as my shoe.

Sorting: hose, nose, rose, chose, close, those, oak, soak; woke, joke, broke, spoke, smoke

Riddle: I am right on the front of your face. Others can see me, but you can not. I rhyme with *rose,* but I am not a flower. What am I? (your nose)

Spelling: nose, rose, chose, close, those

Writing: Students discuss and make a list of things that their noses like to smell: cookies baking, supper cooking, mom's perfume.

-one *Pattern*

Pattern words: bone, alone, phone*

Mixed practice: boat, bone, alone, float, phone

Scrambled sentence: She sat alone by the phone. (Discuss different ways in which this sentence can be reassembled.)

Rhymes:

Little Bo-Peep

Little Bo-Peep has lost her sheep,
        And can't tell where to find them.
Leave them alone, and they'll come home,
        And bring their tails behind them.

Jumping Joan

Here am I,
Little Jumping Joan;
When nobody's with me
I'm all alone.

Functional reading: replica of a phone sign

Sorting: bone, alone, phone, hose, nose, rose, chose, close, those, oak, soak; woke, joke, broke, spoke, smoke

Rhyme riddle: You talk into me but not to me. I rhyme with *bone*. What am I? (phone)

Spelling: bone, alone, phone

Writing: Students make a list of things they like to do when they are alone.

Long-o Unit Review.   On the chalkboard or an overhead, write the long-*o* words presented in this unit. Mix the patterns so students are not simply using the first word as a clue to the other words in that column. Words listed in the sorting exercise can be used for this purpose. If students are not able to read 90 percent of the words, continue to review them until they are able to do so.

Sorting (words should be sorted by rhyming sound): crow, old, goat, cold, boat, load, fold, wrote, smoke, bone, low, grow, broke, row, stole, oak, rose, road, show, pole, alone, soak, note, mole, close, hole, float, slow, hose, nose, woke, coat, sold, toad, joke, roll, hold, know, told, chose, spoke, those, phone

Secret message: Write the words on the lines and read the secret message.

1. Add **n** to **A.** __ __
2. Take the **h** from **hold.** __ __ __
3. Change the **g** in **goat** to **b.** __ __ __ __
4. Add **c** to **an.** __ __ __
5. Take an **e** from **bee.** __ __
6. Take **n** from **an.** __
7. Take the **s** from **homes.** __ __ __ __

_____ _____ _____ _____ _____ _____ _____.

Rhymes:

Fooba Wooba John

Saw a flea kick a tree,
Fooba wooba, fooba wooba,
Saw a flea kick a tree,
Fooba wooba, John.
Saw a flea kick a tree
In the middle of the sea,
Hey, John, ho, John,
Fooba wooba, John.

Saw a crow flying low,
Fooba wooba, fooba-wooba,
Saw a crow flying low,
Fooba wooba John.
Saw a crow flying low,
Miles and miles beneath the snow,
Hey, John, ho, John,
Fooba wooba John.

Saw a bug give a shrug. . . .
In the middle of the rug. . . .

Saw a whale chase a snail. . . .
All around a water pail. . . .

Saw two geese making cheese. . . .
One would hold and the other would squeeze. . . .

Saw a mule teaching school. . . .
To some bullfrogs in the pool. . . .

Saw a bee off to sea. . . .
With his fiddle across his knee. . . .

Saw a hare chase a deer. . . .
Ran it all of seven year. . . .

Saw a bear scratch his ear. . . .
Wonderin' what we're doin' here. . . .

The Goat

There was a man—now please take note—
There was a man who had a goat.
He loved that goat—indeed he did—
He loved that goat, just like a kid.

One day that goat felt frisky and fine,
Ate three reds shirts from off the line.
The man, he grabbed him by the back
And tied him to a railroad track.

But when the train drove into sight,
The goat grew pale and green with fright.
He heaved a sigh as if in pain,
Coughed up those shirts, and flagged the train.

Long-u Patterns

-ule, -use, -uge, -ute, -ew *Patterns*

> *Pattern words:* mule,* use, huge, cute, few
>
> *Mixed practice:* use, us, hug, huge, fake, few, cut, cute
>
> *Scrambled sentence:* The farmer has a few mules.
>
> *Sorting:* mule, use, huge, cute, few, bone, alone, phone, hose, nose, rose, choose, those
>
> *Spelling:* use, huge, few
>
> *Riddle:* My dad is a donkey, and my mom is a horse. I have very long ears. I am not cute, but I work very hard. What am I? (mule)

Writing: Have students make a list of animals that are huge.

Secret message: Write the words on the lines and read the secret message.

1. Drop the **n** from **An.** __
2. Change the **y** in **yule** to **m.** __ __ __ __
3. Add **c** to **an.** __ __ __
4. Change the **m** in **marry** to **c.** __ __ __ __ __
5. Drop the **n** from **an.** __
6. Add an **e** to **hug.** __ __ __ __
7. Change the **t** in **toad** to **l.** __ __ __ __

_____ _____ _____ _____ _____ _____ _____.

■ *R*-Vowel Patterns

-ar *Pattern*

Pattern words: car, far, jar, tar, star*

Mixed practice: car, city, far, fed, tar, tea, star, stop

Scrambled sentence: The jars are in the car.

Rhymes:

Twinkle, Twinkle, Little Star

Twinkle, twinkle, little star,
How I wonder what you are!
Up above the world so high,
Like a diamond in the sky.

Star Light, Star Bright

Star light, star bright,
First star I see tonight,
I wish I may, I wish I might,
Have the wish I wish tonight.

Help! Murder! Police!

Help! Murder! Police!
My mother fell in the grease.
I laughed so hard, I fell in the lard.
Help! Murder! Police!

Reading: Ziefert, H. (1990). *Stitches.* New York: Puffin Books.

Sorting: car, far, jar, tar, star, mule, use, huge, cute, few

Rhyme riddle: What do you call a star that is way up in the sky? (far star)

Spelling: car, far, jar, star

Writing: Have students tell about a time when they went far away or about a place that is far away that they would like to visit.

-ark *Pattern*

Pattern words: park, bark, dark, mark, shark*

Mixed practice: car, bark, far, mark, dark, jar, park

Scrambled sentence: The park closes at dark.

Rhyme:

Bedtime

Down with the lambs
Up with the lark,
Run to bed children
Before it gets dark.

Reading: Cole, J. (1986). *Hungry, hungry sharks.* New York: Random House.

Functional reading: Display a replica of a sign for a park.

Sorting: park, bark, dark, mark, shark, car, far, jar, tar, star, mule, use, huge, cute, few

Rhyme riddle: What do you call a place where sharks play? (shark park)

Spelling: park, bark, dark, mark

Writing: Have students draw a picture of the kind of park in which they would like to play and then write a piece telling about the park.

-arm *Pattern*

Pattern words: arm,* farm, harm

Mixed practice: are, arm, farm, feed, harm, heel

Scrambled sentence: Rain will not harm the farm.

Functional reading: replica of a sign for a farm or a label that uses the word *farm*

Sorting: arm, farm, harm, park, bark, dark, mark, shark, car, far, jar, tar, star

Riddle: Hands need me. If hands did not have me, they could not do anything. My name rhymes with *farms.* What am I? (arms)

Spelling: arm, farm, harm

Writing: Have students write a piece telling how they use their arms. Alter the assignment if any of the students is unable to use his or her arms.

-art, -eart *Patterns*

Pattern words: art, cart,* chart, part, smart, start; heart*

Mixed practice: are, art, car, cart, star, start

Scrambled sentence: Art sat in the cart.

Making words: Distribute the letters: *a, r, s, t, t*

1. Use three letters to make the word *art.*
2. Use the same three letters to make the word *tar.*
3. Add a letter to make the word *star.*
4. Using all the letters, make a word. (*start*)

Sorting: art, cart, part, smart, start; heart, arm, farm, harm

Riddle: I can carry people and things. *Car* is part of my name, but I am not a car. I rhyme with *start.* What am I? (cart)

Spelling: part, start, heart

Writing: Have students write about the smartest animal they know, or about a smart deed that an animal they know has done.

-air, -are, -ere, -ear *Patterns*

Pattern words: air, hair, pair, chair*; care, share, scare, square,*where,* there, bear,* wear, pear

Mixed practice: care, cart, hair, harm, chair, chart, share, scare

Scrambled sentence: A pair of bears scared me.

Rhymes:

Pussy-cat, Pussy-cat

Pussy-cat, pussy-cat, where have you been?
I've been to London to visit the Queen!
Pussy-cat, pussy-cat, what did you there?
I frightened a little mouse under her chair.

Simple Simon

Simple Simon met a pieman
    Going to the fair.
Says Simple Simon to the pieman,
    "Let me taste your ware."

Says the pieman to Simple Simon,
    "Show me first your penny."
Says Simple Simon to the pieman,
    "Indeed I have not any."

Old Chairs to Mend

If I'd as much money as I could spend,
I never would cry old chairs to mend;
Old chairs to mend, old chairs to mend;
I never would cry old chairs to mend.

If I'd as much money as I could tell,
I never would cry old clothes to sell;
Old clothes to sell, old clothes to sell;
I never would cry old clothes to sell.

Reading:

    Arnold, M. (1996). *Quick, quack, quick!* New York: Random House.

    Blocksma, M. (1984). *The best dressed bear.* Chicago: Children's Press.

Functional reading: pears

Sorting: air, hair, pair, chair; care, share, scare, where, there, bear, pear, art, cart, part, smart, start; heart

Rhyme riddle: What do you call a bear that likes to sit? (chair bear)

Spelling: air, hair, pair, chair; care, share, scare, where, there

Writing: Have students draw a picture of and write a piece about a chair that they like. Encourage them to describe the chair and tell why they like it. Students might also create a homophone book in which they depict word pairs such as *hair, hare; pair, pear, stair, stare; where, wear.*

-or, -oor, -ore, -our *Patterns*

Pattern words: or, for; more, sore, tore, wore, score, store*; door,* poor, floor; four,* pour

Mixed practice: for, far, mark, more, tar, tore, poor, part, pour

Scrambled sentence: Open the door to the store.

Rhymes:

It's Raining, It's Pouring

It's raining, it's pouring,
The old man is snoring.
He went to bed and bumped his head.
And he wouldn't get up in the morning.

The North Wind Doth Blow

The north wind doth blow,
And we shall have snow,
And what will poor Robin do then?
Poor thing!

He'll sit in a barn,
And keep himself warm,
And hide his head under his wing.
Poor thing!

It Ain't Going to Rain No More

It ain't going to rain no more, no more,
It ain't going to rain no more;
How in the heck can I wash my neck
If it ain't going to rain no more?

Reading: Ziefert, H. (1997). *The magic porridge pot.* New York: Puffin.

Functional reading: replica of a sign containing the word *store*

Sorting: or, for; more, sore, tore, wore, score, store; door, poor, floor, four, pour, air, hair, pair, chair; care, share, scare, where, there, bear, bark, pear

Rhyme riddle: What do you call a place that sells doors? (door store)

Spelling: for; more, tore, wore, score, store; door, poor

Writing: Have students draw a picture of and write a piece about a store they like to go to. Encourage them to tell what they like about the store. Have students enter *for–four; poor–pour* into the homophone sections of their notebooks, with sentences or drawings to illustrate the meanings of the words.

-orn *Pattern*

Pattern words: born, corn, horn,* torn; warn

Mixed practice: born, boat, corn, coat, tore, torn, warn

Scrambled sentence: My coat is torn.

Rhymes:

The Donkey

Donkey, donkey, old and gray,
Open your mouth and gently bray;
Lift your ears and blow your horn,
To wake the world this sleepy morn.

Little Boy Blue

Little boy blue, come blow your horn;
The sheep's in the meadow, the cow's in the corn.
Where's the little boy that looks after the sheep?
He's under the haystack fast asleep.
Will you wake him? No, not I;
For if I do, he'll be sure to cry.

Red Sky

Red sky at night,
Sailor's delight;
Red sky in the morning,
Sailor's warning.

Reading: Gelman, R. G. (1977). *More spaghetti I say.* New York: Scholastic.

Functional reading: corn, corn flakes

Sorting: born, corn, horn, torn, or, for; more, sore, tore, wore, score, store; door, poor, floor, four, pour

Riddle: I have ears but I can not hear. I rhyme with *horn*. What am I? (corn)

Spelling: born, corn, horn, torn

Writing: Have students write a sentence telling when and where they were born.

-ir, -ur, -urse, -er *Patterns*

Pattern words: sir, stir,* fur, nurse,* purse, her

Mixed practice: sir, sore, store, stir, born, bird

Scrambled sentence: Her kittens were not in their box.

Rhymes:

I'll Sing You a Song

I'll sing you a song,
Though not very long,
Yet I think it as pretty as any.

Put your hand in your purse,
You'll never be worse,
And give the poor singer a penny.

Burnie Bee

Burnie bee, burnie bee,
Tell me when your wedding be?
If it be tomorrow day,
Take your wings and fly away.

Sorting: sir, stir, fur, nurse, purse, her, born, corn, horn, torn

Making words: Distribute the letters: *e, o, r, s, t*

1. Use four letters to make the word *sore.*
2. Change one letter to make the word *tore.*
3. Changing one letter, make the word *rest.*
4. Using all the letters, make a word. (*store*)

Riddle: I have fur. And I can purr. I like to run after birds and rats. My name rhymes with *hat.* What am I? (cat)

Spelling: sir, stir, fur, nurse, her

Writing: Have students tell what they would do if they had a magical purse that never ran out of money.

-urn, -earn, -ire *Patterns*

Pattern words: burn, turn*; earn, learn*; fire, tire,* wire

Mixed practice: sir, sore, store, stir, tire, turn, tore, wire

Scrambled sentence: We learned how to spell *earn.*

Rhyme:

Fire! Fire!

"Fire! Fire!" said Mrs. McGuire.
"Where? Where?" said Mrs. Hare.
"Downtown!" said Mrs. Brown
"Heaven save us!" said Mrs. Davis.

Sorting: burn, turn; earn, learn, sir, stir, fur, nurse, purse

Riddle: I am not a wheel, but I go round and round. I rhyme with *wire.* What am I? (tire)

Spelling: burn, turn; earn, learn

Writing: Students discuss and write about some important or interesting things that they have learned during the past week.

-ird, -eard, -ord, -erd *Patterns*

Pattern words: bird,* third; word*; herd,* heard*

Mixed practice: bird, born, third, torn, were, word, her, herd, heard

Scrambled sentence: I don't know the third word.

Rhyme:

The Mocking Bird

Hush, little baby, don't say a word,
Papa's going to buy you a mocking bird.

If the mocking bird won't sing,
Papa's going to buy you a diamond ring.

If the diamond ring turns to brass,
Papa's going to buy you a looking-glass.

If the looking-glass gets broke,
Papa's going to buy you a billy goat.

If that billy goat runs away,
Papa's going to buy you another today.

Sorting: bird, third; word; herd, heard, burn, turn; earn, learn, sir, stir, fur, nurse, purse

Rhyme riddle: If birds could talk, what would their words be called? (bird words)

Spelling: bird, third, word, heard

Writing: Have students draw a picture of and write a piece about their favorite birds. If possible, have bird books available so that students can have models for their drawings and a source of material for ideas. Encourage students to illustrate and add *herd* and *heard* to their homophone books. Point out that *heard* has an *ear* in it. This can be a reminder for the correct spelling of *heard*.

-ear, -eer *Patterns*

Pattern words: ear,* dear, fear, hear, near; deer,* steer

Mixed practice: fear, for, deer, door, hear, heart, steer, store, stir, turn, tore

Scrambled sentence: The deer came near us.

Rhymes:

Up, Dear Children

Come, my dear children,
Up is the sun,
Birds are all singing,
And morn has begun.
Up from the bed, Miss
Out on the lea;
The horses are waiting
For you and for me!

Fears and Tears

Tommy's tears and Mary's fears
Will make them old
Before their years.

Reading:

Hoffman, J. (1992). *The last game.* Grand Haven, MI: School Zone.

Ziefert, H. (1989). *Dr. Cat.* New York: Penguin.

Sorting: ear, dear, fear, hear, near; deer, steer, bird, third; word; herd, burn, turn; earn, learn

Riddle: What kind of deer is found in letters? (a d-e-a-r dear, as in "Dear Jan")

Spelling: ear, dear, fear, hear, near

Writing: Have students close their eyes and use only their ears. Ask them to notice what they hear. Then have them open their eyes and list all the things they heard. Encourage students to illustrate *dear* and *deer* and add them to their homophone books.

R-Vowel Unit Review.   On the chalkboard or an overhead, write the *r*-vowel pattern words presented in this unit. Mix the patterns so students are not simply using the first word as a clue to the other words in that column. Words listed in the sorting exercise can be used for this purpose. If students are not able to read 90 percent of the words, continue to review them until they are able to do so.

Sorting (words should be sorted by rhyming sound): car, pear, or, corn, air, for, there, art, care, born, arm, burn, heart, bird, cart, park, fur, far, floor, farm, nurse, mark, horn, where, poor, learn, star, jar, more, third, wear, chair, torn, dark, part, sore, tore, wore, word, share, score, store, hair, door, her, smart, pair, harm, turn, purse, sir, chart, start, stir, worn, herd, scare, earn, bark, bear

Secret message: Write the words on the lines and read the secret message.
1. Take away the **p** from **Parks** and put in **Sh.** __ __ __ __ __ __
2. Add **c** to **an.** __ __ __
3. Add **s** to **care.** __ __ __ __ __
4. Add **d** to **an.** __ __ __
5. Add **h** to **arm.** __ __ __ __
6. Take **b** away from **bus.** __ __

_____ _____ _____ _____ _____ _____.

Rhyme:

Wishes

Said the first little chicken
With a queer little squirm,
"I wish I could find
A fat little worm."

Said the second little chicken
With an odd little shrug,
"I wish I could find
A fat little slug."

Said the third little chicken
With a sharp little squeal,
"I wish I could find
Some nice yellow meal."

Said the fourth little chicken
With a small sigh of grief,
"I wish I could find
A little green leaf."

Said the fifth little chicken
With a faint little moan,
"I wish I could find
A small gravel stone."

"Now see here," said their mother
From the green garden patch.
"If you want any breakfast,
Just come here and SCRATCH!"

OTHER-VOWEL PATTERNS

/aw/ Patterns   In some dialects, *caught* and some other words included here with
/aw/ patterns may be pronounced with a short-*o* sound, so that *caught* rhymes
with *hot.* Make adjustments so that instruction fits your students' dialect.

-all *Pattern*

    Pattern words: all, ball,* call, fall, hall, tall, wall, small

    Mixed practice: fall, fear, hear, hall, small, smear

    Scrambled sentence: Throw the small ball.

    Rhymes:

        Jack Hall

        Jack Hall.
        He is so small.
        A mouse could eat him,
        Hat and all.

        Go to Bed Late

        Go to bed late,
        Stay very small.
        Go to bed early,
        Grow very tall.

    Sorting: all, ball, call, fall, hall, tall, wall, small, ear, dear, fear, hear, near; deer

    Rhyme riddle: What do you call a high wall? (tall wall)

    Spelling: all, ball, call, fall, tall, small

    Writing: Have students draw a picture about a game in which a ball is used.
    Then have them write about the picture they drew.

-aw *Pattern*

    Pattern words: saw,* paw, law, claw, draw

    Mixed practice: saw, small, call, claw, law, lead, draw, drop

    Scrambled sentence: Cats' paws have sharp claws.

    Rhyme:

        I Saw Esau

        I saw Esau sawing wood,
        And Esau saw I saw him;
        Though Esau saw I saw him saw,
        Still Esau went on sawing.

    Making words: Distribute the letters: *a, c, l, s, w*

    1. Use three letters make the word *saw.*
    2. Change a letter to make *law.*
    3. Change a letter to make *caw,* as in "The crows caw."
    4. Using all the letters, make a word. (*claws*)

Sorting: saw, paw, law, claw, draw, all, ball, call, fall, hall, tall, wall, small

Rhyme riddle: I have teeth, but I can't eat. But I can cut a piece of wood in two. I rhyme with *paw.* What am I? (saw)

Spelling: saw, draw

Writing: Have students draw a picture of something interesting or special that they saw today or this week. It could be something that was funny or just interesting.

-alk *Pattern*

Pattern words: walk,* talk, chalk

Mixed practice: talk, tall, wall, walk, claw, chalk; hawk

Scrambled sentence: We will talk while we walk home.

Reading: Brenner, B. (1989). *Annie's pet.* New York: Bantam.

Sorting: walk, talk, chalk, saw, paw, law, claw, draw, all, ball, call, fall, hall, tall, wall, small

Riddle: I fly high in the sky, but I am not a plane. I rhyme with *walk.* What am I? (hawk)

Spelling: walk, talk, chalk

Writing: Have students write about the person they most like to talk to.

-aught, -ought, -ost *Patterns*

Pattern words: caught,* taught; ought, bought,* brought; cost, lost*

Mixed practice: bought, ball, brought, call, caught, talk, taught

Scrambled sentence: We brought the lost dog to its owner.

Rhyme:

Two Cats of Kilkenny

There were once two cats of Kilkenny.
Each thought there was one cat too many.
So they fought and they fit,
And they scratched and they bit,
Until, except for their nails,
And the tips of their tails,
Instead of two cats, there weren't any.

Sorting: caught, taught; ought, bought, brought; cost, lost, walk, talk, chalk

Spelling: caught, taught; ought, bought, brought; cost, lost

Riddle: Boys and girls mix me up with *bought.* But *bought* means "buy" in time that has passed. I mean "bring" in time that has passed. I also have one more sound than *bought* does. What word am I? (*brought*)

Writing: Have students draw a picture of something that they lost, either recently or a long time ago. Have them write a piece that tells about the lost item. Model the assignment by drawing a picture of something you lost and writing a brief piece about it.

-ong *Pattern*

Pattern words: long, song,* strong, wrong

Mixed practice: long, lost, wrong, saw, song, strong

Scrambled sentence: The birds sang a long song.

Reading: Rylant, C. (1989). *Henry and Mudge get the cold shivers.* New York: Bradbury Press.

Song:

Oh Where, Oh Where Has My Little Dog Gone?

Oh where, oh where has my little dog gone?
　　Oh where, oh where can he be?
With his ears cut short and his tail cut long
　　Oh where, oh where is he?

Sorting: long, song, strong, wrong, caught, taught; ought, bought, brought; cost, lost, walk, talk, chalk

Riddle: I am a word that you do not like to hear. I rhyme with *song.* I am not right, so I must be _____. (wrong)

Spelling: long, song, strong, wrong

Writing: Students write about some interesting or funny thing that happened to them a long time ago. Model the process by discussing and writing about something that happened to you a long time ago.

/aw/ Pattern Unit Review.   On the chalkboard or an overhead, write the /aw/ pattern words presented in this unit. Mix the patterns so students are not simply using the first word as a clue to the other words in that column. Words listed in the sorting exercise can be used for this purpose. If students are not able to read 90 percent of the words, continue to review them until they are able to do so. Most important, have students read books that contain /aw/ pattern words.

Sorting (words should be sorted by rhyming sound): all, cost, walk, paw, taught, call, talk, saw, ball, fall, lost, hall, tall, law, caught, wall, hawk, small, ought, draw, chalk

Secret message: Write the words on the lines and read the secret message.

1. Take away the **M** from **Me** and put in **W.** __ __
2. Take away the **b** from **bought.** __ __ __ __ __
3. Drop one **o** from **too.** __ __
4. Take away the **s** from **snow** and put in **k.** __ __ __ __
5. Take away the **b** from **bright.** __ __ __ __ __
6. Keep **from** as it is. __ __ __ __
7. Take away the **s** from **song** and put in **wr.** __ __ __ __ __ __

_____ _____ _____ _____ _____ _____ _____.

Long-/oo/ Patterns

-oo, -oon, -une *Patterns*

Pattern words: zoo,* too, boo, moo, moon,* noon, soon, spoon, tune,* prune

Mixed practice: moo, moon, zoo, soon, spoon, too, noon

Scrambled sentence: The zoo opens at noon.

Rhymes:

The Cat and the Fiddle

Hey diddle, diddle,
The cat and the fiddle,
The cow jumped over the moon.
The little dog laughed
To see such sport,
And the dish ran away with the spoon.

The Balloon

"What is the news of the day,
My good Mr. Gray?
They say the balloon
Has gone up to the moon."

Reading: Blocksma, M. (1992). *Yoo hoo, moon.* New York: Bantam.

Functional reading: prunes label

Sorting: zoo, too, boo, moo, moon, noon, soon, spoon, tune, prune, long, song, strong, wrong, caught, taught; ought, bought, brought; cost, lost, walk, talk, chalk

Rhyme riddle: What would you call a zoo for cows? (moo zoo)

Spelling: zoo, too, moon, noon, soon

Writing: Students draw a picture of the moon and write a sentence about the moon.

-ew, -ue *Patterns*

Pattern words: new,* chew, flew, grew; blue,* true, Sue

Mixed practice: new, noon, Sue, soon, blue, boo

Scrambled sentence: The blue plane flew up into the sky.

Rhymes:

Little Betty Blue

Little Betty Blue,
Lost her new shoe.
What will poor Betty do?
Why, give her another,
To match the other,
And then she will walk in two.

The Old Man of Peru

There was an old man of Peru,
Who dreamt he was eating his shoe.
He woke in the night
In a terrible fright,
And found it was perfectly true.

Reading: Ziefert, H. (1997). *The ugly duckling.* New York: Puffin.

Functional reading: beef stew

Sorting: new, chew, flew, grew; blue, true, Sue, zoo, too, boo, moo, moon, noon, soon, spoon, tune, prune

Riddle: I rhyme with *blue.* I am not a lie, so I must be _____. (true)

Spelling: new, flew, grew; blue, true

Writing: Have students draw a picture of something new that they have or something new that they would like to have. Then have them write a piece that tells about their picture.

-oot, -uit *Patterns*

Pattern words: boot,* hoot, toot, shoot; fruit,* suit

Mixed practice: boot, blue, too, toot, suit, Sue, shoot

Scrambled sentence: The roots of the fruit tree grew deep.

Rhyme:

> **Little Boy Blue**
>
> Little boy blue, come blow your horn;
> The sheep's in the meadow, the cow's in the corn.
> Where's the little boy that looks after the sheep?
> He's under the haystack fast asleep.
> Will you wake him? No, not I;
> For if I do, he'll be sure to cry.

Reading:

> Gregorich, B. (1984). *Sue likes blue.* Grand Haven, MI: School Zone.
>
> Witty, B. (1991). *The raccoon on the moon.* Grand Haven, MI: School Zone.

Functional reading: fruit juice, fruit cocktail

Sorting: boot, hoot, toot, shoot; fruit, suit, new, chew, flew, grew; blue, true, Sue

Making words: Distribute the letters: *h, o, o, s, t*

1. Use two letters to make *to,* as in "Go to school."
2. Use three letters to make *too,* as in "I ate too much candy."
3. Use four letters to make the word *hoot.*
4. Using all the letters, make a word. (*shoot*)

Riddle: I can be a banana, a peach, or an apple. I can be a bunch of grapes or a lime. But I can not be green beans or peas. What am I? (fruit)

Spelling: boot, shoot, fruit, suit

Writing: Students draw a picture of their favorite fruits and write a sentence as a caption.

-ool, -ule *Patterns*

Pattern words: cool, fool, pool, tool, school*; rule*

Mixed practice: fool, fruit, toot, tool, school, rule, suit

Scrambled sentence: The new school has a swimming pool.

Rhymes:

> **This Is the Way We Go to School**
>
> This is the way we go to school.
> Go to school, go to school.
> This is the way we go to school,
> On a cold and frosty morning.

> **Mary's Lamb**
> *Sara Josepha Hale*
>
> Mary had a little lamb,
> Its fleece was a white as snow;
> And everywhere that Mary went
> The lamb was sure to go.
>
> It followed her to school one day—
> That was against the rule;
> It made the children laugh and play
> To see a lamb in school.

Reading: Platt, K. (1977). *Big Max in the mystery of the missing moose.* New York: HarperCollins.

Sorting: cool, fool, pool, tool, school, boot, hoot, toot, shoot; fruit, suit

Rhyme riddle: What do you call a pool that is full of cold water? (cool pool)

Spelling: cool, fool, pool, tool, school

Writing: Have students write a piece that tells about their school.

-oom, -oup *Patterns*

Pattern words: boom, broom,* room, bloom, zoom; soup,* group

Mixed practice: boom, boot, bloom, room, root, zoom

Scrambled sentence: He swept the room with a new broom.

Rhyme:

> **Old Woman, Old Woman**
>
> There was an old woman tossed in a basket,
> Seventeen times as high as the moon;
> But where she was going no one could tell,
> For under her arm she carried a broom.
> "Old woman, old woman, old woman," said I,
> Where, oh where, oh where so high?"
> "To sweep the cobwebs from the sky;
> And I'll be with you by and by."

Reading: Dussling, J. (1996). *Stars.* New York: Grosset & Dunlap.

Silverman, M. (1991). *My tooth is loose.* New York: Viking.

Functional reading: names of soups

Sorting: boom, broom, room, bloom, zoom, cool, fool, pool, tool, school, boot, hoot, toot, shoot; fruit, suit

Rhyme riddle: What do you call a broom that sweeps very fast? (zoom broom)

Spelling: boom, broom, room

Writing: Students draw a picture of the room in their homes that they like best, then write a description of the room and tell why it is their favorite.

/ōō/ *Pattern Unit Review.* On the chalkboard or an overhead, write the long-*oo* vowel pattern words presented in this unit. Mix the patterns so students are not simply using the first word as a clue to the other words in that column. Words listed in the sorting exercise can be used for this purpose. If students are not able to read 90 percent of the words, continue to review them until they are able to do so. Most important, have students read books that contain long-*oo* pattern words.

Sorting (words should be sorted by rhyming sound): zoo, new, too, chew, fool, hoot, true, boo, rule, moo, zoom, shoot, group, blue, boot, cool, toot, moon, pool, school, noon, soon, tool, suit, flew, soup, room, boom, spoon, tune, fruit, grew, broom, bloom, prune

Secret message: Write the words on the lines and read the secret message.

1. Keep **The** just as it is. __ __ __
2. Take away the **s** from **suit** and add **fr.** __ __ __ __ __
3. Add **s** to **tree.** __ __ __ __ __ __
4. Take away the **n** from **new** and add **gr.** __ __ __ __ __
5. Take away the **f** from **fall** and put in **t.** __ __ __ __ __

_____ _____ _____ _____ _____.

Short-/oo/ Patterns

-ook *Pattern*

Pattern words: book,* cook, look, took, shook

Mixed practice: cool, cook, broom, book, shook, school, tool, took

Scrambled sentence: Look at the book.

Rhymes:

Fishy-fishy

Fishy-fishy in the brook,
Daddy caught him with a hook.
Mama fried him in the pan,
And baby ate him like a man.

Little Bird

Once I saw a little bird
   Come hop, hop, hop;
So I cried, "Little bird,
   Will you stop, stop, stop?"

I was going to the window
   To say, "How do you do?"
But he shook his little tail,
   And far away he flew.

Reading: Averill, E. (1960). *The fire cat.* New York: Harper & Row.

Sorting: book, cook, look, took, shook, boom, broom, room, bloom, zoom

Riddle: I have many words. And I have stories. But I can not talk. I rhyme with *look.* What am I? (book)

Spelling: book, cook, look, took, shook

Writing: Have students make a list of some good books that they have read.

-ood, -ould *Patterns*

Pattern words: wood,* good, hood, stood; could,* would, should

Mixed practice: could, cook, should, shook, stood, hood, hook

Scrambled sentence: Look at the book.

Rhyme:

Woodchuck

How much wood
Would a woodchuck chuck
If a woodchuck could chuck wood?

Reading: Brenner, B. (1989). *Lion and lamb.* New York: Bantam.

Sorting: wood, good, hood, stood; could, would, should; book, cook, look, took, shook

Riddle: I rhyme with *should* and sound like *would,* but I am not *w-o-u-l-d.* You can knock on me and make things out of me. What am I? (wood)

Spelling: wood, good, could, would, should

Writing: Students draw a picture of something they might make if they had a lot of wood. They then write a brief piece about their drawings. Also have students add *wood* and *would* to their homophone books.

-ull, -ush *Patterns*

> *Pattern words:* pull, full, bull*; push, bush*
>
> *Mixed practice:* pull, push, full, bush, wool
>
> *Scrambled sentence:* The bag is full of wool.
>
> *Rhyme:*
>
> > **Baa, Baa, Black Sheep**
> >
> > Baa, baa, black sheep,
> > Have you any wool?
> > Yes, sir, yes, sir,
> > Three bags full.
> >
> > One for the master,
> > One for the dame,
> > But none for the little boy
> > Who cries in the lane.
>
> *Sorting:* pull, full, bull; push, bush, wood, good, hood, stood; could, would, should
>
> *Rhyme riddle:* What do you call a bull that has had a lot to eat? (full bull)
>
> *Spelling:* pull, full, push, bush
>
> *Writing:* Have students tell what they would do if they had a bag full of money.

/oo/ Pattern Unit Review. On the chalkboard or an overhead, write the short-*oo* vowel pattern words presented in this unit. Mix the patterns so students are not simply using the first word as a clue to the other words in that column. Words listed in the sorting exercise can be used for this purpose. If students are not able to read 90 percent of the words, continue to review them until they are able to do so. Most important, have students read books that contain short-*oo* pattern words.

> *Sorting* (words should be sorted by rhyming sound): book, pull, good, cook, full, took, shook, wood, bush, bull, hood, stood, could, push, would, look, should
>
> *Secret message:* Write the words on the lines and read the secret message.
>
> > 1. Keep **You** just as it is. __ __ __
> > 2. Take away the **w** from **would** and add **sh**. __ __ __ __ __ __
> > 3. Take away **d** from **nod** and add **t**. __ __ __
> > 4. Take away the **b** from **bush** and add **p**. __ __ __ __
> > 5. Take the **f** from **for**. __ __
> > 6. Take away the **b** from **bull** and put in **p**. __ __ __ __
> >
> > _____ _____ _____ _____ _____ _____.

/ow/ *Patterns*

-ow *Pattern*

> *Pattern words:* cow,* how, now, wow
>
> *Mixed practice:* cow, call, hood, how, would, wow
>
> *Scrambled sentence:* The bag is full of wool.
>
> *Rhyme:*
>
> > **Bow, Wow, Wow**
> >
> > Bow, wow, wow,
> > Whose dog art thou?
> > Little Tom Tinker's dog,
> > Bow, wow, wow.

Reading: Oppenheim, J. (1989). *"Not now!" said the cow.* New York: Bantam.

Sorting: cow, how, now, wow, pull, full, bull; push, bush, wood, good, hood, stood

Riddle: I am not later or sooner. I rhyme with *cow* and I am right _____. (now)

Spelling: cow, how, now, wow

Writing: Explain to students that people say, "Wow!" when they want to show that they are happy or surprised. Have them draw a picture of a time when they said, "Wow!" and then write a piece that tells about the picture.

-own *(town) Pattern*

Pattern words: down, town, brown, crown,* clown

Mixed practice: cow, clown, crown, now, not, boat, brown

Scrambled sentence: Take the brown cow to town.

Rhymes:

Jack and Jill

Jack and Jill went up the hill,
To fetch a pail of water;
Jack fell down and broke his crown,
And Jill came tumbling after.

Dickery, Dickery, Dare

Dickery, dickery, dare,
The pig flew up in the air;
The man in brown
Soon brought him down,
Dickery, dickery, dare.

Wee Willie Winkie

Wee Willie Winkie runs through the town,
Upstairs and downstairs in his nightgown,
Rapping at the window, crying through the lock,
Are the children all in bed, for now it's eight o'clock?

Making words: Distribute the letters: *c, n, o, r, w*

1. Use two letters to make the word *ow*.
2. Add a letter to make *cow*.
3. Change a letter to make *now*.
4. Using all the letters, make a word. (*crown*)

Sorting: down, town, brown, crown, clown, cow, how, now, wow

Riddle: I rhyme with *clown*. I am not up, so I must be _____. (down)

Spelling: down, town, brown, clown

Writing: Have students draw a picture of a clown and then write a piece that tells about their picture.

-ound *Pattern*

Pattern words: found, sound, round,* pound, ground

Mixed practice: round, grow, ground, cow, clown, pound

Scrambled sentence: She found her brown hat.

Rhymes:

Wheels on the Bus

The wheels on the bus
Go round and round,
Round and round,
Round and round.
The wheels on the bus
Go round and round,
All over town.

Teddy Bear, Teddy Bear

Teddy Bear, Teddy Bear, turn around,
Teddy Bear, Teddy Bear, touch the ground.

Teddy Bear, Teddy Bear, read the news,
Teddy Bear, Teddy Bear, shine your shoes.

Reading: Raffi. (1988). *Wheels on the bus.* New York: Crown.

Functional reading: a "Lost and Found" sign

Sorting: found, sound, round, pound, ground, down, town, brown, crown, clown

Riddle: You can not see me, but you can hear me. I rhyme with *found.* (sound)

Spelling: found, sound, round, pound, ground

Writing: Have students write a list of the sounds they like best.

-oud, -owd *Patterns*

Pattern words: loud, cloud,* proud, crowd

Mixed practice: low, loud, cloud, clown, cow, crowd, proud

Scrambled sentence: The crowd was loud.

Rhyme:

Windy Nights
Robert Louis Stevenson

Whenever the moon and stars are set,
    Whenever the wind is high,
All night long in the dark and wet,
    A man goes riding by.
Late in the night when the fires are out,
Why does he gallop and gallop about?

Whenever the trees are crying aloud,
    And ships are tossed at sea,
By, on the highway, low and loud,
    By at the gallop goes he.
By at the gallop he goes, and then
By he comes back at the gallop again.

Reading:

Lobel, A. (1975). *Owl at home.* New York: HarperCollins.

Rylant, C. (1987). *Henry and Mudge under the yellow moon.* New York: Bradbury Press.

Sorting: loud, cloud, proud, crowd, found, sound, round, pound, ground, down, town, brown, crown, clown

Riddle: I can be a lot of boys and girls. And I can be a lot of big people, too. I can also be loud. I rhyme with *proud,* but I have a *w* where *proud* has a *u,* and I begin with a *c* instead of a *p.* What am I? (a crowd)

Spelling: loud, cloud, proud, crowd

Writing: Have students write a piece telling about something they are proud of.

-out, -outh, -our, -ouse *Patterns*

Pattern words: out,* shout, mouth, south,* our, hour,* flour, house,* mouse

Mixed practice: out, our, mouth, mouse, south, shout, hour, house

Scrambled sentence: "Go south!" shouted Joe.

Rhymes:

There Was a Crooked Man

There was a crooked man,
And he walked a crooked mile,
He found a crooked sixpence
Against a crooked stile;
He bought a crooked cat,
Which caught a crooked mouse.
And they all lived together
In a little crooked house.

I'm a Little Teapot

I'm a little teapot short and stout:
Here is my handle and here is my spout.
When I get all steamed up, I just shout:
"Just tip me over and pour me out!"

Way Down South Where Bananas Grow

Way down South where bananas grow,
A grasshopper stepped on an elephant's toe.
The elephant said, with tears in his eyes,
"Pick on somebody your own size!"

The Boy in the Barn

A little boy went into a barn,
    And lay down on some hay.
An owl came out, and flew about,
    And the little boy ran away.

A Sunshiny Shower

A sunshiny shower
Won't last half an hour.

What Animals Say

Bow-wow, says the dog,
Mew, mew, says the cat,
Grunt, grunt, goes the hog,
And squeak goes the rat.
Tu-whoo, says the owl,
Caw, caw, says the crow,
Quack, quack, says the duck,
What cuckoos say you know.

Reading:

> Everett, L. (1988). *Bubble gum in the sky.* Mattawah, NJ: Troll.
>
> Hayward, L. (1988). *Hello, house.* New York: Random House.
>
> Vinje, M. (1992). *Hanna's butterfly.* Grand Haven, MI: School Zone.

Sorting: out, shout, mouth, south, our, hour, flour, house, mouse, loud, cloud, proud, crowd, found, sound, round, pound, ground

Riddle: What do you call a mouse that lives in someone's house? (house mouse)

Spelling: out, shout, south, our, house, mouse

Writing: Have students draw a picture of and write a description of their dream houses: houses where they might like to live if they could have any house they wanted.

/ow/ Pattern Unit Review.   On the chalkboard or an overhead, write the /ow / pattern words presented in this unit. Mix the patterns so students are not simply using the first word as a clue to the other words in that column. Words listed in the sorting exercise can be used for this purpose. If students are not able to read 90 percent of the words, continue to review them until they are able to do so. Most important, have students read books that contain /ow/ pattern words.

> *Sorting* (words should be sorted by rhyming sound): cow, found, shout, proud, crown, sound, down, cloud, how, town, mouse, now, south, brown, wow, clown, out, mouth, our, hour, flour, house, loud, crowd
>
> *Secret message:* Write the words on the lines and read the secret message.
>
> 1. Take the **D** from **dog** and put in **F**. __ __ __
> 2. Take the **h** from **his**. __ __
> 3. Take the **n** from **an**. __
> 4. Add **c** to **loud**. __ __ __ __ __
> 5. Keep **close** just as it is. __ __ __ __ __
> 6. Drop and **o** from **too**. __ __
> 7. Keep **the** just as it is. __ __ __
> 8. Add **g** to **round**. __ __ __ __ __ __
>
> _____ _____ _____ _____ _____ _____ _____ _____.

/oy/ Patterns

-oy Pattern

> *Pattern words:* boy,* toy, joy
>
> *Mixed practice:* boy, ball, toy, tall, jay, joy
>
> *Scrambled sentence:* The boy has a new toy.
>
> *Rhyme:*
>
> **The Gingerbread Man**
>
> Smiling girls, rosy boys,
> Come and buy my little toys;
> Monkeys made of gingerbread,
> And sugar horses painted red.
>
> *Sorting:* boy, toy, joy, out, shout, mouth, south, our, hour, flour, house, mouse, loud, cloud, proud, crowd
>
> *Riddle:* You can have fun with me. I can be a ball or a doll. I can be a game or a very small truck. My name rhymes with joy. What am I? (a toy)

Spelling: boy, toy, joy

Writing: Have students draw a picture of the toy they like best and then write a piece telling about the toy.

-oil, -oin, -oice, -oise *Patterns*

Pattern words: oil, boil, join, voice, noise

Mixed practice: oil, our, boy, boil, joy, join, noise

Scrambled sentence: The boiling water was making a noise.

Rhymes:

Tom, Tom, the Piper's Son

Tom he was a piper's son,
He learned to play when he was young;
But the only tune that he could play
Was "Over the hills and far away."

Now Tom with his pipe made such a noise,
That he pleased all the girls and boys;
And they stopped to hear him play,
"Over the hills and far away."

Hot Boiled Beans

Boys and girls come to supper—
Hot boiled beans
And very good butter.

Reading: Witty, B. (1991). *Noises in the night.* Grand Haven, MI: School Zone.

Sorting: oil, boil, join, voice, noise, boy, toy, joy, out, shout, mouth, south

Rhyme riddle: What do you call noise that a crowd of boys make? (boys' noise)

Spelling: oil, join, voice, noise

Writing: Have students make a list of noises that bother them.

/oy/ Pattern Unit Review.   On the chalkboard or an overhead, write the /oy/ pattern words presented in this unit. Mix the patterns so students are not simply using the first word as a clue to the other words in that column. Words listed in the sorting exercise can be used for this purpose. If students are not able to read 90 percent of the words, continue to review them until they are able to do so. Most important, have students read books that contain pattern words.

Sorting (words should be sorted by rhyming sound): boy, oil, toy, boil, joy, join, voice, noise

Secret message: Write the words on the lines and read the secret message.

1. Add **Th** to **at.** __ __ __ __
2. Take the **b** from **boy** and put in **t.** __ __ __
3. Add **s** to **make.** __ __ __ __ __
4. Take **c** from **cloud.** __ __ __ __ __
5. Add **s** to **noise.** __ __ __ __ __ __

_____ _____ _____ _____ _____.

Short-*a* Illustrations

Short-*e* Illustrations

Short-*i* Illustrations

Short-*o* and Short-*u* Illustrations

Short-*u* and Long-*a* Illustrations

Long-*a* and Long-*e* Illustrations

Long-*e*, Long-*i*, and Long-*o* Illustrations

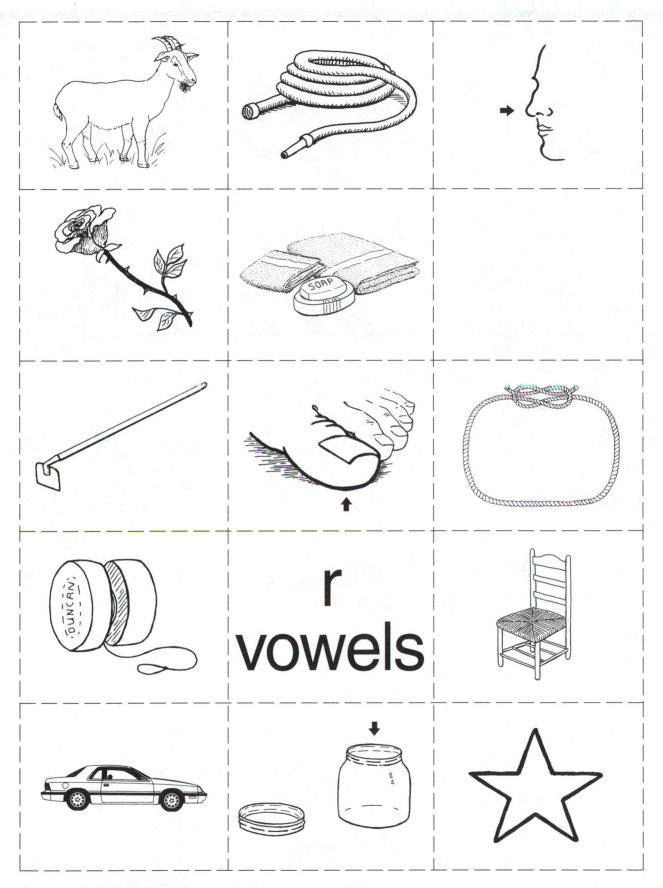

Long-*o* and *r*-Vowel Illustrations

r-Vowel and Other-Vowel Illustrations

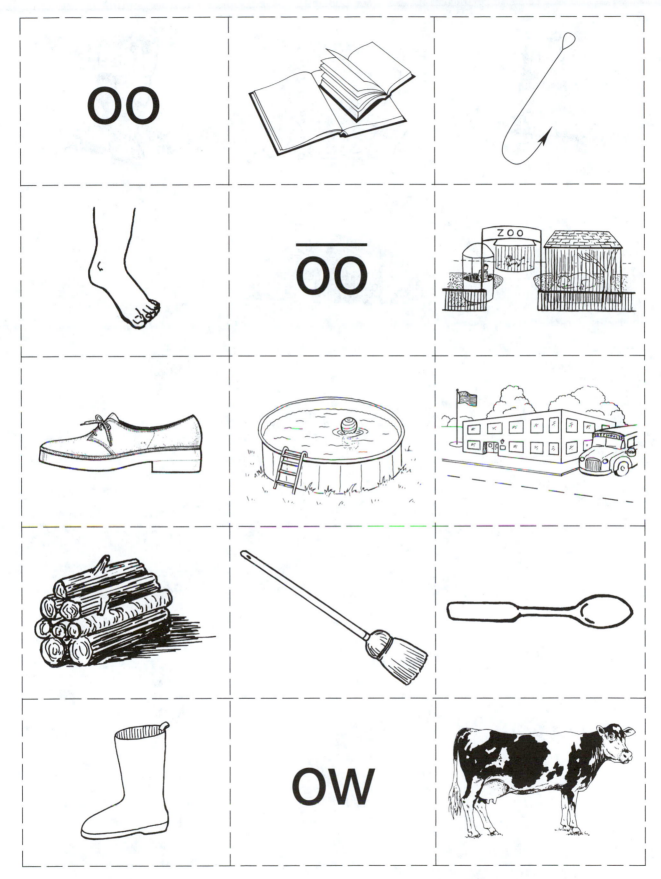

Other-Vowel Illustrations

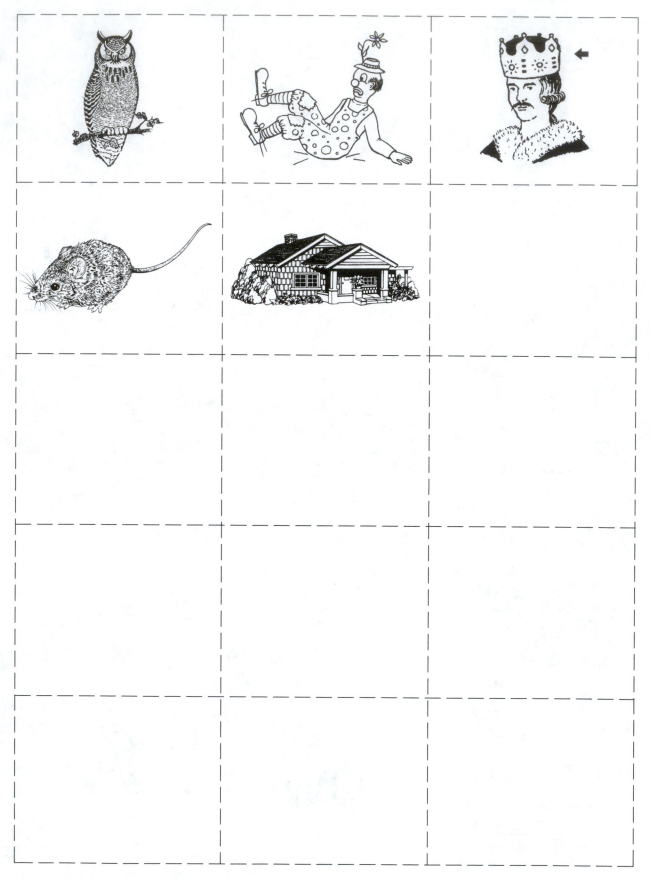

Other-Vowel Illustrations (*continued*)

cat	ran	dad	trap	red
hat	van	had	back	sled
rat	am	mad	pack	led
bat	ham	sad	tack	bell
sat	jam	cap	black	fell
pan	Pam	map	snack	sell
can	Sam	nap	bed	tell
man	bad	snap	fed	yell

Short-a and Short-e Pattern Words

hen	net	nest	slid	hill
men	pet	rest	big	will
pen	lent	pest	pig	spill
ten	sent	test	dig	still
when	tent	did	fig	him
get	went	kid	wig	swim
let	spent	lid	twig	in
met	best	rid	bill	pin

Short-e and Short-i Pattern Words

win	thing	tick	trick	dot
chin	lip	lick	hop	got
twin	tip	quick	mop	hot
king	drip	trick	pop	lot
ring	ship	thick	top	not
sing	trip	pick	drop	pot
wing	kick	sick	shop	shot
bring	pick	stick	stop	spot

Short-i and Short-o Pattern Words

dump	shut	up	gum	lock
jump	duck	cup	hum	rock
junk	luck	pup	drum	block
skunk	truck	us	plum	clock
trunk	lunch	bus	fun	bug
dust	munch	plus	run	dug
just	crunch	but	sun	hug
must	bump	cut	spun	rug

Short-*u* Pattern Words

Chapter 6

SIGHT WORDS

Not all words fall into patterns. Ironically, the words that we meet most frequently in print are those that have the most irregular spellings: *the, of, have.* In addition to being the most frequently occurring words, these are also the oldest. In English, there is a tendency to retain the spelling of a word even though, over the years, the pronunciation of the word may have changed. This preserves the utility of the writing system because it enables us to read texts that were written many years ago. However, it means that the spellings of these older words don't reflect their pronunciations as well as they once did.

A list of high-frequency words is presented in Tables 6.1 and 6.2. Table 6.1 shows these words in order of frequency from 1 through 200. Table 6.2 shows these same words in alphabetical order. The words are drawn from *The Educator's Word Frequency Guide* (Zeno, Ivens, Millard & Rajduvvuri, 1995), which is the most recent large-scale compilation of words used in school texts, children's books, and other materials that students might read.

THE NATURE OF SIGHT WORDS

The term "sight words" is often used to refer to these high-frequency words, especially those like *of* and *the,* whose spellings don't reflect their pronunciations very effectively. "Sight words" also refer to high-frequency words, such as *ball* and *play,* whose spellings do an excellent job of indicating pronunciation but that incorporate advanced patterns.

In addition, the term "sight word" is used to indicate how some high-frequency words are learned: they are simply memorized. Words such as *of* and *the* are best learned through memory, because phonics cues are nonexistent or not effective. Whenever possible, however, high-frequency words should be taught through a phonics approach. Using phonics gives students a hook on which to attach the pronunciation of a printed symbol. Otherwise, students are forced to use nonverbal cues: the length or shape of the word, or some aspect of the word that might be used as a mnemonic aid. For instance, students might remember that *look* is "look" because the two *o*'s look like eyes that are looking. The problem with these cues is that they are rote and arbitrary and so are easily forgotten. In addition, as students learn an increasing number of words in this way, it becomes more difficult to construct distinctive cues (Ehri, 1994).

The term "sight words" has a fourth meaning. It also refers to words that are recognized instantly. Through encountering words and carefully processing them, we create bonds between the words' meanings and their pronunciation and the visual form of the word, so that seeing the word calls up its pronunciation and meaning. Using phonics as memory hooks helps us create these bonds. Eventually, except for unfamiliar names and new words, virtually all printed words become sight words.

TABLE 6.1   High-Frequency Words According to Frequency of Occurrence

1. the	35. when	69. see	103. through	137. such	171. under
2. of	36. we	70. no	104. back	138. here	172. last
3. and	37. there	71. could	105. much	139. take	173. read
4. a	38. can	72. make	106. good	140. why	174. never
5. to	39. an	73. than	107. before	141. thing	175. am
6. in	40. your	74. first	108. go	142. great	176. us
7. is	41. which	75. been	109. man	143. help	177. left
8. you	42. their	76. its	110. our	144. put	178. end
9. that	43. said	77. who	111. want	145. year	179. along
10. it	44. if	78. now	112. lot	146. different	180. while
11. he	45. will	79. people	113. me	147. number	181. sound
12. for	46. do	80. my	114. day	148. away	182. house
13. was	47. each	81. made	115. too	149. again	183. might
14. on	48. about	82. over	116. any	150. off	184. next
15. are	49. how	83. did	117. same	151. went	185. below
16. as	50. up	84. down	118. right	152. tell	186. saw
17. with	51. out	85. way	119. look	153. men	187. something
18. his	52. then	86. only	120. think	154. say	188. thought
19. they	53. them	87. may	121. also	155. small	189. both
20. at	54. she	88. find	122. around	156. every	190. few
21. be	55. many	89. use	123. another	157. found	191. those
22. this	56. some	90. water	124. came	158. still	192. school
23. from	57. so	91. little	125. three	159. big	193. show
24. I	58. these	92. long	126. soon	160. between	194. always
25. have	59. would	93. very	127. come	161. name	195. until
26. not	60. other	94. after	128. work	162. should	196. large
27. or	61. into	95. word	129. must	163. home	197. often
28. by	62. has	96. called	130. part	164. give	198. together
29. one	63. more	97. just	131. because	165. air	199. ask
30. had	64. two	98. new	132. does	166. line	200. write
31. but	65. her	99. where	133. even	167. mother	
32. what	66. like	100. most	134. place	168. set	
33. all	67. him	101. know	135. old	169. world	
34. were	68. time	102. get	136. well	170. own	

When presenting sight words, incorporate phonics cues as much as is feasible. These help readers create bonds between a word's visual form and its pronunciation and meaning. Using phonics reduces the amount of time it takes to learn a new word. Also, incorporate other cues that help students distinguish between words. Present words that have different appearances so that they can be easily distinguished. Don't, for instance, present *what, where, when,* and *which* in the same lesson. However, you might present *then* and *when* at the same time and show how these words have the same internal pattern. This way students have phonics cues which help them store and retrieve the words. Also, build on what students know. If students have had the word *ten* and you are presenting the words *then* and *when,* you might relate *then* and *when* to the *en* in *ten.* You can also help them to see that *the* and *then* begin with the same sound.

Word analysis skills are interdependent. Sight words can't be fully learned until students know basic phonics. But phonics is easier to teach if students know some words at sight. Analogies can only be used on a limited basis if there are only a few comparison words in the student's store of known words. Therefore, readers need broad-based instruction (Ehri & McCormick, 1998).

TABLE 6.2   High-Frequency Words in Alphabetical Order

a	come	how	never	should	until
about	could	I	new	show	up
after	day	if	next	small	us
again	did	in	no	so	use
air	different	into	not	some	very
all	do	is	now	something	was
along	does	it	number	soon	want
also	down	its	of	sound	water
always	each	just	off	still	way
am	end	know	often	such	we
an	even	large	old	take	well
and	every	last	on	tell	went
another	few	left	one	than	were
any	find	like	only	that	what
are	first	line	or	the	when
around	for	little	other	their	where
as	found	long	our	them	which
asked	from	look	out	then	while
at	get	lot	over	there	who
away	give	made	own	these	why
back	go	make	part	they	will
be	good	man	people	thing	with
because	great	many	place	think	word
been	had	may	put	this	work
before	has	me	read	those	world
below	have	men	right	thought	would
between	he	might	said	three	write
big	help	more	same	through	year
both	her	most	saw	time	you
but	here	mother	say	to	your
by	him	much	school	together	
called	his	must	see	too	
came	home	my	set	two	
can	house	name	she	under	

■ WHOLE–PART–WHOLE AND PART–WHOLE APPROACHES

Sight words can be taught through a whole–part–whole approach or through a part–whole approach. In a whole–part–whole approach, students are introduced to the words in the context of a story. In a part–whole approach, students learn the words before encountering them in a story. Neither approach has been shown to be better. Whole–part–whole procedures seem more appropriate for younger students who are reading brief selections. Part–whole procedures may be more suitable for longer selections. However, research does indicate that students should encounter sight words both in context and isolation (Samuels, 1967; Singer, Samuels, & Spiroff, 1973–1974). Seeing words in isolation helps students note the individual elements that make up the word. Seeing words in context helps familiarize students with the meaning and usage of the words and also provides realistic practice. The following section describes steps for presenting sight words in a whole–part–whole lesson. Materials used might be a big book, an experience story, or a portion of a book written on the board.

▦ LESSON USING A WHOLE–PART–WHOLE PROCEDURE TO TEACH SIGHT WORDS

Step 1: Familiarizing Students with the Selection.   A story, rhyme, poem, or song can be used to introduce sight words. In choosing a selection, pick one that students will enjoy so that it can be read over and over again without losing its appeal. From the selection, choose four to five words that you feel are especially valuable for students to learn because they appear over and over again in upcoming selections. For the book *Roll Over! A Counting Song* (Peek, 1980), you might choose the words *they, all, over, out*. Preview the selection by discussing the title and the cover illustration and having students predict what the book will be about. Then read the selection to students, pointing to each word as you do so. Finally, discuss the selection.

Step 2: Rereading the Text with Students.   Reread the text. Invite students to join in. Initially they might join in by reading the refrain, "Roll over! Roll over!" After a second reading, they might chorally read the last two lines: "They all rolled over and one fell out." Eventually, have students read the story on their own.

Step 3: Reading the Story on Their Own.   Have students read the story as independently as possible. If the story has pictures that help identify the words, cover up the illustrations or copy the story on chart paper. That way students focus entirely on the words. Otherwise, they might simply read the pictures.

Step 4: Reassembling the Story.   Copy sentences from the selection on strips of tagboard. Have students reassemble the whole story or—if it is long—portions of it by putting sentences in the right order in a pocket chart. You might select sentences that contain a repeated phrase or the most frequently occurring words. You might also prepare easy or more difficult sentences so that you can provide for individual differences.

   Also have students reassemble single sentences that have been cut up into individual words. This helps students focus on individual words and see how words function in sentences. To focus on the elements in individual words, cut up words into their letters, or use magnetic letters, and have students reassemble the letters into words.

▦ LESSON USING A PART–WHOLE PROCEDURE TO PRESENT SIGHT WORDS

Step 1: Discussing the Meanings of the Words.   This step should only be implemented if the meanings of the sight words are unfamiliar. In general, this will not be necessary because most of the high-frequency words are part of the students' listening and speaking vocabulary. In fact, discussing the meanings of known words wastes valuable instructional time and detracts from the purpose of sight-word instruction, which is helping children rapidly recognize printed versions of frequently occurring words.

Step 2: Presenting the Words in Isolation.   Print each of the new words to be learned on a large card. Show the students each card, but before pronouncing the word on the card, see if the students can read it. If students are able to read a word, discard it and concentrate on the unknown ones. If the word incorporates a phonic element that students know, encourage them to say any parts of the word they know. For instance, students may know the beginning sound of *was* or *way* or the *at* in *that*. Having students identify known parts gives them a foundation on which to build a mental representation of the new word. However, when presenting words such as *once* or *of*, which are highly irregular, do not attempt to have them detect letter–sound relationships. And, except for initial consonants, don't have them seek familiar word parts in words such as *what* and *water*, lest they become confused by the unusual pronunciations that *at* has in these words. As you present the words, point out any features that might help students remember the word—for instance, *are* has an *r; once* begins like *one* but has a *ce* at the end. Also have students spell the words, so they notice individual letters. After presenting and explaining a word, have students read it chorally. As additional words are introduced, have students read the new word and the previously presented words. Continue presenting the words until students recognize them immediately (Bryant, Kelly, Hathaway, & Rubin, 1981).

Step 3: Presenting the Words in Context.   After students can recognize the words rapidly in isolation, present them in the context of short phrases or sentences. Use previously introduced sight words to create phrases and sentences if necessary. In presenting the words *long, know, some, words,* you might present the following:

> some words
> some long words
> I know some long words.

Present the phrases and sentences until students can read them rapidly.

Step 4: Applying the New Words.   Present the story from which the new words were drawn. Discuss the title and the cover and other major illustrations. Then help students find and read the sentences in which the new sight words appear. Based on a discussion of the title, selected illustrations, and the sentence the students read, have them predict what the story might be about and then read to assess their prediction.

Step 5: Reviewing the Words.   From time to time, review sight words that were presented previously. Also provide ample opportunity for practice. Your goal is to develop students' skills so that they recognize high-frequency words immediately. If they have rapid recognition of the most frequently occurring words, they will be able to focus their mental energies on comprehending what they are reading.

ADDITIONAL PRACTICE ACTIVITIES

Many of the same activities used to reinforce patterns can be used to reinforce high-frequency words. Scrambled sentences, sorting, rhymes, riddles, songs, the word wall, homemade books, and children's' books can be used to reinforce sight words. When introducing high-frequency words, introduce the words that occur the most and are the easiest first. A good way to select high-frequency words for introduction is to look over a selection about to be read and choose four or five words that students probably don't know but that are important to an understanding of the story and will probably occur in upcoming selections. The same books used to reinforce patterns can also be used to introduce sight words. In fact, both pattern words and sight words can be introduced at the same time. For instance, after teaching the *-at* pattern in preparation for having students read *Cat on the Mat*, also present the sight words *on* and *the*, because they are an essential part of the book and will occur frequently in upcoming selections.

The rhymes and songs used to introduce patterns can also be used to present high-frequency words. Rhymes and songs, by their nature, contain high-frequency words in addition to pattern or rhyming words.

The best way to develop rapid recognition of high-frequency words or fluency is to read lots of easy materials. Reading materials in which nearly all the words are known builds students' speed of word recognition. Because they are meeting new concepts and experiences, even though the words are easy, students are also building their background of knowledge. Almost any book that is well within the student's grasp can be used to develop sight vocabulary. Listed below are a number of easy books that might be used to develop rapid recognition of high-frequency words.

Appelt, K. (1993). *Elephants aloft.* San Diego, CA: Harcourt. Two elephants take a trip in a hot air balloon to see their Aunt Rwanda. Features sight words: *in, out, across, around, over, under.*

Aruego, J., & Dewey, A. (1979). *We hide, you seek.* New York: Greenwillow. Playing hide-and-go-seek, a clumsy rhino finds the other animals.

Gomi, T. (1977). *Where's the fish?* New York: Morrow, 1977. Readers are asked to find the fish in a series of illustrations.

Hoban, T. (1979). *One little kitten.* New York: Greenwillow. Photos and captions show a kitten's activities.

Inkpen, M. (1994). *Kipper's book of opposites.* San Diego: Harcourt. A dog demonstrates opposites: *in–out, slow–fast, day–night.* Part of the Kipper series.

Lillegard, D. (1984). *Where is it?* Chicago: Children's Press. Boy searches for his red baseball cap.

Maestro, B., & Maestro, G. (1976). *Where is my friend?* New York: Crown. Harriet Elephant looks for her mouse friend. Focuses on position sight words.

McMillan, B. (1991). *Play day, A book of terse verse.* New York: Holiday House. In two-word rhymes and photos, portrays children at play.

Reese, B. (1979). *Sunshine.* New York: Phoenix Learning Resources. Sunshine, the family pet, likes to bark. Containing just 10 different words, this is a very easy book. Part of a series of 10-word books distributed by Phoenix Learning Resources.

Steptoe, J. (1988). *Baby says.* New York: Lothrop, Lee & Shepard. An older brother lets his baby brother play with his blocks.

The fold-and-read books in Appendix B can also be used to reinforce high-frequency words.

USING THE RHYTHM OF LANGUAGE TO FOSTER RAPID RECOGNITION

Word recognition isn't simply a matter of decoding individual words. The words must be organized into phrases, sentences, and stories. When students read, they must recode printed material so as to recapture the rhythm of language. Once students capture the rhythm of the language, they are better able to recognize each of the printed words. It's as though they are carried along by the flow of the language. That's why it is important for students to read lots of connected text, especially selections that are well written and have a natural flow. Reading easy books helps develop that flow. Because of their built-in rhythms and repetitions, reading rhymes is also an excellent way to develop both accuracy and fluency of word recognition. Many of the rhymes used to reinforce word patterns can also be used to practice rapid recognition of high-frequency words. Some especially useful rhymes follow.

The Bear Went over the Mountain

The bear went over the mountain,
The bear went over the mountain,
The bear went over the mountain,
To see what he could see.

Jack Hall

Jack Hall,
He is so small,
A rat could eat him,
Hat and all.

Animals

Can you hop like a rabbit?
Can you jump like a frog?
Can you walk like a duck?
Can you run like a dog?
Can you fly like a bird?
Can you swim like a fish?
And be still like a good child—
As still as this?

A Sailor Went to Sea

A sailor went to sea, sea, sea,
Just to see what he could see, see, see
And all that he could see, see, see
Was the sea, sea, sea.

A-Hunting We Will Go

A-hunting we will go,
A-hunting we will go.
We'll catch a fox
And put him in a box.
And then we'll let him go.

Out

Out goes the rat,
Out goes the cat,
Out goes the lady
With the big green hat.
Y, O, U spells you;
O, U, T spells out!

One, Two, Three

One, two, three, four, five,
Once I caught a fish alive.
Six, seven, eight, nine, ten,
But I let it go again.
Why did you let it go?
Because it bit my finger so.
Which finger did it bite?
The little one upon the right.

Question

Do you love me
Or do you not?
You told me once
But I forgot.

Rain, Rain, Go Away

Rain, rain, go away.
Come again another day.
Little Robert wants to play.

Rain

Rain, rain, go to Spain,
And never come back again.

The Mulberry Bush

Here we go round the mulberry bush,
    the mulberry bush,
    the mulberry bush,
Here we go round the mulberry bush,
On a cold and frosty morning.

This is the way we clap our hands,
    clap our hands,
    clap our hands,
This is the way we clap our hands,
On a cold and frosty morning.

■ Chapter 7

SYLLABIC ANALYSIS

In time, most students eventually learn phonics and become proficient at deciphering single-syllable words. However, a sizable proportion of students have difficulty applying their knowledge of phonics to multisyllabic words. For instance, Alicia, a fourth grader, is able to read *am* and *too* and *cap* and *her* but stumbles over *bamboo* and *chapter,* which incorporate the sounds of these words. Alicia's syllabication skills are weak but could be dramatically improved by building on what she already knows about decoding single-syllable words.

■ TEACHING SYLLABLE PATTERNS

Traditionally, students are taught to decode multisyllabic words by applying generalizations. For instance, students are taught that if a syllable ends in a vowel, that vowel is usually long. Although syllabic generalizations can be useful, a more concrete method of teaching syllabication is to present high-frequency syllabication patterns. Presenting patterns helps students detect and learn to use pronounceable word parts within multisyllabic words. Instead of presenting the open-syllable (*frozen*) generalization, a group of long-*o* multisyllabic words that fit the pattern are introduced. Whenever possible, a one-syllable known word is presented as a contrasting element so that students can relate the polysyllabic pattern to a known single-syllable pattern and also more readily identify the familiar elements in each multisyllabic word, as in the following:

> *no*
> *notice*
> *broken*
> *spoken*
> *frozen*
> *hotel*
> *motel*
> *motor*
> *over*

Reading *no* should help students read *notice,* which should help them read *broken,* which should help them read *spoken* and *frozen,* and so on. The ultimate aim is to teach students to recognize the long-*o* pattern in multisyllabic words so that when they encounter a new word, such as *motor* or *motel,* they see the *mo* as a unit and automatically pronounce it as /mō/, which, in turn, helps them to recognize the whole word or move on to the next syllable.

■ TEACHING STRATEGIES TO STUDENTS

Presenting a series of high-frequency patterns is only part of an effective program of syllabic analysis. Because of the diversity of English spelling, students will encounter patterns that they have not been taught or may even forget patterns that were previously presented. Therefore, they need strategies for coping with multisyllabic words that pose problems for them, just as they need strategies for decoding single-syllable words. Students are shown how to apply the pronounceable word part and analogy strategies to multisyllabic words.

Applying the pronounceable word part strategy to polysyllabic words, students should try to pronounce an unfamiliar multisyllabic word syllable by syllable. In general, students would pronounce the first syllable, then the second, and so on. However, if they are unable to pronounce the first syllable, they might try their luck with a subsequent syllable. The pronunciation of a medial or ending syllable may trigger the pronunciation of the entire word. For instance, pronouncing the *tent* in *content* might spark the pronunciation of the whole word.

If the pronounceable word part strategy doesn't work, then students should try the analogy strategy. The strategy works much the same way when used with multisyllabic words as it does with single-syllable words. However, instead of making just one comparison, it may be necessary to make two or three. A student stumbling over the word *shampoo* uses the analogous words *ham* and *too* to sound it out. The word *fever* is sounded out by comparing its two syllables to *he* and *her*.

▓ STEPS FOR DECODING MULTISYLLABIC WORDS

Listed below is a series of steps that students might take when confronting a multisyllabic word that is unfamiliar in print.

1. Say each part of the word, or say as many parts as I can.
2. If I can't say a part, think of a word that is like the part I can't say and then try to say that word part. (If I can't do 1 or 2, then go to 5.)
3. Put the parts together to make a word.
4. Ask: "Is this a real word? Does it make sense in the story?" (If not, try again or go to 5.)
5. Say "blank" for the word. Read to the end of the sentence. Ask myself: "What word would make sense here?"

Unfortunately, these strategies don't work all the time. There are some syllables for which no analogies can be found. In addition, the pronunciation of a vowel is often altered when it is found in a syllable, especially one that is unaccented. For instance, the *be* in *belong* is no longer analogous to *he*, because the long *e* has become a schwa (buh-LONG). Students need to be taught to make adjustments in pronunciation when applying the strategies. Students should also be taught to use the glossary or dictionary when other strategies don't work.

In making comparisons, students can think up their own analogy words or can use the analogy words presented in a Model Words list. The Model Words list is composed of single-syllable model words that accompanied single-syllable patterns previously taught and multisyllabic model words, such as *action* and *future*, that have been introduced. As a pattern is introduced, add it to the Model Words list. If students have already mastered single-syllable patterns, they can build on this knowledge to attack multisyllabic words, because most multisyllabic words are composed of two or more patterns found in single-syllable words (*farm-er, win-dow*). Basically, instruction consists of showing students how to use what they already know to attack apparently unfamiliar words. A sample Model Words list is presented in Table 7.1.

SCOPE AND SEQUENCE OF THE PROGRAM

Although there are more than 200 syllable patterns, only about 100 of these occur with a high degree of frequency. The most useful 95 patterns, together with example words to illustrate those patterns, are presented in the Syllable Pattern Resources at the end of this chapter. Patterns were chosen on the basis of frequency of occurrence and ease of learning. Emphasis is on two-syllable patterns. However, a number of three- and four-syllable words and patterns are included in the program. The easiest and most frequently occurring patterns should be presented early in the program and include compound word patterns (*sunshine, baseball*), the schwa-*a* pattern (*ago, away*), and the -*ar* (*garden*), -*en* (*happen*), and -*er* (*over*) patterns. Later in the program more advanced elements, such as -*tion* (*action, nation*) and -*ture* (*future, nature*) are introduced. A suggested sequence for presenting the patterns is given in Table 7.2.

It is suggested that at least three patterns a week be presented. The patterns can be introduced on Monday and then reinforced during the week. Students' mastery of the patterns could be assessed on Friday.

TABLE 7.1   Advanced Model Words

-*a*	table
-*a* (schwa)	ago
-*ab*	cab, cabin
-*an*	pan, panic
-*ap*	nap, napkin
-*ar*	car, far, farmer
-*at*	cat, caterpillar
-*e*	me, meter
-*e* (schwa)	telephone
-*e* (i)	demand
-*en*	ten, tender
-*er*	her, hermit
-*et*	net, netting
-*i*	I, tiger
-*i* (schwa)	similar
-*im*	swim, swimmer
-*ion*	mill, million
-*tion*	act, action
-*in*	pin, win, winter
-*is(s)*	miss, mister
-*it*	hit, hitter
-*o*	no, hotel
-*o* (schwa)	opinion
-*ob*	rob, robber
-*or*	or, order
-*u*	music
-*u* (schwa)	upon
-*um*	sum, summer
-*un*	sun, sunny
-*ur*	fur, furry
-*ture*	future

TABLE 7.2   Scope and Sequence of Multisyllabic Patterns

High-Frequency Patterns

Compound word patterns
Schwa-*a*
-*en*, -*o*, -*er*
-*ar*, -*at*, -*it*
-*in*, *is(s)*, -*un*
be-, *re*-, -*or*
-*a*, -*y* = /ē/, -*ey*, -*ble*
-*i*, -*ur*, -*um*
-*ic(k)*, -*et*, -*im*

Short-Vowel Patterns

-*ab*, -*ad*, -*ag*, -*ang*
-*am*, -*an*, -*ant*, -*ap*
-*ent*, -*el(l)*
-*ep*, -*es*, -*ev*
-*id*, -*ig*, -*il(l)*
-*ob*, *oc(k)*, -*od*
-*ol*, -*om*, -*on*
-*op*, -*ot*, -*age*
-*ub*, -*uc(k)*, -*ud*
-*uf*, -*ug*, -*up*
-*um*, -*us*, -*ut*, -*uz*

Long-Vowel and -*ture* Patterns

-*e*, -*ee*, -*ea* = /ē/
-*ide*, -*ire*, -*ise*, -*ive*, -*ize*
-*ade*, -*aid*, -*ail*, -*ale*, -*ain*, -*ate*
-*ope*, -*one*, *oke*, -*u*, -*ture*

Other-Vowel and Miscellaneous Patterns

-*al*, -*au*, -*aw*
-*ea* = /e/, *i* = /ē/, *i-e* = /ē/
-*tion*, -*sion*, -*y* = /ī/
-*oi*, -*oy*
-*ou*, -*ow*
-*oo*, -*ove* = /oo/, -*u* = /oo/
-*ook*, -*oot*, -*ood*, -*ul(l)*

MULTISYLLABIC PATTERNS LESSON

When introducing multisyllabic patterns that incorporate patterns found in single-syllable words, stress how the multisyllabic patterns are built on single-syllable patterns. Also provide ample opportunity for students to apply their skills and strategies. Emphasize the use of pronounceable word part and analogy strategies when students encounter multisyllabic words.

Step 1: Introducing the Pattern.   Write *tie* on the board and have students read it. Then write *tiger* under it, saying the syllables as you write them. Write the separate syllables in contrasting colors, or underline them so students can discriminate them more easily. Contrast *tie* and *tiger* so that students see the similarities. Then have students read *tiger*. Present the following words in this same way: *spider, tiny, title, pilot, Friday.* Then have all the words read.

Step 2: Formulating a Generalization.   Lead students to see that *i* often has a long-*i* vowel sound when it comes at the end of a syllable. Create a Model Words chart, if you don't already have one. (A Model Words chart displays a model word for each pattern taught. If students have difficulty with a word, they refer to the chart and find a model word or words that follow the same pattern as the word they are attempting to read.) Pointing out that *tiger* is the model word for the -*i* pattern, have students add it to their Model Words chart. Later, if students have difficulty with a word containing an -*i* syllable, encourage them to say each part of the word or as many parts as they can and then reconstruct the word. If necessary, they can use *tiger* or other model words to help them.

Step 3: Guided Practice.   Possible practice activities include the following:

Guess the Word.   Cut words into separate syllables. Display the first syllable, and, if you wish, provide a semantic clue. Have students try to guess what the whole word is. Then display the second syllable. If it is a two-syllable word, have them put the two syllables together and say the word and see if their guess was correct. If the word has three or more syllables, have them put the first two syllables together and make a new guess if they wish. Continue in this fashion until the whole word has been assembled. For the word *volunteer,* for example, you would display *vol* and invite a student to pronounce it and guess what the whole word might be. Other students should be encouraged to add their predictions. In this way, they are exposed to a number of words that follow the pattern. After writing predictions on the board, add the second syllable, *un,* and invite a student to read the second syllable and add it to the first. At this point students can stick with their original predictions or make new ones. After writing their predictions on the board, display *teer,* have a student read it, and then add it to *vol-un* and read the whole word. The class then compares their predictions with the target word.

Assembling Scrambled Syllables.   Make words by putting together two of the three syllables in each row. On the lines, write the words that you make.

1.	ny	um	ti	_____
2.	be	der	spi	_____
3.	tle	ti	er	_____
4.	lot	ly	pi	_____
5.	ger	mur	ti	_____

You could also put syllables on separate cards and have students form words by putting syllables together.

Completing Sentences.   Underline the word that fits the sense of the sentence better.

1. The (tiger, tiny) is a big cat.
2. The (silent, spider) slowly spun its web.
3. What is the (tiger, title) of the book that you are reading?
4. I will see you next (Frisbee, Friday).
5. The (tinny, tiny) dog had a loud bark.

Step 4: Application.   Provide students with frequent opportunities to make use of this strategy by reading basal stories, trade books, periodicals, and real-world materials. Except at very beginning levels, virtually all books and other materials contain multisyllabic words. As materials grow harder, the proportion of multisyllabic words increases. If students are reading books at the appropriate level, then the proportion of multisyllabic words presented in the text should not be overwhelming. To ensure that students have an opportunity to apply syllabication skills, examine the text to be read and note major multisyllabic patterns incorporated. Select two or three major patterns that you feel might give students problems, and teach them. Following this procedure ensures that students will have the opportunity to apply their skills in the context of their reading.

Step 5: Expansion of Patterns.   Expand the pattern to include more advanced words: *silent, final, minus.* You might also combine the long-*i* pattern with the *-ant* pattern. Write *ant* on the board. Then show how you would use long-*i* syllables to create new words.

    ant
giant
reliant
defiant

Step 6: Review.   From time to time, review the patterns and model the process of using them. When students encounter difficult words, encourage them to seek out pronounceable word parts or use the model words to help them decode the words. Provide assistance as needed.

ADDED REINFORCEMENT ACTIVITIES

READING SYLLABLE RIDDLES

Have students read syllable riddles similar to the following. The purpose of the exercise is to help them detect the separate syllables in words. Once students catch onto the way the riddles are formed, encourage them to compose syllable riddles of their own.

What kind of a tie has stripes and growls? (a **tig**er)
What's a good day for cooking? (a **Fri**day)
What kind of point makes you feel bad? (a disap**point**ment)
What kind of a car do people laugh at? (a **car**toon)
What kind of a rock can be shot into space? (a **rock**et)

◼ REAL-WORLD APPLICATIONS

Use signs, labels, sets of directions, and other real-world reading materials to reinforce patterns. To provide practice for the $i = /\bar{e}/$ pattern, for example, you might display and have the class read a label from a box of uncooked **spaghetti,** a sign in the library indicating **magazines,** a newspaper ad for **radios,** a label from a can of **zucchini,** and the markings on a **police** car.

◼ MUSIC

Since song lyrics are usually divided into syllables, have students read or sing songs that contain polysyllabic patterns that you wish to reinforce. This is an especially valuable activity in the beginning stages of instruction in decoding polysyllabic words. If students sing the words, they should be looking at them as they sing them so they have the opportunity to see how the polysyllabic words are divided into syllables.

Pop! Goes the Weasel

All a-round the mul-berr-ry bush the mon-key chased the wea-sel,
The mon-key thought t'was all in fun,
Pop! goes the wea-sel.

A pen-ny for a spool of thread,
A pen-ny for a nee-dle,
That's the way the mon-ey goes
Pop! goes the wea-sel.

Ruf-us has the whoop-ing cough,
Poor Sal-ly has the mea-sles,
That's the way the doc-tor goes,
Pop! goes the wea-sel.

Skip to My Lou

Lost my part-ner, what'll I do?
Lost my part-ner, what'll I do?
Lost my part-ner, what'll I do?
Skip to my Lou, my dar-lin'.
Skip, skip, skip to my Lou,
Skip, skip, skip to my Lou,
Skip, skip, skip to my Lou,
Skip to my Lou, my dar-lin'.

Yankee Doodle

Yan-kee Doo-dle came to town a-rid-ing on a po-ny
Stuck a feath-er in his cap and called it mac-a-ro-ni.
Yan-kee Doo-dle, keep it up! Yan-kee Doo-dle, dan-dy,
Mind the mu-sic and the step and with the girls be hand-y.

◼ RHYMES

Rhymes are also an excellent way to reinforce syllable patterns. Rhymes that might be used to provide practice with multisyllabic words are presented in the Syllable Pattern Resources section.

■ SPELLING

Teaching students to spell multisyllabic words helps them to focus on key elements in the word. It also helps them remember the patterns that make up the words. As long as words are carefully chosen so that the words introduced are those that would most likely be needed in students' writing, then teaching students to spell the words should also improve their overall spelling ability. Suggested spelling words are provided in the Syllable Pattern Resources section.

■ SYLLABLE SORTS

Sorting also helps students become aware of the syllables in words. Sorting is an excellent technique for helping students discover the key concept of open and closed syllables. The teacher can point out and explain the difference between open and closed syllables, but having students discover it for themselves is much more effective. To foster the discovery process, provide students with a mixture of open-syllable and closed-syllable words in an open sort, so that students are led to discover how the words are the same and how they differ and why. Words such as the following might be presented: *dinner, diner, bitter, biter, winner, whiner, tinny, tiny, latter, later, hopping, hoping, robber, robot, picnic, pilot, broken, broccoli.* As with other sorting activities, choose words that are known to students. After students have sorted the words, have them explain how and why they sorted the words as they did. Since the sort is an open one, they may have sorted the words in several ways. If they didn't notice the long-vowel/short-vowel distinction, encourage them to see if there are other ways in which they could sort the words. Lead students to see, if they haven't already discovered it, that one group of words has long vowels and the other group has short vowels and that the long vowels are open (end the syllable) and the short vowels are closed (syllable ends with a consonant). Another way of looking at it is that long vowels are followed by one consonant (*tiger*) and short vowels are followed by two consonants (*trigger*). Have students suggest other words that follow these patterns and find open and closed syllables in their reading.

To reinforce specific vowel patterns, have students sort long- and short-*a* multisyllabic words, long- and short-*e* multisyllabic words, long- and short-*i* multisyllabic words, long- and short-*o* multisyllabic words, and long- and short-*u* multisyllabic words. There are a number of exceptions to the open and closed syllable patterns (*wagon, robin*), so have students include a third column for items that don't seem to fit. Long- and short-*e* multisyllabic words might be sorted as is shown in Figure 7.1.

The sort shows that *e* vowels generally follow the generalization, but there are a number of apparent exceptions, including *record*, which has a variable pronunciation depending on whether it is used as a verb or a noun. Sorting helps students discover the regularities as well as the variability of the spelling system.

Sorts can also be constructed for specific patterns. For instance, you can set sorts in which students contrast words ending in *-tion, -ion,* or *-sion.* Sorts can also be set up to contrast various spellings within the short-*u* or another pattern: *-um, -us, -up, -uff,* for example. Or sorts can be set up to contrast words ending in *-able* with those ending in *-ible.* To set up sorts, choose elements that your students have some knowledge of but have not mastered. Or reinforce elements that you have just taught. Use words that students are likely to know, so they can focus on determining underlying regularities rather than being caught up in decoding the words. Words listed in the Syllable Pattern Resources section, which follows, illustrate many of the most frequently occurring syllable patterns and should be helpful in setting up sorts.

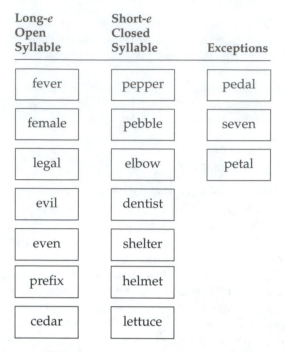

Long-*e* Open Syllable	Short-*e* Closed Syllable	Exceptions
fever	pepper	pedal
female	pebble	seven
legal	elbow	petal
evil	dentist	
even	shelter	
prefix	helmet	
cedar	lettuce	

FIGURE 7.1 Sample Sort for Long-*e* and Short-*e* Vowels

APPLICATION TO SELECTIONS BEING READ

After the class has read a selection containing multisyllabic words, choose four or five multisyllabic words that appeared in the piece and that illustrate a particular pattern. Help students read the words and lead them to see what the common pattern is. When teaching new multisyllabic vocabulary words, instead of simply pronouncing the words, invite students to attempt to use their skills to say them. This provides them with practice and gives the teacher an opportunity to see how well students can apply their skills.

PHONEMIC RESPELLINGS

Also use books and magazines that respell words phonemically. Model and explain the process of using the phonemic respellings. As part of the postreading discussion, have students pronounce the words and read the passages in which they appear.

WRITING

In addition to group writing activities, encourage students to write individual stories that incorporate newly learned words.

INTEGRATION WITH OTHER SUBJECTS

From time to time, relate the new patterns to science, social studies, music, or another subject area. When introducing multisyllabic words in subject matter areas, instead of pronouncing words for students, encourage them to use their newly learned strategies to decode the words.

▤ WORD OF THE DAY

Display a long but decodable word each day and encourage students to work out its pronunciation. Feature words that are in students' listening vocabularies but that they may not recognize in print.

▤ INCIDENTAL TEACHING

When students are about to read a story, trade book, or selection from a content area text, search out from the selection two or three dominant syllable patterns that might pose problems for students, and present these to the class. Also, as students encounter difficult multisyllabic words in their reading, remind them to use the strategies and patterns they have been taught.

▤ USE OF CONTEXT

Context and reading for meaning are important parts of the program. Constructing meaning is the ultimate aim of all reading and should be emphasized throughout. When students decode a word, they should check to see that the word they have reconstructed is a real word and fits the context in which it appears. For some words, the pronounceable word part and analogy strategies don't work, so students will need to rely on context, morphemic analysis, and dictionary skills.

▤ SYLLABLE PATTERN RESOURCES

This Syllable Pattern Resources section provides possibilities for teaching and reinforcing 95 highly useful syllable patterns. Included are some or all of the following: a listing of words that might be used to illustrate the syllable, scrambled syllables, spelling words, rhymes, songs, riddles, real-world materials that use the pattern, and suggestions for using the new words in writing. Sample application words are also listed. After learning a group of patterns, students are presented with application words that incorporate the patterns just taught. Students are then asked to decode the words. This gives students practice in applying patterns and fosters skill in the use of the pronounceable word part and analogy strategies. If students are reading materials on the appropriate level, the patterns suggested should occur naturally in their materials. One way of matching syllable instruction with students' reading is to analyze the selection students are about to read and search for dominant multisyllabic patterns. Then teach those patterns. This will require making some adjustments in the suggested scope and sequence.

Syllable patterns are presented in groups of three. Lessons are arranged in units as follows: high-frequency patterns, short-vowel patterns, long-vowel patterns, and *r*- and other-vowel patterns. The patterns are in approximate order of difficulty.

▤ HIGH-FREQUENCY PATTERNS

Compound-Words Pattern

Pattern words: some, someone, sometime, something, somewhere; day, daylight, daytime, daybreak, daydream; out, outside, outdoor, outline, outfield

Scrambled words: ball base in, one even some, day out side, self my where, time door lunch

Application words: outgrow, outlaw, sunbeam, sundown, infield

Rhyme:

The Snowman

Once there was a snowman
    Stood outside the door
Thought he'd like to come inside
    And run around the floor;
Thought he'd like to warm himself
    By the firelight red;
Thought he'd like to climb up
    On that big white bed.
So he called the North Wind, "Help me now I pray.
    I'm completely frozen, standing here all day."
So the North Wind came along and blew him in the door,
    And now there's nothing left of him
But a puddle on the floor!

Syllable riddle: What kind of a house is easy to pick up? (a **light**house)

Spelling: someone, sometime, something, anyone, anything, outside, inside

Writing: Students make as many words as they can by putting the following words together: *in, out, side, door, up, down, sun, way.*

Schwa-a Pattern

Pattern words: go, ago, away, alone, awake, asleep; round, around, along, alive, apart, about; agree, again, against, among, across

Scrambled words: sleep a read, a go play, head a next, over a round, a long lamp

Application words: awake, amazing, alone, along, apart

Rhyme:

Taking off

The airplane taxis down the field
And heads into the breeze,
It lifts its wheels above the ground,
It skims above the trees,
It rises high and higher
Away up toward the sun,
It's just a speck against the sky
—And now it's gone!

Syllable riddle: As she was leaving, what did the first circle say to the second circle? (I'll see you **around**.)

Spelling: ago, away, alone, about, around, along, across, again, against, asleep

Writing: Students use these three words in a sentence: *ago, away, about.*

-en, -o, -er Patterns

Pattern words: pen, open, happen, enter, twenty, plenty; no, notice, broken, spoken, frozen, motor; her, under, ever, never, other, brother, mother

Scrambled words: ken spo er, zen er few, ter bro ken, pen o ter, en ver o

Application words: farmer, number

Rhymes:

Wishes

Said the first little chicken,
With a queer little squirm,
"Oh, I wish I could find
A fat little worm!"

Said the next little chicken,
With an odd little shrug,
"Oh, I wish I could find
A fat little bug!"

Said the third little chicken,
With a sharp little squeal,
"Oh, I wish I could find
Some nice yellow meal!"

Said the fourth little chicken,
With a small sigh of grief,
"Oh, I wish I could find
A green little leaf!"

Said the fifth little chicken,
With a faint little moan,
"Oh, I wish I could find
A wee gravel-stone!"

"Now, see here," said the mother,
From the green garden-patch,
"If you want any breakfast,
You must come and scratch."

Elephant

The elephant carries a great big trunk.
He never packs it with his clothes.
It has no lock and it has no key,
But it takes it wherever it goes.

A Mouse in Her Room

A mouse in her room woke Miss Dowd.
She was frightened and screamed very loud.
    Then a happy thought hit her—
    To scare off the critter,
She sat up in bed and meowed.

Spelling: open, happen, twenty, plenty, ago, over, under, ever, never, other, brother, mother

Functional reading: frozen fish label, "Open" sign

Syllable riddle: What letter can you write with? (an **o**pen)

Writing: Students use these three words in a sentence: *broken, motor, ever.*

-ar, -at, -it *Patterns*

Pattern words: car, garden, sharpen, farmer, market, partner; at, matter, batter, scatter; it, sitter, kitten, kitchen, pitcher

Scrambled words: a gar den, ter mat o, en o ver, har bit ten

Application words: bitter, clatter, chatter, market

Spelling: garden, farmer, matter, kitten, kitchen

Functional reading: garden shop sign

Rhyme:

Little Raindrops
Jane E. Browne

Oh, where do you come from,
    You little drops of rain,
Pitter patter, pitter patter,
Down the window pane?

They won't let me walk,
    And they won't let me play,
And they won't let me go
Out of doors at all today.

Syllable riddle: What kind of a den has a lot vegetables? (a **gar**den)

Writing: Students use these three words in a sentence: *pitcher, chatter, batter.*

-in, -is(s), -un *Patterns*

Pattern words: win, winter, window, dinner, finish; miss, mister, mistake, tennis; sun, under, until, hunter, thunder, hundred

Scrambled words: ner din a, un in til, ter sis o, per whis ar, thun it der

Application words: thinner, winner

Spelling: winter, dinner, finish, sister, whisper, under, until, hundred, mistake

Functional reading: frozen dinner label

Syllable riddle: When is it wrong to take something? (when it is a **mis**take)

Writing: Students use these four words in a sentence: *dinner, finish, tennis, until.*

Rhyme:

If You Should Meet a Crocodile

If you should meet a crocodile,
Don't take a stick and poke him;
Ignore the welcome in his smile,
Be careful not to stroke him.
For as he sleeps upon the Nile,
He thinner gets and thinner;
And whenever you meet a crocodile,
He's ready for his dinner.

be-, re-, -or *Patterns*

Pattern words: be, became, beside, below, begin, belong; remind, report, reward, refuse, receive; or, order, morning, corner, forty, before

Scrambled words: fore be re, a ner cor, un mind re, gin be de, port en re

Application words: farmer, number

Spelling: became, below, begin, belong, report, receive, before, morning, forty

Syllable riddle: What kind of mind do you need when you forget? (a **re**mind)

Writing: Students use these three words in a sentence: *before, morning, remind.*

-a, -y = /ē/, -ey, -ble *Patterns*

Pattern words: pay, paper, baby, famous, favorite; sun, sunny, funny, dusty, shady; key, turkey, monkey, donkey, honey, money; a, able, table, cable, bubble, mumble

Scrambled words: dy la en, ble ta un, by at ba, dy san re, key tur er

Application words: major, windy, bubble, candy

Functional reading: honey label

Rhymes:

The Mulberry Bush

Here we go round the mulberry bush,
    the mulberry bush,
    the mulberry bush,
Here we go round the mulberry bush,
On a cold and frosty morning.

This is the way we clap our hands,
    clap our hands,
    clap our hands,
This is the way we clap our hands,
On a cold and frosty morning.

One Potato, Two Potato

One potato, two potato
Three potato, four,
Five potato, six potato,
Seven potato, MORE.

Syllable riddle: What kind of a key do we eat on Thanksgiving? (a **tur**key)

Spelling: paper, baby, famous, sunny, funny, money, table

Writing: Students make a list of their favorite famous people.

-i, -ur, -um *Patterns*

Pattern words: tie, tiger, spider, tiny, title, Friday; fur, furry, hurry, turkey, turtle, purple; sum, summer, number, pumpkin, stumble

Scrambled words: ber en num, ble stum or, be der spi, ny en ti, ple pur y

Application words: trumpet, tumble, tidy, burden, murder

Rhymes:

Bed in Summer
Robert Louis Stevenson

In winter I get up at night
And dress by yellow candle-light.
In summer, quite the other way,
I have to go to bed by day.

I have to go to bed and see
The birds still hopping on the tree,
Or hear the grown-up people's feet
Still going past me in the street.

And does it not seem hard to you,
When all the sky is clear and blue,
And I should like so much to play,
To have to go to bed by day?

There Was a Young Lady of Niger

There was a young lady of Niger,
Who smiled as she rode on a tiger.
They returned from the ride
With the lady inside,
And the smile on the face of the tiger.

Humpty Dumpty

Humpty Dumpty sat on a wall
Humpty Dumpty had a great fall.
All the king's horses and all the king's men
Had scrambled eggs for breakfast.

Poor Old Lady, She Swallowed a Fly

Poor old lady, she swallowed a fly.
I don't know why she swallowed a fly.
Poor old lady, I think she'll die.

Poor old lady, she swallowed a spider.
It squirmed and wriggled and turned inside her.
She swallowed the spider to catch the fly.
I don't know why she swallowed a fly.
Poor old lady, I think she'll die.

Poor old lady, she swallowed a bird.
How absurd! She swallowed a bird.
She swallowed the bird to catch the spider,
She swallowed the spider to catch the fly,
I don't know why she swallowed a fly.
Poor old lady, I think she'll die.

Poor old lady, she swallowed a cat.
Think of that!
She swallowed a cat.
She swallowed the cat to catch the bird,
She swallowed the bird to catch the spider,
She swallowed the spider to catch the fly,
I don't know why she swallowed a fly.
Poor old lady, I think she'll die.

Poor old lady, she swallowed a dog.
She swallowed the whole hog when she swallowed the dog,
She swallowed the dog to catch the cat,
She swallowed the cat to catch the bird,
She swallowed the bird to catch the spider,
She swallowed the spider to catch the fly,
I don't know why she swallowed a fly.
Poor old lady, I think she'll die.

Poor old lady, she swallowed a cow.
I don't know how she swallowed the cow.
She swallowed the cow to catch the dog,
She swallowed the dog to catch the cat,
She swallowed the cat to catch the bird,
She swallowed the bird to catch the spider,
She swallowed the spider to catch the fly,
I don't know why she swallowed a fly.
Poor old lady, I think she'll die.

Poor old lady, she swallowed a horse.
She died, of course.

Functional reading: pumpkin pie label

Syllable riddle: What kind of a tie has stripes and growls? (a **ti**ger)

Spelling: tiger, tiny, title, spider, Friday, hurry, purple, summer, number

Writing: Students use these three words in one sentence: *hurry, pumpkin, turkey.*

▪ SHORT-VOWEL PATTERNS

-ic(k), -et, -im *Patterns*

Pattern words: pick, picnic, attic, nickel, pickle, chicken; let, leter, better, lettuce, settle, metal; tick, ticket, pocket, rocket, bucket, magnet, jacket; swim, swimmer, chimney, limit, improve, simple

Scrambled words: en chick er, el et nick, um ket mar, ple sim at

Application words: ticket, popsickle, settler, pimple, improve

Rhyme:

Lucy Locket

Lucy Locket lost her pocket,
Kitty Fisher found it;
Not a penny was there in it,
Only ribbon round it.

Songs:

Polly, Put the Kettle on

Pol-ly, put the ket-tle on, Pol-ly, put the ket-tle on,
Pol-ly, put the ket-tle on, We'll all have tea.

Su-key, take it off a-gain, Su-key, take it off a-gain,
Su-key, take it off a-gain, They've all gone a-way.

Wabash Cannonball

From the great At-lan-tic O-cean,
To the wide Pa-cif-ic shore,
From the queen of flow-ing moun-tains
To the south-land by the shore,
She's might-y tall and hand-some,
And quite well known by all;
She's the might-y com-bi-na-tion of the
Wa-bash Can-non-ball.

Listen to the jin-gle,
The rum-ble and the roar,
As she glides a-long the wood-land,
Through the hills and by the shore.

Hear the might-y rush of the en-gine,
Hear that lone-some call,
You're trav'-ling through the jun-gles
On the Wa-bash Can-non-ball.

Functional reading: frozen chicken label, pickles label

Syllable riddle: What kind of a rock can be shot into space? (a **rock**et)

Spelling: chicken, nickel, pickle, letter, lettuce, settle, metal, ticket, limit, improve, simple

Writing: Students use these three words in one sentence: *limit, picnic, ticket.*

-ab, -ad, -ag, -ang *Patterns*

Pattern words: cab, cabin, cabbage, rabbit, habit, absent; sad, saddle, paddle, shadow, ladder, address; bag, baggy, wagon, dragon, magnet, magazine; sang, anger, angry, tangled

Scrambled words: dle pad at, on wag on, ad bit rab, lad hab der, pat net mag

Application words: tablet, hanger, baggage, admit

Spelling: absent, cabin, shadow, ladder, address, magazine, magnet, sang, angry

Functional reading: magazines sign

Syllable riddle: What kind of a net is used to pick up metal? (a **mag**net)

Writing: Students use these three words in one sentence: *cabin, dragon, shadow.*

-am, -an, -ant, -ap *Patterns*

Pattern words: am, hammer, scramble, camel, camera; can, candy, handy, handle; ant, giant, distant, instant; nap, napkin, happy, happen, captain, chapter

Scrambled words: ter an chap, er hap pen, dy e can, un stant in, tant dis hap

Application words: ambulance, hammer, animal, trapper, capture

Rhyme:

> **There's Music in a Hammer**
>
> There's music in a hammer.
> There's music in a nail.
> There's music in a kitty cat,
> When you step upon her tail.

Functional reading: candy sign, shampoo label

Syllable riddle: What kind of an ant is very large? (a **gi**ant)

Spelling: candy, giant, distant, happy, happen, captain, chapter

Writing: Students use these three words in one sentence: *chapter, distant, address.*

-ent, -el(l) *Patterns*

Pattern words: went, event, prevent, cement, invent, experiment; yell, yellow, elbow, elephant, jelly, welcome

Scrambled words: en jel ly, ant vent e, ter shel is, vent em in, bow el im

Application words: hello, seldom, consent

Rhymes:

> **What Is Pink?**
>
> *Christina Rossetti*
>
> What is pink? A rose is pink
> By the fountain's brink.
>
> What is red? A poppy's red
> In its barley bed.
>
> What is blue? The sky is blue
> Where the clouds float through.

What is white? A swan is white
Sailing in the light.

What is yellow? Pears are yellow,
Rich and ripe and mellow.

What is green? The grass is green,
With small flowers between.

What is violet? Clouds are violet
In the summer twilight.

What is orange? Why, an orange,
Just an orange!

Two Little Kittens

Two little kittens, one stormy night,
Began to quarrel, and then to fight;
(one had a mouse, the other had none),
And that's the way the quarrel begun.

"I'll have that mouse," said the biggest cat;
"You'll have that mouse? We'll see about that!"
"I *will* have that mouse," said the eldest son,
"You *shan't* have the mouse," said the little one.

I told you before 'twas a stormy night,
When these two little kittens began to fight;
The old woman seized her sweeping broom,
And swept the two kittens right out of the room.

The ground was covered with frost and snow,
And the two little kittens had nowhere to go;
So they laid them down on the mat at the door,
While the old woman finished sweeping the floor.

Then they crept in, as quiet as mice,
All wet with the snow, and as cold as ice;
For they found it was better, that stormy night,
To lie down and sleep than to quarrel and fight.

Functional reading: jelly label

Syllable riddle: What kind of a bow bends the arm? (an **el**bow)

Spelling: event, prevent, yellow, elbow, jelly, welcome

Writing: Students use the following words in one sentence: *elephant, museum, welcome.*

-ep, -es, -ev *Patterns*

Pattern words: pep, pepper, peppermint, September, shepherd, separate; less, lesson, address, success, yesterday, restaurant; seven, several, never, clever, every

Scrambled words: er en nev, ant dress ad, en clev er, herd shep ble, in les son

Application words: ever, clever, rescue, level, message, accept

Functional reading: restaurant sign, peppermint candy label

Syllable riddle: What kind of a cape does the letter *s* wear? (an **es**cape)

Spelling: September, separate, address, success, yesterday, restaurant, seven, several, every

Writing: Students use these three words in one sentence: *lesson, September, several.*

-id, -ig, -il(l) *Patterns*

Pattern words: rid, riddle, middle, hidden, midnight; wig, wiggle, giggle, signal, figure; pill, pillow, silver, silly, building, children

Scrambled words: an chil dren, dle mid en, gle um wig, at den hid, ly sil it

Application words: digger, kidding, midday, million, riddle

Rhymes:

Higgledy, Piggledy, See How They Run
Kate Greenaway

Higgledy, piggledy! see how they run!
Hopperty, popperty! what is the fun?
Has the sun or the moon tumbled into the sea?
What is the matter, now? Pray tell it me!

Higgledy, piggledy! how can I tell?
Hopperty, popperty! hark to the bell!
The rats and the mice even scamper away;
Who can say what may not happen today?

The Ostrich Is a Silly Bird
Mary E. Wilkins Freeman

The ostrich is a silly bird,
    With scarcely any mind.
He often runs so very fast,
    He leaves himself behind.

And when he gets there, has to stand
    And hang about till night,
Without a blessed thing to do
    Until he comes in sight.

The Cat and the Fiddle

Hey, diddle, diddle,
The cat and the fiddle,
The cow jumped over the moon.
The little dog laughed
To see such sport,
And the dish ran away with the spoon.

Spelling: middle, hidden, midnight, signal, figure, silly, building, children

Writing: Have students make a list of things that make them giggle.

-ob, oc(k), -od *Patterns*

Pattern words: rob, robber, robin, problem, probably, hobby, gobble; doc, doctor, pocket, chocolate, rocket, hockey; cod, body, model, modern, product, somebody

Scrambled words: in rob ow, ey hock od, ject ar ob, im el mod, tor doc us

Application words: cobbler, bobble, locket, socket, anybody

Rhyme:

> **I Don't Suppose**
>
> I don't suppose
> A lobster knows
> The proper way
> To blow his nose,
> Or else perhaps
> Beneath the seas,
> They have no need
> to sniff and sneeze.

Functional reading: chocolate candy label

Syllable riddle: What kind of a bird steals? (a **rob**in)

Spelling: problem, probably, doctor, chocolate, body, modern, product, some-body

Writing: Students use these three words in a sentence: *chocolate, gobble, probably.*

-ol, -om, -on *Patterns*

Pattern words: doll, dollar, follow, holiday, jolly; mom, momma, comma, comment, promise; monster, monument, honest, honor, concrete

Scrambled words: est hon ble, un jol ly, le ment com, lar col et, com ma al

Application words: volcano, responsible

Rhymes:

> **A Diller, A Dollar**
>
> A diller, a dollar,
> A ten o'clock scholar;
> What makes you come so soon?
> You used to come at ten o'clock,
> And now you come at noon.

> **Miss Polly Had a Dolly**
>
> Miss Polly had a dolly that was
>   sick, sick, sick.
> So she sent for the doctor
>   quick, quick, quick.
> The doctor came with his bag
>   and hat
> He knocked at the door with a
>   rat tat tat.
>
> He looked at Miss Dolly and
>   shook his head,
> He said, "Miss Polly, put her
>   straight to bed."
> He wrote on some paper for a
>   pill, pill, pill,
> "I'll be back in the morning with my
>   bill, bill, bill."

Syllable riddle: What kind of a doll is worth 100 cents? (a **doll**ar)

Spelling: dollar, follow, holiday, common, promise, honest, honor, comment, volcano

Writing: Students use these three words in a sentence: *holiday, monument, promise.*

-op, -ot -age *Patterns*

Pattern words: shop, shopper, popular, opposite, copy; rot, rotten, gotten, bottom, bottle, robot; cab, cabbage, bandage, damage, message, baggage, garbage

Scrambled words: on y cop, con vil lage, ar cot ton, sage em mes, tom bot op

Application words: luggage, chopper, cotton

Rhyme:

The Postman

The whistling postman swings along.
   His bag is deep and wide,
And messages from all the world
   Are bundled up inside.

The postman's walking up our street.
   Soon now he'll ring my bell.
Perhaps there'll be a letter stamped
   In Asia. Who can tell?

Functional reading: cabbage sign

Syllable riddle: What kind of a cab is a vegetable? (a **cab**bage)

Spelling: copy, popular, opposite, bottom, bottle, robot, damage, message, garbage

Writing: Students use these three words in a sentence: *cabbage, rotten, garbage.*

-ub, -uc(k), -ud *Patterns*

Pattern words: rub, rubber, bubble, stubborn, subject, public; luck, lucky, chuckle, success, product; mud, muddy, buddy, study, puddle, huddle, sudden

Scrambled words: ble bub en, ab dle pud, le ur buck, suc cess id, den sud em

Application words: blubber, bucket, muddle, cuddle, study

Rhyme:

The Little Turtle
Vachel Lindsay

There was a little turtle.
He lived in a box.
He swam in a puddle.
He climbed on the rocks.

He snapped at a mosquito.
He snapped at a flea.
He snapped at a minnow.
And he snapped at me.

He caught the mosquito.
He caught the flea.
He caught the minnow.
But he didn't catch me.

I Love You

I love you, I love you,
I love you divine,
Please give me your bubble gum,
You're sitting on mine.

Functional reading: bubble gum

Syllable riddle: What kind of a den can a bear get into in a hurry? (a **sud**den)

Spelling: rubber, stubborn, subject, public, success, sudden, study, lucky, chuckle

Writing: Students use these three words in a sentence: *lucky, muddy, puddle.*

-uf, -ug, -up *Patterns*

Pattern words: stuff, stuffy, muffin, suffer, buffalo; bug, buggy, ugly, suggest, struggle; pup, puppy, puppet, supper, upper

Scrambled words: pet pup up, ger strug gle, per sup pent, ly gest sug, age fin muf

Application words: fluffy, guppy, muggy, muppet

Rhymes:

The Squirrel

Whisky, frisky,
Hippity hop.
Up he goes
To the tree top.

Whirly, twirly.
Round and round,
Down he scampers,
To the ground.

Furly, curly,
What a tail!
Tall as a feather,
Broad as a sail.

Where's his supper?
In the shell,
Snappy, cracky,
Out it fell.

As I Was Standing in the Street

As I was standing in the street
As quiet as could be,
A great big ugly man came up
And tied his horse to me.

Functional reading: muffins label

Spelling: suffer, muffin, suggest, struggle, puppy, supper, upper

Syllable riddle: What kind of a pet is made of wood, cloth, or plastic? (a **pup**pet)

Writing: Students use these three words in a sentence: *muffins, suggest, supper.*

-um, -us, -ut, -uz *Patterns*

Pattern words: hum, humble, fumble, grumble, stumble; muss, mustard, muscle, custom, customer, discuss; but, button, butter, mutter, gutter; fuzz, fuzzy, puzzle, muzzle, buzzer, buzzard;

Scrambled words: ug tom cus, ty dus is, ton ent but, ter but al, zle op puz

Application words: flutter, discussion, tumble

Rhyme:

> **The Brook**
> Grumbling, stumbling,
> Fumbling all the day;
> Fluttering, stuttering,
> Muttering away;
> Rustling, hustling,
> Rustling as it flows,
> This is how the brook talks,
> Bubbling as it goes.

Functional reading: mustard, butter labels

Syllable riddle: What kind of a bird makes a noise like a fly? (a **buzz**ard)

Spelling: muscle, custom, customer, discuss, butter, puzzle

Writing: Students use these three words in a sentence: *customer, mutter, puzzle.*

-e, -ee, -ea = /e/ *Patterns*

Pattern words: secret, fever, female, even, equal; see, bee, beetle, needle, indeed, succeed, agree, agreement; sea, season, reason, beaver, eager, easily

Scrambled words: one tle bee, son rea ic, gle gre ea, ob suc ceed, peat ant re

Application words: eagle, repeat

Syllable riddle: What kind of a male is not a man or a boy? (a **fe**male)

Spelling: season, reason, easily, eaten, repeat, leader, beetle, indeed, succeed, agree

Writing: Students use these three words in a sentence: *easily, indeed, leader.*

-ide, -ire, -ise, -ive, -ize *Patterns*

Pattern words: side, beside, decide, divide, provide; tire, entire, require, admire, umpire; wise, surprise, exercise, advise, disguise; drive, arrive, alive, survive; prize, realize, recognize, memorize, apologize

Scrambled words: un side be, et vise ad, tire en ic, re de cide, ub vive sur

Application words: require, inspire, advertise, retire

Syllable riddle: What kind of a side can you use to help you make up your mind? (a **de**cide)

Spelling: beside, divide, decide, entire, realize, surprise, alive

Writing: Students use these three words in a sentence: *realize, disguise, surprise.*

-ade, -aid, -ail, -ale, -ain, -ate *Patterns*

Pattern words: made, parade, invade, lemonade, centigrade; tail, detail, trailer, airmail, available; male, female; rain, contain, obtain, explain, complain; gate, locate, hesitate, hibernate, appreciate

Scrambled words: on fraid a, lo cate ad, rade pa ic, ab tain ob, main um re

Application words: calculate, appreciate, exaggerate, persuade, remain

Functional reading: lemonade label

Syllable riddle: What kind of a grade is very cool? (0 degrees **centi**grade)

Spelling: afraid, detail, female, contain, explain, obtain, hesitate, appreciate

Writing: Students use these three words in a sentence: *appreciate, lemonade, contain.*

-ope, -one, -u, -ture *Patterns*

Pattern words: hope, antelope, envelope, telescope; phone, telephone, microphone; use, music, human, museum; future, nature, adventure, creature

Scrambled words: ture fu idse, ang one ry, ture nat en, uz ture crea, er con ang, ken bro ar

Rhyme:

> **Whole Duty of Children**
> *Robert Louis Stevenson*
>
> A child should always say what's true
> And speak when he is spoken to,
> And behave mannerly at table:
> At least as far as he is able.

Syllable riddle: What kind of an ant looks like a deer? (an **ant**elope)

Spelling: envelope, telescope, telephone, anger, angry, future, nature, adventure, creature

Writing: Students use these three words in a sentence: *tangled, creature, telephone.*

-al, -au, -aw *Patterns*

Pattern words: all, also, already, although, altogether, walrus; cause, saucer, author, August, autumn, caution, daughter; draw, drawing, awful, crawling, strawberry

Scrambled words: ust ike Aug, age umn aut, aw ful up, cer ap sau, ways al au

Application words: auditorium, sausage, automobile, faucet

Spelling: also, although, always, autumn, author, awful, drawing

Rhyme:

> **The Sausage**
>
> The sausage is a cunning bird
> With feathers long and wavy;
> It swims about the frying pan
> And makes its nest in gravy.

Functional reading: August (on calendar), sausage label

Syllable riddle: What kind of a wall has whiskers? (a **wal**rus)

Writing: Students use these three words in a sentence: *always, author, drawing.*

-ea = /e/, i = /ē/, i-e = /ē/ *Patterns*

Pattern words: sweat, sweater, weather, feather, meadow; treasure, measure, pleasure, pleasant; radio, easier, period, spaghetti, appreciate; magazine, submarine, gasoline, vaccine, limousine, police

Scrambled words: on er weath, i tax air, ic lice po, sure trea re, ant pleas en

Application words: happiness, wealthy, threaten

Rhymes:

Weather

Whether the weather be fine,
Or whether the weather be not,
Whether the weather be cold,
Or whether the weather be hot,
We'll weather the weather
Whatever the weather
Whether we like it or not.

Yankee Doodle

Yankee Doodle came to town,
 Riding on a pony.
He stuck a feather in his cap
 And called it macaroni.

Functional reading: spaghetti label, macaroni label

Syllable riddle: What kind of a marine spends a lot of time under water? (a **sub**marine)

Spelling: weather, measure, easier, police, pleasant

Writing: Students use these three words in a sentence: *police, treasure, meadow.*

-tion, -sion, -y = /ī/ *Patterns*

Pattern words: act, action, addition, station, invention, information; question, mention, suggestion; confuse, confusion, conclusion, occasion; reply, supply, deny, magnify

Scrambled words: ques des tion, sup tion ply, tion able ac, tion visi men, con ny de

Application words: explosion, persuasion, destination

Song:

Wabash Cannonball

From the great At-lan-tic O-cean,
To the wide Pa-cif-ic shore,
From the queen of flow-ing moun-tains
To the south-land by the shore,
She's might-y tall and hand-some,
And quite well known by all;
She's the might-y com-bi-na-tion of the Wa-bash Can-non-ball.

Listen to the jin-gle,
The rum-ble and the roar,
As she glides a-long the wood-land,
Through the hills and by the shore.

Hear the might-y rush of the en-gine,
Hear that lone-some call,
You're trav'-ling through the jun-gles
On the Wa-bash Can-non-ball.

Functional reading: railroad station sign, information sign

Syllable riddle: Which word needs more than one man? (**men**tion)

Spelling: action, addition, invention, information, question, mention, reply

Writing: Students make a list of their favorite inventions.

-oi, -oy *Patterns*

Pattern words: point, poison, disappoint, disappointment, noisy, avoid, moisture, joy, enjoy, destroy, royal, loyal, voyage

Scrambled words: joy en um, voy sur age, void be a, y pro nois, al ment roy

Application words: rejoice, appointment, moisture, oyster

Functional reading: poison label

Syllable riddle: What kind of a point makes you feel bad? (a disap**point**ment)

Spelling: point, noisy, enjoy, destroy, loyal, voyage

Writing: Students write about a voyage that they would enjoy. They tell where they would like to go and why they would like to go there.

-ou, -ow *Patterns*

Pattern words: round, around, about, announce, announcement, thousand; mount, amount, mountain, fountain, surround, compound; cow, power, flower, allow, allowance

Scrambled words: ble er pow, round sur ar, per bout a, thous sand tru, nounce move an

Application words: foundation, boundary, doubtful, shower

Rhymes:

The Seasons

Spring is showery, flowery, bowery;
Summer is hoppy, croppy, poppy;
Autumn is wheezy, sneezy, freezy;
Winter is slippy, drippy, nippy.

The Cow
Robert Louis Stevenson

The friendly cow, all red and white,
    I love with all my heart:
She gives me cream with all her might,
    To eat with apple-tart.

She wanders lowing here and there,
    And yet she cannot stray,
All in the pleasant open air,
    The pleasant light of day;

And blown by all the winds that pass
    And wet with all the showers,
She walks among the meadow grass
    And eats the meadow flowers.

The City Mouse and the Garden Mouse
Christina Rosetti

The city mouse lives in a house;
    The garden mouse lives in a bower,
He's friendly with the frogs and toads,
    And sees the pretty plants in flower.

The city mouse eats bread and cheese;
    The garden mouse eats what he can;
We will not grudge him seeds and stalks,
    Poor little, timid, furry man.

Functional reading: Flowers-for-sale sign

Syllable riddle: Which word has a lot of sand? (thou**sand**)

Spelling: around, about, announce, amount, mountain, surround, thousand, flower, allow, power

Writing: Students use the following three words in one sentence: *allowance, announce, thousand.*

-oo, -ove = /$\overline{oo}$/, -u = /$\overline{oo}$/ *Patterns*

Pattern words: too, bamboo, shampoo, cartoon, raccoon, balloon; prove, improve, improvement, approve, remove, movements; Sue, super, studio, truly, tuna

Scrambled words: sham ut poo, per su er, car un toon, pre ly tru, oo move re

Application words: kangaroo, noodles, future, musical

Rhyme:

I Raised a Great Hullabaloo

I raised a great hullabaloo
When I found a large mouse in my stew,
Said the waiter, "Don't shout
And wave it about,
Or the rest will be wanting one, too."

Functional reading: tuna label, shampoo label, noodles label

Syllable riddle: What kind of a car makes people laugh? (a **car**toon)

Spelling: balloon, improve, approve, remove, super, student, truly, tuna

Writing: Students use the following three words in one sentence: *shampoo, super, truly.*

-ook, -oot, -ood, -ul(l) *Patterns*

Pattern words: book, bookstore, workbook, cookbook, lookout; foot, football, footprint, footstep, barefoot; hood, neighborhood, childhood, goodness, wooden; bull, bulldozer, bulletin, bullfrog, bully; full, cupful, helpful, careful, thankful, awful

Scrambled words: ful care ble, steps foot oint, wood en tion, aug hood child, ful y help

Application words: cheerful, wakeful, cookout

Functional reading: bookstore sign

Syllable riddle: What can be printed with feet? (**foot**prints)

Spelling: thankful, careful, neighborhood, goodness, football

Writing: Students use the following three words in one sentence: *bookstore, cookbook, helpful.*

Chapter 8

USING CONTEXT

Because use of context speeds decoding and vice versa, students should be encouraged to read for meaning and should constantly ask themselves as they read: "Does this make sense?" Materials should be carefully selected so that they promote the use of context. Well-written, carefully organized text that has a natural flow to it is best. For beginning readers, materials that use familiar, repeated elements are especially helpful. Most important, the text should be on the proper level. If there are too many unknown words, students are unable to use context. When too many words are unknown, students are unable to make sense of the text and so no context is constructed.

CHANGING ROLE OF CONTEXT CLUES

In beginning reading, picture clues play an essential role. Since beginning readers' word recognition skills and store of sight vocabulary is limited, the author conveys much of the meaning of a selection through illustrations. Some beginning reading materials use illustrations in such a way that no reading is required. A counting book, for instance, might show five dogs to go along with the caption "five dogs." A student could "read" the caption "five dogs" by simply looking at the illustration.

Although most youngsters make use of picture clues, some may need to be prompted to use them. One youngster, reading about a tiger, stumbled over the word *tiger* even though there was an illustration of a tiger at the top of the page. The teacher prompted the use of the picture clue by asking: "What does the picture show?" When the student replied, "tiger," and realized that the picture revealed the identity of the word, the teacher prompted the use of phonics as a cross-check by asking: "What else tells you that the word is *tiger*? What letter does the word *tiger* begin with? What letter does it end with?" Since the student knew initial and final consonants, he was able to respond correctly.

In addition to providing a cross-check, the prompting also fostered the use of decoding skills. Picture clues are transitory. As texts become longer and more complex, picture clues become less useful. The teacher was preparing the student for a time when picture clues would no longer be effective. Prompting children to use initial consonants fosters the use of a phonics strategy so that as the usefulness of picture clues begins to fade, phonics clues naturally take over.

Often, picture clues provide a partial clue, which can be complemented by phonics strategies. For instance, the illustration may be ambiguous—the reader can't tell if horses or ponies are being shown in an illustration. By using initial consonants to complement information from the illustration, the reader can determine that the caption says *pony* because it begins with the letter *p*.

The nature of context clues changes as students grow older. In the early stages of reading, virtually all the words that students read are in their listening vocabularies. At about grade 4, the nature of reading changes (Chall, 1996). As reading becomes more content-centered, students encounter words that are not in their listening vocabularies. Context clues are now used to help them ascertain the meanings of unfamiliar words. The emphasis in this text is on using context clues to help get the pronunciations of words that are in students' listening vocabularies but not their reading vocabularies. However, as readers progress, they need to be able to use context clues to derive the meanings of unfamiliar words.

TEACHING CONTEXT CLUES

Just as with other skills, context clues should be taught directly. Model how you would go about using context to figure out the identity of an unknown word. Show students that sometimes it is necessary to go beyond the blank in order to figure out the unknown word. If students are unable to use their decoding skills to figure out a hard word, teach them to reread the whole sentence but say "blank" when they come to the unknown word. Explain that they should ask themselves: "What word would fit here? What word would make sense here?" After figuring out what word might fit, they should then reread the sentence with the word in it and see if it fits. If not, they need to try again.

Along with learning how to use context, students should learn when to use it. For instance, they need to see that decoding strategies won't work with words like *of*, *one*, or *once*, so they need to use context with words of this type. And if they have tried phonics and that hasn't worked, they should try context. After teaching the use of context clues, review this strategy from time to time. Also use prompts to guide students in their use of strategies.

IMPORTANCE OF PHONICS

Although phonics and context clues should be integrated, phonics clues are generally more effective. When students encounter a difficult word, they should first see if there is any part they can say or, if not, if it is like a word they know. If they can't reconstruct the word through the use of pronounceable word parts or analogy, they should then use context. Once students have used phonics or context to construct a word, they should insert the word in the sentence, reread it, and see if it makes sense. If students used context as a clue, they should also use phonics as a cross-check. If they reconstructed an unfamiliar word as being *yell*, noting that it begins with *y* and ends with *ll* confirms their response.

USING PROMPTS

Throughout the text, there have been sample lessons on using pronounceable word part and analogy strategies. However, students also need to be taught when and where to use each strategy and how to integrate strategy use. This can be done through direct instruction, which might include modeling when and where to use strategies and through prompting. Prompting is an effective technique because it is an ongoing procedure that can be used as students encounter difficult words.

Listed in Table 8.1 are a number of prompts that can be used to direct students to an effective use of strategies. Most of the prompts have been presented previously. However, several prompts have not been discussed: sound-by-sound decoding, monitoring/checking, affirmation, starter prompt, and assessment prompt. Although the pronounceable word part and analogy strategies are preferred, the sound-by-sound strategy is occasionally used by students, especially those who are struggling with their reading and having difficulty chunking parts of words. Using this prompt, the teacher leads students who are unable to use the pro-

TABLE 8.1   Word Analysis Prompts

Strategy	When Used	Prompt
Pronounceable word part	Unknown word contains a part student can say: *am* or *amp* in *champ*	Can you say any part of that word?
Analogy	Unknown word is like a word student knows: unknown word *grain* is like known word *rain.*	Is this word like any word that you know?
Sound by sound	Student is unable to chunk word. Works out word sound by sound: /s/-/p/-/e/-/l/: spell.	Can you say the first sound, the next sound, the next sound?
Context	Student is unable to use phonics clues, but the text provides usable context clues.	What would make sense here? Read to the end of the sentence and see what word would fit.
Monitoring	Student checks to see whether the word pronounced is a real word and fits the context of the selection (actually, students should monitor for meaning whenever they read)	Is that a real word? Does that make sense? Does that sound right?
Affirmation	Teacher wishes to reinforce the student's correct use of a strategy	I like the way you used a part of the word that you knew to help you say the whole word.
Assessment	Teacher wants to see what strategies the student is using	How did you figure out that word?
Starter	Student is unable to use any of the strategies to decode an unknown word	Could the word be _____?

nounceable word part or analogy strategies to reconstruct a word sound by sound. When the student encounters a word such as *net,* which is phonically regular, the teacher asks: "What is the first sound, the next sound, the last sound? Can you put all the sounds together? What word do you make when you put all the sounds together?" Gradually, students who work out the pronunciation of words sound by sound should be led to use chunks of the word as is done with the pronounceable word part and analogy strategies.

Monitoring/checking helps students become aware of the meaning of what they read and notice when the text stops making sense or a word doesn't fit. Student self-correction of errors, especially those that change the meaning of a sentence or selection, is a sign that the student is monitoring for meaning. If the student fails to note or correct a misreading, the teacher asks such questions as: "Does that make sense? Does that sound right? Try that again." Sometimes, none of the prompts works. The student doesn't seem to be able to use any of the strategies. When that happens, use a starter prompt (Clay, 1993b). In a starter prompt, you supply the difficult word but do so in question form: "Is the word *brave*?" This is better than simply telling students the word, because it does require a response and involves the student in reexamining the word.

Affirmation prompts help students reflect on their strategy use. After having successfully worked out the pronunciation of a difficult word, the teacher provides specific feedback, which is reinforcement for a job well done but also brings to students' consciousness the awareness of a strategy that they have been using, perhaps without thinking much about it. "I like the way you used a part of the word that you could say to help you pronounce the whole word," or "I like the way you noticed that the word *sunk* didn't make sense and you corrected it." To gain insight into students' use of strategies, use an assessment prompt. After they have decoded a difficult word, ask such questions as, "How did you figure out that word?" or "How did you know that word was *weigh*?"

Of course, the initial reaction to a misreading should be no reaction. If a student has misread a word, give him a chance to correct himself. Let him read to the end of the sentence, or in some cases the end of the paragraph. If he is monitoring for meaning, chances are he will note that the text doesn't make sense and will self-correct. By not jumping in, the teacher provides the student with the opportunity to apply his monitoring strategy. If the misreading is not corrected, or if the student is unable to correct it, then use the appropriate prompt.

If the student makes minor miscues such as substituting *this* for *that* or omitting *a* or *the* and similar non-meaning-changing miscues, simply ignore these. If the student is making a high proportion of miscues, it may be that the material is too difficult. Try easier material and/or give more preparatory assistance.

ONGOING, SYSTEMATIC INSTRUCTION

In addition to using prompts to foster the use of strategies, it is also important to provide ongoing instruction in the use of decoding strategies. As noted earlier, whenever a phonic or syllabic element is introduced, students should be taught how to apply the pronounceable word part or analogy strategy when they encounter a word containing that element. Students should also be taught how to use context clues. On a continuing basis, at least once a week, students should be given challenge words and asked to decode them. Challenge words are words that students have not seen before but that incorporate previously taught elements. For instance, *pat* and *chat* would be challenge words because they incorporate the familiar *-at* pattern but were not presented when the *-at* pattern was introduced and did not appear in materials that students read. Often, challenge words can be lifted from selections that students are about to read. Presenting words in isolation forces the use of a sounding-out strategy. To foster the use of context or the integration of context and phonics, it is important to present words in context. You might present sentences such as "Joe and I had a chat about his new cat" and encourage the use of both phonics and context. For students working on multisyllabic words, present sentences in which they are invited to integrate syllabic analysis and context: "Which **invention** changed our lives more, TV or the car?"

Chapter 9

SPELLING

Although there is some overlap between spelling and reading, spelling places greater demands on visual memory, especially the ability to visualize words. Gentry (1997) refers to this ability as the "spelling gene." Far from being a rote memory skill, spelling is conceptual. Spelling is based on three principles: alphabetic, orthographic, and meaning or morphemics (Henderson & Templeton, 1986). On its most basic level, English spelling is alphabetic or phonemic. Letters represent sounds. In the word *pet,* for instance, the letters *p-e-t* represent the sounds /p/, /e/, /t/. However, in a large number of words there is no one-to-one relationship between the word's letters and its sounds. The orthographic or word pattern principle means that spelling is frequently determined by the patterning of letters within a word. For instance, the *e* marker at the end of a word indicates that a vowel is long rather than short, as in *pet/Pete.*

According to meaning, the third principle, words that have similar meanings have similar spellings, even if their pronunciations differ. For instance, the italicized letters in the following word pairs have different pronunciations even though the letter in each pair is the same: comp*e*te/comp*e*tition, ser*e*ne/ser*e*nity. Spellings have been kept the same to show the similarity in meanings. As students' knowledge of spelling develops, they learn first the alphabetic principle, then the orthographic principle, and finally, the meaning principle. Their understanding of the spelling system dictates the strategies they use to spell words. Novice readers and writers use a sounding-out strategy. They spell what they hear. As they encounter vowel digraphs (*boat, beat*) and final-*e* markers (*lake, time*), they begin to use a visual strategy. They picture the spelling of the words. They may also begin to use rules or generalizations to help them spell words. Later still, they use their knowledge of roots and affixes as a spelling strategy.

Recognizing that spelling is developmental but poses special problems for many students, Building Words stresses instruction and practice in spelling at every level. Building Words takes full advantage of the fact that spelling and reading can be mutually reinforcing, especially in the early stages. Words are easier to spell if the learner has encountered them in reading. On the other hand, spelling can foster the learning of the alphabetic system and the retention of printed forms of words. After a pattern has been introduced as a phonics element, the most useful words in the pattern should be introduced as spelling words. Each single-syllable and multisyllabic pattern presented in the Vowel Pattern Resources section and the Syllable Pattern Resources section is accompanied by a suggested list of spelling words that incorporate the pattern taught.

GEARING INSTRUCTION TO STAGES

Spelling instruction should, of course, be geared to students' basic understanding of the spelling system. Students who have not learned to spell short-vowel words will not profit from instruction in spelling long-vowel words. In addition, students who have not yet learned to use sound strategies will not be able to implement visual or meaning strategies. In general, spelling instruction should follow the same general sequence as was recommended for reading. However, students are taught to decode elements before being taught to encode or spell them. To make sure that students are being instructed at the appropriate level, administer the Spelling Placement Test, presented in Chapter 3.

▨ PREALPHABETIC STAGE

In the prealphabetic stage, which is also known as the prephonemic stage, students have not yet discovered that letters represent sounds. However, these students may realize that print carries meaning and that they can write a story. They may use drawings, letterlike forms, letters chosen at random, or a combination of letters and numbers to write their stories. Gradually, students discover that letters represent sounds. Often, this essential discovery is made in kindergarten. However, a small percentage of students may enter first grade not yet having made that discovery. A factor in making the switch from random spelling to spelling by sound is the child's confidence and willingness to take a risk. In their 8-year study of spelling, Hughes & Searle (1997) found a number of students who were unwilling to attempt to spell words even though they had more extensive knowledge of letters and letter-sounds than some students who had already made the transition to the early alphabetic stage. Instruction should be complemented by encouragement.

▨ ALPHABETIC STAGE

In the alphabetic stage students develop the understanding that the sounds in words are represented by letters. This development parallels their growing concept of *word*. Children who are beginning to represent the beginning sounds of words are also showing the ability to point to the separate words as a line of print is being read and point to the beginning and ending of a word (Hughes & Searle, 1997). Apparently their growing awareness of how the writing system works and how a line of print is read encourages them to attempt to spell words. At the very beginning stages, students may spell a whole word with just the initial consonant. Just because students represent a whole word with a single letter doesn't mean that they are not aware of all the sounds in a word. At first the task of thinking what letter represents each sound may simply be too overwhelming to students (Hughes & Searle, 1997). Later, students add the final consonant so that *car* is spelled KR, and, later still, they begin spelling vowel sounds. Through reading instruction and experimentation with writing, students may learn some of the initial consonants but need instruction on some of the less frequently occurring consonants and those, such as /k/, /s/, and /j/, that have more than one major spelling. Digraphs, especially *ch*, also pose difficulties. As students progress toward the middle or end of the alphabetic stage, they are ready for instruction in spelling short-vowel words.

In Hughes and Searle's study, most students were well into the alphabetic stage by the end of first grade. Those who weren't continued to lag behind their peers throughout the elementary school years and were poor spellers in sixth grade. Early intervention may prevent poor spelling in later years.

Instruction during this stage should focus on introducing essential phonic elements, such as initial and final consonants, consonant digraphs, short-vowel patterns, and high-frequency clusters. After students have been taught a word pattern or other phonics element, they should be taught how to spell that element. Students are taught to spell the -*ill* pattern after they have learned to read it. They should also be taught to spell high-frequency words, such as *the, are, was, there,* that they have encountered in their reading and that they will need in their writing. Activities might include learning to stretch out sounds, sorting, reading, using the word wall, and, of course, lots of opportunities to write.

WORD PATTERN STAGE

In the word pattern stage, students move beyond simple one-sound, one-letter correspondence and begin to see final-*e* (*made*) and vowel-team patterns (*maid*). At this point, students need to move from relying on spelling a word according to the way it sounds to considering also the way a word looks. In addition to thinking about the sounds in a word, students have to look at a word they have written and ask themselves, "Does that look right?" Increasingly, spelling becomes visual and conceptual. During this stage, students learn to spell long-vowel words (*beat, bake*), *r*-vowel words (*whirl, scar, scare*), and other-vowel words (*crawl, song, stood, spool*) conventionally. They also become proficient at spelling initial and final clusters (*branch*) and preconsonantal nasals (*junk*).

As they first enter the word pattern stage, students are aware on a global level that a word does not look right. They have a sense that the word does not have quite enough letters, so they add a letter here or there as in SING for *sign* or YAER for *year*. Gradually, they learn to focus on the part of the word that does not look right and may try several spellings before they select the one that looks like it is spelled correctly (Hughes & Searle, 1997).

Activities at this level include maintaining a word study notebook in which students keep a running list of new words they have learned, patterns they are studying, weekly spelling lists, personal spelling lists, and lists of highly useful spelling words (high-frequency words, days of the week, months of the year, spelling demons, homophones and homographs). There might also be a place to record words that have an interesting sound, meaning, or history.

Instruction at this stage might focus on alternative ways of spelling long-vowel, *r*-vowel, and other-vowel patterns. Many of the spellings are governed by the element's placement in the word. For instance, some vowel digraphs, such as *ai/ay* and *ou/ow,* are said to be in complementary distribution (Venezky, 1965). The *ai* and *ou* spelling of /$\bar{a}$/ and /ow/ appear in beginning and medial positions (aid, out) but not in word-final position. When in word-final position, the *ay* (ray) and *ow* (cow) spellings are used. Other examples of vowels in complementary distribution are listed in Table 9.1. Rather than attempting to present all the spellings of long-vowel, *r*-vowel, and other-vowel words, stress should be placed on learning the major spellings, especially those that occur in high-frequency words or words that students will most likely be called upon to write.

MULTISYLLABIC PATTERN STAGE

Once students are well on their way to mastering the spelling of single-syllable words, they are ready to enter the multisyllabic stage (also known as syllable juncture) (Bear, Invernizzi, Johnston, & Templeton, 1996). A sign that students are entering this stage is their concern with doubling the final consonant of words such as *stopping* and *runner* and dropping the final *e* from words such as *choking* and *making* (Bear et al., 1996). Instructional focus at this stage is on spelling key syllable

TABLE 9.1   Vowels in Complementary Distribution

Initial/Medial	Final
ai (paid)	*ay* (pay)
au/aw (author, awful)	*aw* (law)
oy/oi (oyster, noise)	*oy* (toy)
ou/ow (out, owl)	*ow* (how)

patterns, with special attention to the two major patterns, open (*hotel*) and closed syllables (*robber*). Doubling of final consonants (*winning*) and dropping the final *e* (*whining*) should be emphasized. Rules for creating plurals should also be covered.

Word sorts can be used to highlight a comparison of open and closed syllables, words that double the final consonant versus those that don't, words in which the final *e* is dropped, and also words in which the final *y* is changed to *i* versus final-*y* words that don't change.

■ MORPHEMIC ANALYSIS STAGE

In the final stage, morphemic analysis, focus is on the relationship between meaning and spelling. As students examine prefixes, suffixes, and bases or roots, they learn that for many words, meaning affects spelling. Thus *electric* and *electricity* have similar spellings so that meaning is preserved, even though pronunciation of the *-ic* portion of the words differ. Likewise, in *walked, prayed,* and *wanted,* the spelling of the *-ed* past-tense marker is the same even though the pronunciation of *-ed* is different in each of the three words (Wilde, 1992). Instruction should highlight the meaning connection so that students understand better why some words are spelled the way they are. Instruction should also highlight the effect of adding prefixes and suffixes. Word sorts can help students describe some of the principles that underlie such perplexing decisions as when to use *-ible* versus when to use *-able* spelling or when to use the *-ir, -im, -in,* or *-il* prefix. At this stage students should focus on or even spell the base word first and then add prefixes or suffixes. For instance, students will not compose misspellings such as *realy* or *unecessary* if they have focused on *real* or *necessary* as the base word and then added the suffix *-ly* or the prefix *un-* (Snowball & Bolton, 1999).

■ FORMAL VERSUS INFORMAL INSTRUCTION

Should a spelling program be informal and incidental, so that elements are presented when the need arises, or should the program be formal and systematic, with essential elements being taught on a regular basis? The answer is "yes." Instruction should be both informal and formal. Elements should be taught as the need arises. However, because some essential elements may be neglected or may not be taught at all or may not be taught in sufficient depth, the program should be systematic. For the primary grades, daily instruction is advocated. Gentry and Gillet (1993) recommend spending 15 minutes a day on spelling and suggest the following schedule:

Monday—Students develop a list of words for study.

Tuesday, Wednesday, Thursday—Students are actively engaged in workshop-type activities. These include sorting, playing spelling games, working with the dictionary, working on patterns, word wall, secret word, making words, and secret message, or proofreading.

Friday—Students are tested on their words. Because many of the words may be personally chosen, you might arrange for pairs of students to test each other.

■ CHOOSING WORDS FOR SPELLING

Which words should be included in a spelling program? Counting technical words, there are more than a million words in printed English. However, only a few thousand of these are used with high frequency. The first 5,000 words account for 90 percent of the words used in writing (Gentry & Gillet, 1993). The first 100 account for 50 percent of the words that elementary school students will write (Snowball & Bolton, 1999). It makes sense, then, to teach high-frequency words such as *the, is, of, are,* and *when,* which will occur over and over again in writing. This is similar to the principle of teaching sight words in reading.

However, learning to spell is more than just memorizing a list of words. Since spelling is conceptual, it is important that students discover the principles that underlie the alphabetic system. Therefore, just as in reading, it is important to present words in patterns. As Gentry and Gillet (1993) note, "children learn to spell pattern by pattern, not word by word" (p. 89). Thus, each week's list should contain at least some words that share a common element. This might be four or five words from the *-at* pattern. However, the words should also be ones that students are most likely to use in their writing. (The advantage of learning a pattern such as the *-at* pattern is that students can then use their knowledge to spell other *-at* words.) As part of suggested activities for reinforcing each single-syllable and multisyllabic pattern (see the Vowel Pattern Resources section and the Syllable Pattern Resources section), Building Words presents suggested pattern spelling words. To these suggested pattern words, add high-frequency spelling words. A listing of 200 high-frequency spelling words adopted from Gentry and Gillet (1993) is presented in Table 9.2. A listing of words suggested in the Vowel Pattern and Syllable Pattern Resources sections is presented in Table 9.3. A listing of high-frequency and irregularly spelled words is contained in Table 9.4.

TABLE 9.2   High-Frequency Spelling Words

about	call	for	is	next	see	up
after	came	found	its	nice	she	try
again	can't	friend	it's	night	should	two
all	car	from	just	no	so	us
also	cat	get	know	not	some	very
always	charge	give	let	now	something	want
am	children	go	like	of	sometimes	wanted
an	class	good	little	off	started	was
and	clean	got	live	old	still	water
another	come	had	look	once	take	way
anything	could	happen	long	one	team	we
are	Dad	happy	lot	only	tell	well
around	day	has	love	or	that	went
as	did	have	made	other	the	were
at	didn't	he	make	our	their	what
back	different	help	man	out	them	when
bad	do	her	many	over	then	where
be	doesn't	here	me	people	there	while
because	dog	him	Mom	play	they	who
bed	don't	his	money	put	thing	why
before	down	home	more	ran	think	will
best	eat	homework	morning	really	this	with
better	even	house	most	right	thought	work
big	every	I	mother	run	time	world
boy	family	I'm	much	said	to	would
brother	father	if	my	saw	told	year
bus	favorite	in	name	say	too	you
but	first	into	new	school	took	your
by	food					

TABLE 9.3   Spelling Patterns

Level One: Short-Vowel Patterns	Level Two: Long-Vowel Patterns	Level Three: R-Vowel and Other-Vowel Patterns
Short-*a* patterns *-at* cat, sat, at, that *-an* can, man, an, ran *-am* am, jam *-ad* had, bad, mad, sad *-ag* bag, flag *-ap* map, snap *-ack* back, black, pack	**Long-*a* patterns** *-ake* cake, take, wake, lake, shake, snake *-ame* came, name, same, game *-ate, -ait* ate, date, late, hate; wait *-ave* gave, save, wave, brave *-ade, -aid* made, grade, paid *-ace* face, race, place *-age* age, page, cage *-ale, -ail* whale; tail, sail, mail *-ain, -ane* rain, train; plane *-ay* day, may, say, stay, play	**R-vowel patterns** *-ar* car, far, jar, star *-ark* park, bark, dark, mark *-arm* arm, farm, harm *-art, -eart* part, start, heart *-air, -are, -ere, -ear* air, hair, pair, chair; care, share, scare; where, there *-or, -ore, -oor, -ore, -our* for; more, tore, wore, score, store; door, poor *-orn* born, corn, horn, torn *-ir, -ur, -urse, -er* sir, stir; fur; nurse; her *-urn, -earn, -ire* burn, turn; earn, learn *-ird, -eard, -ord, -erd* bird, third; word; heard *-ear, -eer* ear, dear, fear, hear, near
Short-*e* patterns *-ed* bed, red *-ell* tell, well, yell *-en* ten, men, when *-et* get, let, pet, set, wet, yet *-end* end, send, bend *-ent* cent, went, sent *-est* best, nest, rest	**Long-*e* patterns** *-e, -ee, -ea, -ey* he, me, she; see, free, tree, three *-eep* keep, sleep, jeep, sheep *-een, -ean* green, seen; mean, clean *-eet, -eat* feet, meet, sweet; heat *-eal, -eel* feel, meal, real *-ead, -eed* read; need, feed *-eam* dream, cream, stream	**/aw/ patterns** *-all* all, ball, call, fall, tall, small *-aw* saw, draw *-alk* walk, talk, chalk *-aught, -ought, -ost* caught, taught; ought, bought, brought; cost, lost *-ong* long, song, strong, wrong
Short-*i* patterns *-it* it, sit, little *-in* in, win, skin *-ill* will, hill *-id* did, hid, kid *-ig* big, pig, dig *-ing* ring, sing, thing, bring *-ip* ship, trip, slip *-ick* pick, sick, trick *-ish* dish, fish, wish	**Long-*i* patterns** *-ie, -igh* pie, lie; high *-ight* night, light, might, right *-ike* bike, like, hike *-ide* hide, ride, side, wide *-ime, -yme* time, dime, lime *-ine* nine, line, mine, shine *-ice* ice, nice, rice, twice *-ile, -ife* mile, smile, while, life *-ite* bite, quite, white *-y* my, cry, sky, why, fly	**/o͞o/ patterns** *-oo, -oon, -une* zoo, too; moon, noon, soon *-ew, -ue* new, flew, grew; blue, true *-oot, -uit* boot, shoot; fruit, suit *-ool, -ule* cool, fool, pool, tool, school *-oom, -oup* boom, broom, room
Short-*o* patterns *-op* hop, top, shop *-ot* lot, hot, not, spot *-ock* block, clock	**Long-*o* patterns** *-o, -oe* no, go, so *-ow* low, grow, show, slow, know *-oat, -ote* goat, boat, coat; note, wrote *-oad* toad, load, road *-ole, -oll* hole, pole; roll *-old* old, gold, cold, fold, hold, sold, told *-oak, -oke* woke, joke, broke, spoke *-ose* nose, rose, chose close, those *-one* bone, alone, phone	**/oo/ patterns** *-ook* book, cook, look, took, shook *-ood, -ould* wood, good; could, would, should *-ull, -ush* pull, full; push, bush
Short-*u* patterns *-ug* bug, rug, hug *-un* fun, run, sun *-ut* but, cut, shut *-up* up, cup, puppy *-ub* cub, rub, tub *-ump* bump, jump, dump *-unk* junk, skunk, trunk *-us(s), -ust, -uck* us, bus; must, just; truck	**Long-*u* patterns** *-ule, -use, -uge, -ute, -ew* mule; use; huge; flute; few	**/ow/ patterns** *-ow* cow, how, now, wow *-own* down, town, brown, clown *-ound* found, sound, round, pound, ground *-oud, owd* loud, cloud, proud; crowd *-out, -outh, -our, -ouse* out, shout; south; our; house, mouse
		/oy/ patterns *-oy* boy, toy, joy *-oil, -oin, -oice, -oise* oil, join, voice, noise

TABLE 9.3   Continued

Levels Four and Five: Syllable Patterns

High-frequency patterns
Compound words someone, sometime, something, anyone, anything, outside, inside
Schwa-*a* ago, away, alone, about, around, along, across, again, against, asleep
-en, -o, -er open, happen, twenty, plenty; ago; over, under, ever, never, other, brother, mother
-ar, -at, -it garden, farmer; matter; kitten, kitchen
-in, is(s), -un winter, dinner, finish; sister, mistake, whisper; under, until, hundred
be-, re-, -or became, below, begin, belong; report, receive; before, morning, forty
-a, -y = /e/, -ey, -ble paper, baby, famous; sunny, funny; money; table
-i, -ur, -um tiger, tiny, title, spider, Friday; hurry, purple; summer, number

Short-vowel patterns
-ic(k), -et, -im chicken, nickel, pickle; letter, lettuce, settle, metal, ticket; limit, improve, simple
-ab, -ad, -ag, -ang absent, cabin; shadow, ladder, address; magazine, magnet; sang, angry
-am, -an, -ant, -ap hammer; candy; giant, distant; happy, happen, captain, chapter
-ent, -el(l) event, prevent; yellow, elbow, jelly, welcome
-ep, -es, -ev September, separate; address, success, yesterday, restaurant; seven, several, every
-id, -ig, -il(l) middle, hidden, midnight; signal, figure; silly, building, children
-ob, -oc(k), -od problem, probably; doctor, chocolate; body, modern, product, somebody
-ol, -om, -on dollar, follow, holiday, volcano; common, comment, promise; honest, honor
-op, -ot, -age copy, popular, opposite; bottom, bottle, robot; damage, message, garbage
-ub, -uc(k), -ud rubber, stubborn, subject, public; success, lucky, chuckle; sudden, study
-uf, -ug, -up suffer, muffin; suggest, struggle; puppy, supper, upper
-um, -us, -ut, -uz custom, customer; muscle, discuss; butter; puzzle

Long-vowel patterns
-ee, -ea = /ē/ season, reason, easily, eaten, repeat, leader; beetle, indeed, succeed, agree
-ide, -ire, -ise, -ive, -ize beside, divide, decide; entire; surprise; alive; realize
-ade, -aid, -ail, -ale, -ain, -ate afraid; detail; female; contain, explain, obtain; hesitate, appreciate
-ope, -one, -oke, -u, -ture envelope, telescope; telephone; broken, spoken; future, nature, adventure, creature

Other-vowel patterns
-al, -au, -aw also, although, always; autumn, author; awful, drawing
-ea = /e/, i = /e/, i-e = /ē/ weather, measure, pleasant; easier, police
-tion, -sion, -y = /ī/ action, addition, invention, information, question, mention; confusion, conclusion, occasion, explosion, persuasion; supply, deny, magnify, reply
-oi, -oy point, noisy; enjoy, destroy, loyal, voyage
-ou, -ow around, about, announce, amount, mountain, surround, thousand; flower, allow, power
-oo, -ove = /o͞o/, -u = /o͞o/ balloon; improve, approve, remove; super, student, truly, tuna
-ook, -oot, -ood, -ul(l) book, bookstore, workbook; football; neighborhood, goodness; thankful, careful

A third source of words are those that the students have a specific need to learn. These might be words that they are misspelling in their writing, words that they will need in upcoming writing tasks, or words that they may need to write as part of content-area learning.

How many words should be presented each week? Young students and those experiencing difficulty with spelling might be presented with just five words a week. Older students and adept learners might be given ten or more (Gentry & Gillet, 1993). Commercial programs generally present twenty to twenty-five words a week. However, on average, students know about 65 percent of the words in their spelling books before the words are presented for study, so in reality they are faced with learning only ten or fewer new words.

TABLE 9.4   High-Frequency Spelling Words

Grade One	Grade Two		Grade Three		
a	about	where	above	its	truth
all	after	who	again	juice	until
any	around	work	against	kept	wash
are	ask	would	alive	knee	wasn't
as	because		almost	knew	watch
came	been		always	knock	we've
come	behind		another	know	which
do	beside		became	large	while
done	both		become	later	winter
for	brother		before	learn	won
from	children		beginning	leave	won't
give	could		better	lesson	word
go	cover		between	letter	write
gone	didn't		birth	lion	wrong
has	dog		birthday	listen	wrote
have	don't		both	love	year
he	door		build	lucky	yellow
I	down		busy	March	yesterday
is	egg		buy	month	you're
many	every		by	more	you've
me	eye		can't	morning	young
mom	father		candy	move	
my	found		child	never	
of	funny		circle	north	
on	great		circus	often	
one	happy		city	other	
said	house		close	outside	
saw	into		color	own	
she	laugh		dance	part	
some	milk		does	peach	
they	money		doesn't	pencil	
to	mother		dollar	ready	
two	nothing		early	scare	
was	off		earth	sew	
we	once		eight	shouldn't	
were	only		enter	since	
what	over		even	soft	
yes	people		felt	sorry	
you	pretty		Friday	south	
your	pull		friend	speak	
	push		front	sports	
	put		fruit	square	
	says		girls	stairs	
	should		grandmother	store	
	start		group	such	
	their		guess	sure	
	these		half	thank	
	three		head	there	
	today		hear	they're	
	took		here	think	
	upon		horse	third	
	very		hour	though	
	want		I'd	too	
	warm		inside	touch	
	water		isn't	tried	
	what		it's	true	

TABLE 9.4   Continued

Grade Four		
across	else	quarter
addition	enjoy	reason
address	enough	reach
afraid	entrance	realize
ahead	except	return
almost	extra	rule
already	family	scared
America	famous	science
American	fearful	scream
among	field	search
angry	finish	season
animal	first	second
attack	follow	secret
August	forest	sentence
author	forgot	several
awful	glove	shoulder
balloon	ground	silver
baseball	grown	steak
believe	handle	straight
body	heart	strength
bottle	height	strong
bounce	herself	sugar
break	himself	surprise
brought	history	taught
built	hundred	teacher
caught	idea	thought
center	interest	thousand
chance	invent	threw
change	invention	through
character	island	thumb
charge	January	together
chief	library	travel
clothes	lonely	truly
contest	magic	Tuesday
cough	mouth	turkey
country	movies	understand
county	mystery	United States
couple	nation	visit
cousin	neighbor	wagon
cried	nephew	wear
daughter	number	Wednesday
dead	o'clock	weigh
December	offer	weight
decided	order	whatever
department	ought	whenever
depend	pair	whether
desert	perfect	whole
difference	person	woman
different	phone	wonder
dinner	piece	worry
double	planet	worse
doubt	please	wreck
dozen	present	wrist
during	probably	weather
either	prove	
eleven	purple	

Grade Five			
ability	create	important	pollution
absent	creature	impossible	popular
accident	cruise	improvement	population
active	damage	increase	possible
actually	dangerous	insist	promise
admire	deaf	jewel	president
adventure	deliver	journal	problem
advertise	describe	journey	quiet
although	description	knowledge	rear
answer	deserve	language	receive
anxious	dessert	laughter	record
apartment	diary	length	relative
appear	difficult	local	remember
argument	direction	lunar	repair
arrange	discover	machine	reply
attempt	distant	major	respond
aunt	division	male	responsibilities
autumn	dough	marriage	responsibility
avenue	effort	mayor	rough
average	election	measure	separate
aware	electric	memory	serious
balance	empty	mention	slept
banana	enclose	message	soldier
beautiful	enemy	metal	stomach
berry	equal	million	subject
borrow	excellent	minute	succeed
bother	excite	mirror	suffer
bought	excitement	mistake	television
breakfast	exercise	mountain	terrible
breath	expect	multiply	theater
breathe	experience	needle	thief
bury	explain	neither	thorough
business	expression	niece	throughout
calendar	favorite	normal	tongue
captain	female	notice	tough
capture	figure	novel	toward
carried	finally	obey	treasure
carrot	finger	object	trouble
certain	fond	occasion	unusual
champion	forward	ocean	vacation
cheerful	freeze	office	vegetable
choice	frighten	opinion	victory
choose	fuel	opposite	view
clue	garbage	ounce	voyage
collect	gather	paragraph	warn
comfortable	general	parent	whistle
company	germ	pause	width
compare	government	peace	witness
complain	guide	pedal	youth
complete	guilty	perhaps	zero
condition	happiness	persuade	
connect	holiday	pleasant	
consent	honest	pleasure	
continue	horrible	poem	
correct	hospital	polar	
courage	hungry	police	

SPELLING SCOPE AND SEQUENCE

The scope and sequence of spelling instruction should be similar to one for instruction in phonics for reading. As a general rule, however, only words that students can read are included in spelling instruction. Short-vowel patterns are introduced after a number of initial consonants have been learned. Digraphs and some clusters are then taught, followed by long-vowels, *r*-vowels, other vowels, and additional clusters. Although some high-frequency multisyllable words will have been taught earlier, the focus then shifts to multisyllabic words followed by an introduction of words in which morphemic elements are emphasized. A characteristic of the scope and sequence in spelling is that the demands made by students' writing are emphasized. A sample scope and sequence for spelling instruction is presented in Table 9.5. Recommendations for the teaching of specific spelling words can be found in the resources sections of Chapters 6 and 8.

SPELLING STRATEGIES

Just as students are taught to use decoding strategies when they encounter difficult words, they should also be shown how to use spelling strategies when they are called on to spell a difficult word. The strategies include best spelling, thinking how it sounds, thinking how it looks, thinking of a word like this one, trying it out, thinking of its parts, using a rule, using a reference, and asking for help (Wilde, 1992; Snowball & Bolton, 1999).

Best spelling means that students spell the word as best they can and later check the correctness of the spelling. This strategy is especially useful and, in fact, highly desirable when students are writing and don't want to interrupt the flow of the writing process. In thinking how it sounds, students say the word slowly and try to write the word sound by sound. This works especially well when the word in question is highly predictable. In thinking how it looks, the student tries to picture the word. This works well for high-imagery words or words such as *of* and *once* that don't lend themselves to a think-how-it-sounds strategy. In thinking of a word like this one, students use a known word to help them. In trying it out students have a go at a word. If a word doesn't look right, they write it again, and per-

---

TABLE 9.5   Scope and Sequence for Spelling Instruction

Level 1	Level 4
Beginning consonants	Multisyllabic words
Short-vowel patterns	Doubling of final consonant
Consonant digraphs	Dropping of final *e*
High-frequency clusters	Advanced contractions
High-frequency words	Easy prefixes
	Easy suffixes
Level 2	Easy roots
Long-vowel patterns	
Clusters	**Level 5**
High-frequency words	Multisyllabic words
	Review of doubling of final consonant
Level 3	Review of dropping of final *e*
r-Vowel patterns	Medium prefixes
Other-vowel patterns	Medium suffixes
Compound words	Medium roots
Contractions	
Easy multisyllabic words	

haps even a third or fourth time and choose the version that looks correct. Students should not erase words that they believe might be misspelled. If they do, they won't be able to compare possible spellings to see which one looks correct. In the think-of-its-parts strategy, students think of the base word and then think of the affixes that are being added. For instance, when spelling *comedian*, students might have a sense that it should be written with two *m*'s (*commedian*). However, thinking of the base and the prefix that was added should help them resist this impulse. In the use-a-rule strategy, students might drop the final *e* (*hoping*) or double the final consonant (*stopped*) or apply another useful spelling generalization. In the use-a-reference strategy, students use spelling notebooks, a dictionary, a list of spelling words that have been posted, a spell checker, an electronic speller, their texts, or another appropriate source. If all else fails, students can ask for help from a friend, a teacher, or a parent.

Teach strategies directly. As you write on the board, model the process of sounding out a word by stretching out its sounds or attempting to visualize a word or trying out spellings. Also use prompts. Some prompts that might be used are listed in Table 9.6.

STUDY TECHNIQUE FOR LEARNING SPELLING WORDS

In addition to learning how to use spelling strategies, students also need to learn how to study spelling words. Effective studying involves examining the word closely, pronouncing the word, saying the letters that make up the word, visualizing the word, and writing the word. The steps of an adapted version of the Fitzgerald

TABLE 9.6   Spelling Prompts

Strategy	When Used	Prompt
Best spelling	Student hesitates while writing a piece because she is unsure of the spelling of a word.	Spell the word as best you can and check it after you have finished writing.
Think how it sounds	Student is having difficulty spelling a word that has a predictable spelling.	Say the word slowly. Stretch it out. What sound do you hear first? What sound do you hear next?
Think how it looks	Student is having difficulty spelling a word that contains letters not directly predictable from its sounds.	Can you picture the word? Can you think where you might have seen that word before? Can you see it in your mind? How does it look?
Analogy	Student is having difficulty spelling a word that sounds and looks like a word that she can spell.	Is the word like any word that you know how to spell? How do you spell (known word)? How do you spell (unknown word)?
Rule	Student is having difficulty when adding *ed* to words like *hope* and *stop*.	Does it follow a rule? Is there a rule that would help you spell the word?
Proofing	Student has misspelled words in her written piece.	Do the words have all their sounds? Do they look right?
Affirmation	Teacher wishes to reinforce the student's correct use of a strategy.	I like the way you stretched the word out and thought about each of its sounds.
Assessment	Teacher wants to see what strategies the student is using.	How did you figure out how to spell that word?

(1951) method, which has been in use for more than four decades but is still widely recommended, are listed below.

1. Look at the word carefully.
2. Pronounce the word. Be sure to say each sound in the word.
3. Spell the word to yourself.
4. Close your eyes and try to see the word in your mind.
5. Cover the word, say it, and write it.
6. Check the spelling.
7. Repeat the steps if the word is misspelled.

STUDENTS WHO HAVE SPECIAL DIFFICULTY WITH SPELLING

For most students, spelling develops in tandem with decoding and overall reading. Students who can read on a third-grade level can usually spell third-grade words. Unfortunately, some students make slow progress in both reading and spelling. They need extra help in both areas. However, some students who are proficient readers are poor spellers. They lack what Gentry (1997) terms the "spelling gene." They have serious difficulty visualizing words, which is the main characteristic of average and good spellers. They generally continue to spell by ear rather than by eye, continue to misspell easy words, and are inconsistent. They may spell *off* correctly in the first paragraph but misspell it in the second paragraph. Poor spellers may also have particular difficulty with sounds that are hard to detect, such as the second sound in a cluster: the *t* in *stop* or the *r* in *brave*. They also have difficulty with sounds such as /l, /r/, /m/, and /n/ when they are in the middle of a word or at the end. The inflectional endings *-s* and *-ed* also pose problems for poor spellers and are frequently omitted (Moats, 1995). These difficulties seem to be rooted in a weakness in phonological processing. Because of a weakness in processing sounds, words may not be clearly coded or stored.

In addition to having difficulty with detecting subtle sounds in words and spelling them correctly, poor spellers often have difficulty with orthographic patterns such as representing long vowels with a digraph, as in the *oa* spelling of long *o* in *goat* or the final-*e* spelling of long *o* in *hope.*

Because poor spellers may have a weakened phonological system, emphasis should be placed on detecting sounds in words. At the earliest levels, emphasize the individual sounds of words and their spellings, especially when dealing with such items as clusters (*stand*), which are difficult to detect. When introducing a word such as *stand*, help students focus on each sound in the word. Say each sound, /s/, /t/, /a/, /n/, /d/, and have students say them with you. Students might trace or write the word to help them detect and remember the letters and sounds in the word. Students in the alphabetic stage might say each sound as they trace each letter. However, students in the word pattern stage and beyond are beginning to chunk words and to see patterns in words. They might say the word or each syllable as a whole as they trace it. Steps for a tracing technique that have been adapted from Fernald (1943) are listed below.

STEPS FOR TRACING SPELLING WORDS

Step 1: Students say the word as a whole.

Step 2: Students in the alphabetic stage say each sound as they trace the word. If they are learning *dig,* students say, "dig, /d/, /i/, /g/, dig." If they are in the word pattern stage students say the whole word or say the word syllable by syllable. For the word *nation,* the student would say, "nation, na, tion, nation," and trace the word or syllable as he says it. The student continues to trace the word until he believes he can write it from memory.

Step 3: Student writes the word from memory and checks her spelling versus the correct spelling. If the student can write the word correctly twice, she goes to the next word. If not, she continues to trace.

Tracing and saying words focuses students' attention and it helps them to become aware of the separate sounds or sound patterns in a word. Tracing can also be a helpful technique for students who have poor visual memory for words. In addition to tracing the words, students should also practice picturing them in their minds. And they should be encouraged to use mnemonic devices.

Struggling readers and writers also need to be provided with words on their spelling level, not their reading level. Spelling generally lags behind reading, especially as students move into the middle grades. A student reading on a third-grade level may still be struggling with second-grade spelling. Struggling readers should also be encouraged to use a spell checker. A number of inexpensive electronic devices that are designed to assist both proficient and struggling spellers are available from Franklin (800-266-5626). These devices help students look up words that they can only partially spell, help with homophones, and provide practice activities.

INDIVIDUALIZING SPELLING INSTRUCTION

One way of individualizing spelling is for students to create spelling journals. On the inside cover of their journals, students might write or paste a list of the steps for studying spelling words. In the rest of the journal students write words to be learned. These can be dictated words from the word or syllable patterns they are learning (see Vowel Pattern Resources and Syllable Pattern Resources sections), high-frequency words, words that they need to write a piece they are currently working on, special-interest words, or words from subject-matter areas. An excellent source of words is those that have posed problems for them in their writing. Words to be learned are written in the left-hand column of notebook pages that have been divided into columns as shown in Figure 9.1. It is essential, of course,

Words	Hard Parts	Helpful Hints	Quizzes			
friend	friend	i before end				
hear	hear	Need an ear to hear				
when	when					

FIGURE 9.1   Sample Page from Spelling Notebook

that students write the correct spellings in their journals. They can do this by checking class lists, dictionaries, spell checkers, or getting help from the teacher. In a second column, students rewrite the word but circle parts of the word that are tricky or difficult. This might be the *ie* in *friend* or the *ean* in *ocean*. Students might also write a mnemonic to help them remember the difficult part of a word. The mnemonic might be supplied by the teacher or invented by the students. The mnemonic for *friend* might be "*friend* has an *i* and an *end* at the end" (Education Department of Western Australia, 1994). Five columns can be drawn to the right of the list of spelling words. These can be used to check daily quizzes.

Working with a partner of similar spelling ability, students quiz each other and check off each word spelled correctly. Transfer is a problem for poor spellers. Often they spell words correctly on a quiz but then misspell them in their writing. Taking several quizzes fosters automatic learning so skills are more likely to transfer. After a word has been spelled correctly on three consecutive quizzes, it is counted as being mastered (Education Department of Western Australia, 1994). If after five quizzes a student is still unable to spell a word correctly, you may ask the student to use a tracing technique to learn the word.

TEACHING SPELLING

Spelling should be closely tied in to students' writing. In their study of good and poor spellers, Hughes and Searles (2000) found that good spellers were writers. Writing provides students with a reason to be concerned about spelling and also with opportunities to apply spelling skills. As Hughes and Searle note,

> Writing also creates a purpose for learning to spell by developing a sense of audience. When writers care about what they are writing, and about how their ideas are received by readers, they are more apt to understand how readers are influenced by correct and incorrect spellings. As a consequence, committed writers are more likely to strive to become good spellers. (p. 204)

In addition to recognizing the importance of good spelling as part of their writing, good spellers also took greater responsibility for working out spelling problems. They were more apt to look up a word or try a spelling strategy as opposed to asking a peer, parent, or teacher for help. Good spellers were also better at proofreading. They were more likely than poor spellers to notice a word that did not look right. Good spellers were more likely to try several spellings when their original try did not look quite right and then choose the one that seemed to be correct. Good spellers had a highly developed sense of what looked right and what did not. This may have been because of their experience with orthographic knowledge, which is their awareness of which letters should appear together (Stahl, Osborne, & Lehr, 1990) and is fostered by wide reading. Poor spellers, on the other hand, relied heavily on the way words sound. One student spelled *irresponsibility* as *irrisponsibility* even though she had written the words *responsible* and *responsibility* correctly. Apparently, she failed to use the meaning connection and, instead, relied on the lower-level sound system.

Whole-class or whole-group methods are used to model study techniques and spelling strategies, including proofreading. They are also used to introduce spelling words that are appropriate for the whole group or class. Based on a pretest, a spelling lesson generally begins with students attempting to spell the new words.

The teacher dictates from five to ten words. The teacher says the word, uses it in a sentence, and says the word once more. Students attempt to spell the word. Students should be encouraged to say the word slowly as they attempt to spell it, and to emphasize each sound as they say it. Use and encourage students to use a spelling pronunciation. For instance, even though the middle syllable of *difference* is omitted in normal pronunciation, encourage students to include it so that they say "dif-FER-ence." Explain that this is not the way the word is pronounced in ordinary speech, but pronouncing it the way it is spelled as they study or get ready to write the word will help them learn to spell it.

After the words have been dictated, the teacher supplies the correct spellings. As the teacher goes over the correct spellings, she highlights similarities among the words, points out hard parts, and provides a mnemonic or any information about the word's history that might help students spell the word correctly. For instance, when introducing words such as *knock, knit,* and *knight,* explain that at one time these words were pronounced with a /k/ sound, so that *knee* was pronounced /knē/. Students might try saying the words the way they were once pronounced. Hopefully, the information that *knee* was once pronounced with a /k/ sound will help students to remember to include the *k* when spelling these words. Students compare their spellings with the correct spellings and enter the correct spelling of each word in their notebooks. As students compare their misspellings with the correct spellings, they should note parts of the words that they got wrong. These parts could be circled in the second column and given special attention. Students then study words and engage in a variety of workshop activities as explained earlier. They also take practice quizzes.

The first word that students should be taught to spell is their names. After that, present some easy high-frequency words and the most useful words from the phonics patterns. In general, students should only be taught to spell words that they can read. Patterns are especially useful elements because once students can spell one pattern word, they can build on that knowledge to spell other words in that pattern. For instance, once students can spell *cat,* they should be able to learn to spell *rat, hat, sat,* and other *-at* words fairly easily. To show students how to use their knowledge of one word to spell other words, ask, "If you can spell *cat,* then what others can you spell?" (Snowball & Bolton, 1999). Lead them to see that *hat* and other *-at* words are spelled just like *cat* except for the first letter. Using this same principle of building on what students know, show them how if they can spell a base word, they can spell its inflected forms. If they can spell spell *jump,* they can spell *jumps, jumping,* and *jumped.*

■ SPELLING GENERALIZATIONS

Except for final *e,* phonics generalizations are not very useful. However, spelling generalizations can be a significant aid, especially if students participate in constructing the generalizations. Students develop a deeper understanding of regularities in the spelling system if they derive their own conclusions. This can be achieved by having students observe how words are spelled and through sorting. For instance, when students are grappling with adding *ed* to words, have them list words from their reading that end in *ed* (Snowball & Bolton, 1999). Students might list words such as the following: *helped, stopped, jumped, dripped, placed, cheered, passed, hopped, hated, cried, planned, yelled, pinned, baked, chopped, wanted, dried, tied.* Working with you or in small groups, students note what the base word in each item is and how it is changed when *ed* is added. As an alternative, you might supply a similar listing from students' reading and writing and have them sort the words. Initially, you may want to present only single-syllable words in which the final consonant stays the same (*helped, jumped*) and words in which it is doubled (*stopped, planned*). Later, include words ending in final *e* (*hated, baked*) and final *y* (*cried, tried*), multisyllabic words (*committed, occurred*), and words ending in *c* (*mimicked, picnicked*). Also present words ending in *ing, er,* and *est.* If you select the words, it is easier to regulate the level of difficulty of the task. Some common spelling generalizations are listed below.

Adding Suffixes

- When a word ends in *e*, drop the *e* when adding an ending beginning with a vowel: *hoped, hoping, prettier.*
- When a word ends in *oe*, do not drop the final *e* when adding an *ing*: *hoeing.*
- When a word ends in a single consonant preceded by a single vowel, double the final consonant before adding an ending beginning with a vowel: *hopped, hopping, bigger, biggest.* This also applies to multisyllable words if the final syllable is accented: *committed, committing, occurred, occurring.*
- When a word ends in *y* preceded by a consonant, change the *y* to *i* and add *ed*: *cried, hurried, tried.* When a word ends in *y* preceded by a vowel, add *ed*: *played.*
- Keep the *y* when adding *ing* to words of one syllable that end in *y*: *crying, trying.*
- When a word ends in *c*, add a *k* when adding an ending beginning with a vowel: *picnicked, trafficked.*

Forming Adverbs

- To form an adverb, add *ly* to the base word: *really, lovely.*
- When a word ends in *y*, change the *y* to *i* when adding *ly*: *noisily.*
- When a word ends in *ic*, add *al* before adding *ly*: *automatically.* There are some exceptions: *publicly.*
- When adding *ly* to words that end in *e*, keep the *e* for most words: *sincerely.* The *e* is dropped in words such as *truly, possibly.*

Forming Plurals by Adding es

- Add *es* to form the plural of words ending in *ch, sh, s, x, z: churches, bushes, glasses, boxes.*

Adding the Suffixes able and ible

- The suffix *able* is added to whole words: *acceptable, dependable.*
- The suffix *ible* is added to partial words: *horrible, visible.*
- There are some exceptions: *distractible, incomprehensible.*

PROOFREADING

Proofreading is an essential component of spelling instruction and also a key part of the writing process. As students proofread, they check for capitalization, punctuation, and usage errors, and they also apply spelling skills and strategies by correcting misspelled words. Proofreading is attitudinal as well as cognitive. Just as you want students to take ownership of their writing, you also want them to be responsible for correcting errors in their writing. One way of doing this is by building students' confidence in their proofreading ability. Set proofreading goals that students can attain and hold students to them. Also provide specific instruction and lots of practice in proofreading strategies.

Model how you go about proofreading. Show students how you slow down your pace when you proofread, and read a piece aloud to yourself so that you can hear whether the words sound right. Also carefully inspect the words to see whether they look right. Demonstrate how you might put a ruler under the line you are examining so that you focus on that part of the text. Show how you might circle words that do not look right and use a reference to check their spelling.

Show, too, how you might use a spell checker. Explain that the spell checker will often provide a number of possible spellings. Demonstrate how you go about choosing the right one. Also note that the spell checker can't check a word if it is too far off the mark. Explain, too, that the spell checker will not be able to tell if you have used the wrong homophone, such as using *hair* for *hare*, and will not flag this as an error. Most spell checkers have only a limited number of proper nouns in their dictionaries. When using a spell checker, students might copy troublesome words into their spelling notebooks for later studying. Encourage the use of talking spell checkers if these are available. Because they read the piece aloud, talking spell checkers will help students detect dropped endings that they otherwise might not have noticed.

Other helpful proofreading tools are word walls, handbooks of style that contain sections on the proper use of confusing word pairs, such as *accept* and *except*, spelling notebooks, electronic and hard-copy dictionaries, booklets of words frequently used in students' writing, and atlases and almanacs.

If students are writing on a specific topic, it is helpful to compose a list of words that they might use but whose spelling might be difficult. If students are writing about recycling, for instance, you might introduce such words as *garbage, waste, recycling, environment, landfill*, and *pollution*.

To further demonstrate proofreading, copy a rough draft of a student's composition and, with the students' help, proofread and correct it. Use a sample piece from a previous class so as not to embarrass anyone, or create a composite piece that features elements that the class is having difficulty with. Also encourage peer proofreading. We have a tendency to read what should be on a page rather than what is there, so it is helpful to have someone else read our papers. However, students should understand that the ultimate responsibility for proofreading rests with them. Bring in examples of errors from newspapers, magazines, and other print sources. Encourage students to spot the errors and correct them. This will help build the habit of proofreading. If possible, invite a reporter from the local paper or a local writer to discuss proofreading and techniques they use.

With the class, create a proofreading checklist. As new mechanical items are introduced, such as spelling and capitalizing the months of the year, add these to the list. Often students will spell words correctly on a spelling quiz but will misspell them in written pieces. Hold students responsible for words that have been taught. Remind them that they should take special note of words that they have studied and should double-check to make sure that these are spelled correctly. Students should use their spelling notebooks as a proofreading reference. Some students may even spell the same word in two different ways in a piece of writing. Suggest that they note which looks more correct and check their choice in a reference.

All of us have spelling demons, words that we continue to misspell even though we have studied them and looked them up countless times. Discuss your demons and how you handle them. Students might keep a list of their demons and use the list as a part of their proofreading tools. To help students focus on troublesome words, review and post a short list of words likely to cause problems: *there, their, its, it's*. If you notice that students are having difficulty with particular words in their rough drafts, you can include these words in the focused list or in the weekly spelling lists.

Although correct spelling is desirable, do not overemphasize it; students' writing can suffer when they are worried about spelling. Instead, stress the importance of content and expression. When composing, students' main concern should be on getting their thoughts down. Spelling and other mechanical issues can be addressed during the proofreading stage. To keep focussed on the message, students should spell as well as they can and may circle words that they are unsure of for later checking. They might also try several spellings and choose the one that looks most correct. Giving it a try and seeing how it looks are strategies used by successful spellers (Hughes & Searle, 1997).

Be on the lookout for students who restrict the words they use in their writing to those they can spell. This is a strategy that struggling spellers frequently use, but it hampers their writing development. Stress the importance of what they have to say and how they say it, and provide extra assistance with spelling.

ASSESSING SPELLING

To assess students' spelling progress, check students' partner quizzes each week. You may also want to administer a spelling test periodically. Because transfer is essential, also check students' written pieces.

INTEGRATING SPELLING AND READING INSTRUCTION

Although writing words and decoding them are different tasks, they can, with careful planning, be used to reinforce each other. The key is to gear instruction to the students' stage of development and to plan instruction so that spelling instruction builds on what students learn as they encounter new words and patterns in their reading.

Chapter 10

ORGANIZING AND IMPLEMENTING A PROGRAM FOR BUILDING WORD ANALYSIS SKILLS AND STRATEGIES

Building Words can be implemented in a number of ways. It can be used with all students or just those students who need more intensive instruction or additional practice. It can be used as the core word analysis program or a supplementary program to complement a basal or children's book approach. It can be used with the whole class, with a small group, or for one-on-one instruction. Building Words is highly effective when used as the core word analysis program. All students benefit from a carefully sequenced program in decoding and spelling when accompanied by ample opportunity to read and write for real purposes. It is also helpful if all students are able to use the key strategies emphasized in building literacy: pronounceable word parts, analogy, and context. Learning is accelerated when all the school's staff are teaching the same strategies and using the same terminology. If it is not used as the core program, Building Words should be carefully coordinated with the core program.

SETTING OBJECTIVES

An effective program of literacy development begins with a statement of general goals, which are translated into specific objectives. The objectives should be those that are most likely to result in maximum improvement in literacy. The objectives should include a clear statement of what you expect students to be able to do and standards of performance. Possible objectives for building literacy are listed below. These objectives and the suggestions for assessing them should be adapted to fit the specific needs of your students.

Objective 1.   Students will achieve a grasp of basic word analysis skills and strategies: phonics, sight words, syllabification, and contextual clues.   Given the elements in isolation or a series of words containing the basic elements in question, students can pronounce them with 80 percent accuracy. (Elements include consonants, digraphs, clusters, short-vowel, long-vowel, *r*-vowel, and other-vowel patterns).

> ***Assessment***
> - Word Pattern Survey, Syllable Survey
> - Quiz in which 10 to 20 target items are presented

- Performance on Benchmark Passages Inventory
- Observations of students' reading of material in which the target element appears

Objective 2. When they encounter difficult words, students will use appropriate strategies to decode the word. Students attempt to use the appropriate strategy 80 percent of the time. (The success rate of correctly decoding the word will usually be somewhat lower than the rate of attempting the strategy. The important point is that students apply strategies. Strategies include pronounceable word part, analogy, sound by sound, picture clue, context.)

Assessment
- Observations of students' reading
- Response to Student Decoding Interview
- Performance on a running record or Benchmark Passages Inventory

Objective 3. Students will learn to spell key phonic elements and high frequency words.
Assessment
- Performance on periodic quizzes on words taught
- Response to Student Spelling Interview
- Observations of students' attempts to spell words
- Analysis of written work

Although the focus of Building Words is on developing word analysis skills and strategies, the following objectives should be a part of a balanced program of literacy instruction. The ultimate goal of word analysis instruction is to fully develop students' abilities to read and write and to foster a love of reading.

Objective 4. Students will read a variety of materials incorporating the phonics or syllabification analysis elements taught as evidenced by:
- Reading at least 20 minutes a day in school
- Reading at least 20 minutes a day out of school
- For students on levels 1 and 2, reading at least 25 books a year
- For students on levels 3 and 4, reading at least 10 books a year

Assessment
- Record of books and other materials read in class
- Record of books read at home
- Log of time spent reading
- Observations of students

Objective 5. Students will demonstrate overall growth in their reading as evidenced by:
- Ability to read increasingly more difficult books with at least 95 percent word recognition and 75 percent comprehension
- Performance on Benchmark Passages Inventory
- Performance on benchmark books

Objective 6. Students will demonstrate overall growth in their writing as evidenced by:
- Longer, more complex sentences
- More varied vocabulary
- Longer, more fully developed pieces
- Attempting a variety of writing forms
- More accurate spelling, capitalization, and punctuation

Assessment
- Observations
- Checklists
- Analyses of written pieces
- Record of written pieces or portfolio

DIRECT, SYSTEMATIC INSTRUCTION

Objectives need to be translated into instructional techniques. Students need direct, systematic instruction geared to their strengths. High-quality instructional techniques emphasized in this text feature Word Building; guided reading including text walk; shared reading; language experience, including shared writing and interactive writing; and sorting.

BUILDING ON WHAT STUDENTS KNOW

Techniques used and content presented need to build on what students know, which is the essence of Word Building. Students also need to be taught strategies that they can apply on their own so they become independent, competent learners. For struggling readers, the failure cycle needs to be broken.

AS AN INTERVENTION PROGRAM

Although Building Words works well as a classroom program and, if carefully implemented, can prevent most reading and writing problems, it is especially effective for struggling readers and writers. Instruction is explicit and systematic and geared to students' literacy levels and stages of development. Often struggling readers and writers need additional practice. Building Words provides suggestions for a variety of practice activities and a number of books and other materials at each level so that students have lots of opportunities to implement skills and strategies through real reading and writing for real purposes, which provide the most effective practice of all.

Intervention can be conducted by the classroom teacher or by a specialist or, better yet, by the classroom teacher and specialist working together. If conducted by a specialist, it can be a pull-out or within-class program or a combination of the two. If possible, intervention should be conducted within the classroom. Regardless of where it is conducted, intervention should be carefully coordinated with the classroom program.

SELECTING STUDENTS

Select students with the greatest needs in reading and writing. However, when first implementing the program, also select those students who are most likely to benefit from it. You may want to focus on students whose attendance is dependable and who are cooperative. Once you have experience with the program, you can begin to work with more challenging students.

SIZE OF GROUP

Students make the most progress when taught one on one. In many situations, however, one-on-one instruction is not practical. If because of time and staffing constraints it is necessary to work with groups of students, keep the groups to a reasonable size. A group of five or six is the maximum that can be taught effectively. However, the more serious the difficulties, the smaller the group should be.

SCHEDULING INSTRUCTION

Intervention instruction is most beneficial when it is additive, when it is in addition to the instruction already provided. Students who are behind need more instructional time if they are expected to catch up. Before school, after school, and summer programs are recommended. However, if this is not practical, arrange intervention sessions when they fit best into the daily schedule. You might hold intervention sessions when the rest of the class is engaged in sustained silent reading, working at learning centers, taking part in literature circles, or working on individual or group projects. Students who are not given intervention assistance need to know that you are busy at that time, so they should work independently and hold questions until later. If other professionals are working in the room with you, you might want to work out an arrangement in which the other professionals spend time with the rest of the class while you work with the intervention group.

Intervention groups should be scheduled every day, if possible, but not less than three times a week. Sessions can last from 20 to 45 minutes, with 40 minutes being the recommended duration. Including both regular classroom and intervention instruction, students in grades 1 through 3 should have a total of at least 90 minutes of literacy instruction each day. Students in grades 4 and 5 should have at least 60 minutes.

The pacing of instruction should be brisk. Emphasis should be placed on the skills and strategies that have the highest payoff and on activities that provide the best practice of these skills and strategies.

PARTS OF A BUILDING WORDS LESSON

A Building Words lesson should include certain key elements. As a minimum, there should be a review of past material, an introduction or extension of a new skill or strategy, and opportunity to apply that skill or strategy. The parts of a daily lesson are described below.

Review (2 to 5 minutes).   Review previous pattern. Read or reread a verse, song, poem, riddle, or other brief selection that incorporates a pattern previously presented. Also discuss the take-home selection read the previous night.

Introduction or Extension of New Pattern or Strategy (5 to 10 minutes). Introduce a new pattern or extend a pattern previously presented. Build the pattern as explained in the sample lessons. If time allows, provide guided practice by having students sort pattern words, unscramble a sentence, and read a rhyme or other brief selection that contains the pattern.

Reading a New Selection Containing the Pattern (6 to 15 minutes).   For younger students or older students reading on a very low level, use a text walk. For older students use a less structured procedure such as guided reading or KWL. The selection should be on the students' instructional level (95 percent of the words are known) and should incorporate the new pattern.

Spelling/Writing (5 to 10 minutes).   Introduce or review spelling words related to the new pattern and/or compose a sentence or brief selection using one or more of the new pattern words. The sentence or brief selection is dictated by the group and scribed by the teacher. Students copy each word on a 3" by 5" card, mix the cards up, and place them in an envelope. As a home assignment, students reassemble the scrambled sentence. As students become more proficient, drop this activity. By the time students have learned the short-vowel patterns, writing and reassembling sentences will have lost much of its value (Morris, 1999). Instead, as time allows, have students write a piece on a topic of their choosing. The piece might be developed over a number of sessions. In addition to the time spent on writing during their Building Words lessons, students need a full program of writing development in which they write letters, narratives, and various kinds of expository pieces.

Conclusion of Session (2 to 5 minutes).   The session ends with a riddle or a gamelike activity, such as a mystery word, that incorporates the new pattern. Students also choose or are given a take-home selection to read. The take-home selection can be a children's book, a booklet that you or the students have made, a fold-and-read booklet, an experience story, or a periodical.

■ MANAGING THE LESSON

One-on-one sessions work well because instruction can be geared to the specific needs of the learner. When groups of students are taught, needs become more diversified. Insofar as possible, select students who have common needs. Since the focus of Building Words is on developing word analysis skills and strategies, use students' decoding skills as a basis for grouping. Place all the students who have difficulty with long vowels, for instance, in the same group. It is not necessary that all have exactly the same level of knowledge. For students who have very limited knowledge of long vowels, the lessons will be an introduction to new skills. For those who have some knowledge of long vowels, the lessons will be an extension or review.

If necessary, adjust the demands of the reinforcement activities. Rhymes, riddles, songs, and other practice activities should be on the appropriate level of difficulty. However, if they are a bit too hard for just one or two members of a group, share-read them with the whole group. Similarly, if you are using multiple copies of a book for application reading, use a text walk to give students thorough preparation for reading the book. Or you might provide each student with a book written on her level. A sample lesson in which the *-oad* pattern is presented to a group of five students of somewhat varying abilities is presented next.

Sample Lesson: Teaching the **-oad** Pattern to a Small Group

Review (2 to 5 minutes).   Review the *-oat* pattern, which was introduced in a previous lesson. The class share-reads or sings "Papa's Going to Buy You a Diamond Ring." Long-*o* words in the song are emphasized. Students briefly discuss the selection they read the night before.

Introduction or Extension of New Pattern or Strategy (5 to 10 minutes).   The *-oad* pattern is introduced. Students sort words into *-oad* and *-oat* patterns.

Reading a New Selection Containing the Pattern (6 to 15 minutes).   Using a text walk, the teacher introduces *Toad on the Road* (Schade, 1992). Students are invited to read the title, which contains two *-oad* pattern words, and to predict what Toad might do in the story. The teacher then walks students through the story picture by picture. Explaining that Toad loves to drive, the teacher asks a volunteer to find the word *drive.* Turning to the next page, the teacher explains that Toad is a careful driver and asks a volunteer to point out the word *careful.* The teacher proceeds through the rest of the story in similar fashion, highlighting the story and focusing on words and phrases that might pose problems: *traffic light, car wash, sip and slurp, chew and munch, roof rack, magic shows,* and *Ferris wheels.* The conclusion of the selection is not analyzed, so that students have the opportunity to read some of the text completely on their own and will have the satisfaction of seeing how the selection ends. As part of the text walk, students are provided with a purpose for reading. They can predict what will happen, or you can give them a purpose for reading. For this selection, students might predict where Toad and his friends are going.

After reading the selection silently, the students discuss their predictions and talk over the rest of the story. Students reread orally passages that verify, clarify, or amplify their responses. Each student might also be asked to read aloud his favorite part.

Spelling/Writing (5 to 10 minutes).   Students are introduced to the spelling words: *toad, load, road.* Students complete a spelling sort containing *-ow, -oad,* and *-oat* words. If time allows, the class composes a group (or individual) story about a class trip on the road: "Our Class on the Road."

Conclusion of Session (2 to 5 minutes).   Students take home a copy of *Toad on the Road* to reread, or another book in the Toad series, or another text that reinforces the *-oad* pattern. Students conclude the session by singing "I've Been Working on the Railroad" as the teacher points to each word of the song, which has been written on the chalkboard or is being shown on a transparency.

COORDINATED PROGRAM

The intervention program should be closely coordinated with the school's program. The school's program should be of high quality. A highly effective literacy program is the best way to prevent literacy learning problems. A high-quality program also builds on the gains that students make in a successful intervention program. Gains made in an intervention program are in danger of being lost unless they are nurtured in a high-quality classroom program.

STAFFING

The staff is the heart of the program. Staff should be well versed in the program and dedicated. The program can be taught by the classroom teacher, by a specialist working in or out of the classroom, or by well-trained and well-supervised paraprofessionals or volunteers. If paraprofessionals or volunteers are used, they need to be carefully supervised. In-service sessions should be held on a regular basis to keep up with the latest developments in the field, to test new ideas, to share ideas, to work out problems, and to discuss new materials. Supervision with feedback or coaching sessions is especially helpful. If outside help is not available, assess your program as objectively as you can. Use the Building Literacy Self-Assessment Checklist (Table 10.1) as a guide for coaching or self-assessment sessions.

MONITORING PROGRESS

It is important to monitor progress; otherwise, students may move on to long-vowel patterns before they have mastered short-vowel patterns and become overwhelmed. The best way to assess students' progress is to observe their daily work.

TABLE 10.1   Building Literacy Self-Assessment Checklist

	Yes	No	Partially	Plans for Implementation
New pattern is carefully introduced.				
Materials being read incorporate the new pattern.				
Materials are on the appropriate level.				
Reinforcement activities are varied and effective.				
Reinforcement activities include sorting and/or other high-payoff activities.				
Students attempt to apply strategies.				
Students are given appropriate prompts and feedback.				
Students read materials at home that incorporate pattern.				
Patterns are reviewed as necessary.				
Teacher builds on what students know.				

Ask such questions as: After reading a selection, is the student able to retell it or answer questions about it? If comprehension is lacking, the selection might be too hard. There may be too many unknown words in the selection. Also ask: How does the student do with Word Building? Does the student participate? Does the student seem to be learning the new patterns? How successful is the student at putting together scrambled sentences? How successful is the student at sorting patterns and reading rhymes and riddles? How successful is the student at completing take-home activities? After discussing take-home selections, have each student read a favorite sentence or passage. Note the accuracy of students' reading and the strategies they use when they encounter difficult words. If students are missing one word out of every ten, the selection is probably too hard. You might want to check further to make sure the students are being given material at the right level. Also note what students do when they encounter a word that fits a pattern that has been taught but that was not included among the words presented when the pattern was taught. If students are able to decode the word, this suggests that they are applying skills.

Some erroneous responses and false starts are to be expected. Otherwise, the material and activities may not be challenging enough. Some prompting and reteaching may be necessary. However, if nearly every skill needs to be retaught and prompting seems to be necessary for nearly every response, then the student's program might be at too high a level. Some adjustments may need to be made. It is important that students be instructed at a point where they are successful most of the time.

While observation provides a wealth of information, it is somewhat subjective. On a weekly basis, try to obtain objective assessments of students' work. These assessments might include the following:

- An oral quiz on the pattern and sight words taught. Test all of the words or a sampling of ten of them. Performance that is less than 80 percent suggests the need for reteaching and added practice.
- A dictated quiz on the week's spelling words. Performance below 90 percent suggests the need for some reteaching or additional studying.
- A sample of students' oral reading. Have students read a 100-word sample orally. Word recognition should be 95 percent. Comprehension should be 75 percent. Suggestions for assessing students' oral reading are presented in Appendix A.

PERIODIC EVALUATION

In addition to conducting ongoing assessment activities, provision should also be made for evaluating students' progress at key points. This could be at the end of a unit, quarter, semester, or after students have completed a significant block of learning, such as after all the short-vowel patterns have been presented. For this cumulative type of evaluation, the following might be used.

- Examining performance on the Benchmark Passages Inventory. The benchmark inventory passages, which include two passages on each level and are presented in Appendix A, were written specifically for Building Words. They incorporate key elements from the major stages of the program and so provide trustworthy information about students' performance.
- Examining performance on benchmark books. Instead of or along with the Benchmark Passages Inventory, you might use actual children's books to serve as a benchmark. Applying the same standards as you do for the Bench-

mark Passages Inventory, have students read selected passages and retell the story or respond to comprehension questions that you compose.

Other evaluative measures include

- Giving the Word Pattern Survey as a posttest.
- Giving the Syllable Survey as a posttest.
- Assessing samples of students' work collected in a portfolio.
- Giving the Elementary Spelling Inventory as a posttest.
- Giving the Spelling Placement Test as a posttest.
- Using results of district-wide, state-wide, or national performance and/or norm-referenced tests of reading and writing. These tests might not address the specific objectives of this program and/or may not assess strategies in the way they were taught. However, test results should provide general information about students' overall achievement in reading and writing. See the section on Objectives for additional suggestions for evaluation.

Whatever devices are used to monitor and evaluate students' progress, it is important that this information be used to provide assistance as needed and to make necessary adjustments. The first step in the evaluation process is to define objectives. The final step is to use the results of the evaluation to improve the program.

PARENTAL AND COMMUNITY INVOLVEMENT

Parents can provide invaluable support for the school's literacy program. They can foster voluntary reading by encouraging their children to read and helping them obtain books. They can also help develop a positive attitude toward reading and writing and set aside a time and place for studying. The community can provide volunteers, needed financial resources, and overall support. Some businesses, for instance, give their employees time off to tutor in local schools. And some provide free ice cream, pizza, or other incentives for voluntary reading programs.

AMPLE OPPORTUNITY TO READ AND WRITE

All readers and writers, but especially those who are struggling, also need lots of opportunities to read and write. This means that they should be provided with a wide variety of books and other reading materials on the appropriate level and lots of meaningful writing activities that are challenging but not overwhelming.

CHECKLIST FOR EVALUATING YOUR LITERACY PROGRAM

A strong program in word analysis, such as that presented in Building Words, should be complemented by an equally strong program in comprehension. Students should read the finest in children's literature and develop their writing skills. Students should have the opportunity to make full use of and extend the decoding and spelling skills fostered by Building Words. How does your literacy program shape up? Table 10.2 is a checklist designed to help you evaluate the effectiveness of your literacy program and to identify areas of strength as well as areas of weakness, so that you can make plans for improvements.

TABLE 10.2   Building Literacy Evaluation Checklist

	Yes	No	Somewhat	Plans for Improvement
Objectives are clearly stated.				
Focus is on high-payoff skills and strategies.				
Program builds on what students know.				
Direct, systematic instruction is provided.				
Pacing is brisk.				
Ample time is provided for reading and writing.				
Reading, writing, and spelling are related.				
Progress is continuously monitored.				
Intervention program is coordinated with class program.				
Students are placed at appropriate levels.				
Materials on appropriate levels are available.				
Parents and community are involved.				

■ Appendix A

BENCHMARK PASSAGES INVENTORY

■ PLACING STUDENTS

Placing students at the right level is essential for the success of this program. If students are given materials that are too difficult, they will be frustrated, and reading will be seen as an impossible, unhappy task. If materials are too easy, students may be bored and progress will be hampered. The Benchmark Passages Inventory is a streamlined informal reading inventory designed to place students in the appropriate level text. In the Benchmark Passages Inventory, students read, orally and silently, paragraphs that gradually increase in difficulty. As they read orally, you note their errors. After they read a passage orally or silently, you ask five to eight comprehension questions. Based on students' ability to read passages orally and their comprehension on oral and silent passages, you determine their reading levels.

Two benchmark passages are provided for each level, one to be read orally and one to be read silently. Because first-grade reading encompasses tasks of differing difficulty, ranging from reading books in which there is just one sentence per page to reading brief chapter books, first-grade reading has been divided into three levels as follows:

Easy first grade—incorporates sight words and short vowels.

Middle first grade—emphasizes long-vowel patterns but includes some other-vowel and *r*-vowel patterns

Ending first grade—includes all the single-syllable vowel patterns but has a concentration of other-vowel and *r*-vowel words and some multisyllable words.

Others levels assessed by the Benchmark Passages Inventory include second through sixth grades. Regardless of how levels are obtained, verify students' placement by observing their performance. If a student seems to be struggling, move him down a level. If, on the other hand, the student doesn't seem to be challenged, boost him up a level.

■ ADMINISTERING THE BENCHMARK PASSAGES INVENTORY

If you have not already done so, administer the Word Pattern Survey or the Syllable Survey. These yield estimated reading levels and can be used to determine where to start administering the Benchmark Passages Inventory. Using Tables A.1 and A.2, determine the student's estimated reading level. Start the inventory by

TABLE A.1   Placement Chart for Word Pattern Survey

Total Score	Estimated Instructional Level
0–5	Beginning reading
	Retest with Beginning Consonant Correspondences Survey
6–10	Sight word
11–20	Easy first grade
21–30	Middle first grade
31–45	Ending first grade
46–60	Grade 2
61–80	Grade 3; give Syllable Survey

TABLE A.2   Placement Chart for Syllable Survey

Total Score	Estimated Instructional Level
1–20	Grade 2
21–39	Grade 3
40–45	Grade 4
46–50	Grade 4+

administering the passage that is one level below the one indicated by the Word Pattern or Syllable Survey. If, for instance, the student obtained a score of between 46 and 60 on the Word Pattern Survey, which translates into second-grade level, start the inventory by administering the passage that is on the ending first-grade level.

After deciding on a starting point, show the student the student copy of the Benchmark Passages Inventory and explain that you would like her to read some stories out loud to you. Explain, too, that as she reads, you will be writing down some notes. Tell her that after she has read a story you will ask her some questions about it. Explain that there may be some hard words in the story but she should just do the best that she can.

Each selection has a brief introduction. After reading the introduction, ask the student to read the oral selection out loud to you. Then, using the symbols noted in Figure A.1, record the student's misreadings on the teacher marking copy of the Benchmark Passages Inventory provided at the end of this appendix. Indicate words that are mispronounced, inserted, omitted, or that the student asked you to supply. All of these count as misreadings. However, misreadings that are self-corrected do not count as errors.

After the student has read the selection, ask the comprehension questions that follow the selection. Write the student's response, so you can double-check its accuracy later if necessary. Do not give any assistance, but if the student does not give you enough information to evaluate the response, you can request additional information. Say to the student, "Can you tell me more about that?"

After the student has read and answered questions on the oral selection, administer the silent selection. Explain to the student that she is to read the story to herself. Tell her that after she has read a story you will ask her some questions

a ~~strange~~ animal *(strong)*	Mispronounced word
a ~~strange~~ animal	Omitted word
a strange *(mean)* animal	Inserted word
a (strange) animal	Word supplied by teacher
a ~~strange~~ animal *(strong ✓)*	Self-correction (not counted as an error)

FIGURE A.1   Marking Symbols

about it. Continue testing until the student's word recognition is 90 percent or less on the oral selection. If time is limited and you can't give the full inventory, administer only the oral selections.

DETERMINING READING LEVELS

To determine a student's reading level, consider both percentage of word recognition and comprehension. Enter both percentages for each level on a Benchmark Passages Inventory Summary Sheet. A sample summary sheet is presented in Figure A.2. A blank summary sheet is presented in Figure A.3. From these percentages, you will obtain three levels: the independent, the instructional, and the frustration. The independent level is the level at which the student achieves 99 percent word recognition and 90 percent comprehension. It is the level where the student can read on her own without any help from the teacher. The instructional level is the highest level at which the student achieves 95 percent word recognition and 75 percent comprehension. It is the level at which the student can read if given some help from the teacher. The frustration level is the point at which word recognition is 90 percent or less or comprehension is 50 percent or less. The material at this level is so difficult that the student can't handle it even if given instructional help. In Building Words, the student should be operating on the instructional level.

How well should a student be able to read? You may obtain an estimate of the student's reading potential by using the Benchmark Passages Inventory as a listening test. Once the student has reached the frustration level, read the selections beyond that level to her. After reading a selection, ask the comprehension questions just as you did when the student was reading the passages. Read two passages at each level and average the scores. Continue until the student's comprehension is less than 50 percent on two levels. The listening level is the highest point at which the student can understand 75 percent of the selections that are read to her, which means that she can answer 75 percent of the questions asked about the selections that were read to her. The listening level is an estimate of the student's language development and indicates the level at which the student might be expected to read if she had the necessary decoding skills.

INTERPRETING THE INVENTORY

In addition to providing estimated reading levels, the Benchmark Passages Inventory can also be used to yield valuable information about the student's word analysis and comprehension. As students read orally, note the kinds of strategies they use to decode difficult words. Do they sound them out letter by letter, do they use pronounceable word parts, do they use context, do they quickly give up and ask for help? Also note the kinds of phonic elements that present problems. Note how they do with each major type of pattern: short vowel, long vowel, *r*-vowel, other vowel. Note, too, how they do with clusters and multisyllable words. After administering the inventory, analyze the errors. For a more thorough analysis, use the Miscue Analysis form presented in the next section.

Also take a look at students' comprehension. How does comprehension compare to word analysis? If word analysis is 95 percent or higher, then comprehension should be 70 to 75 percent or higher. Ask yourself: What kinds of questions did the student do well with? What kinds of questions posed problems? What role is vocabulary playing? Is the student missing questions because of limited vocabulary? What role does background of experience play? Is the student missing questions because of limited background knowledge? How about thinking skills? Is the student missing questions because he is not applying thinking skills?

Name Jonah Maxwell   Grade   4   Date Nov. 15

School P.S. 72   Examiner's Name   T. G.

Benchmark Passages Inventory Summary Sheet

Level	Word Recognition		Comprehension				Listening		
			Oral	Silent	Avg.		Pass. 1	Pass. 2	Avg.
Easy first	100		100	100	100				
Middle first	98		100	100	100				
End of first	100		100	80	90				
Second	96		80	80	80				
Third	95		80	80	80				
Fourth	92		80	60	70				
Fifth	90		60	60	60				
Sixth							80	80	80

Levels

Independent _____1_____

Instructional _____3_____

Frustration _____5_____

Listening Capacity _____6_____

Summary of Strengths & Needs

Strong listening and language skills. Good overall comprehension. Needs work with decoding advanced multisyllabic patterns.

Scoring Criteria

	Word Recognition		Comprehension
Independent	99%	and	90%
Instructional	95%	and	75%
Frustration	90%	or	50%
Listening Capacity			75%

FIGURE A.2   Sample Benchmark Passages Inventory Summary Sheet

Name _____   Grade _____   Date _____

School _____   Examiner's Name _____

Benchmark Passages Inventory Summary Sheet

Level	Word Recognition		Comprehension Oral	Silent	Avg.		Listening Pass. 1	Pass. 2	Avg.
Easy first									
Middle first									
End of first									
Second									
Third									
Fourth									
Fifth									
Sixth									

Levels   Summary of Strengths & Needs

Independent   _____

Instructional   _____

Frustration   _____

Listening Capacity   _____

Scoring Criteria

	Word Recognition		Comprehension
Independent		and	
Instructional		and	
Frustration		or	
Listening Capacity			

FIGURE A.3   Blank Benchmark Passages Inventory Summary Sheet

MISCUE ANALYSIS

To gain insight into students' knowledge of phonics elements and use of decoding strategies, analyze their errors or miscues. Students use both phonics and context to decode words, and they should be using these systems in parallel fashion. To determine how they are using these systems, analyze their word-recognition errors, or miscues, using a modified miscue analysis. A sample Miscue Analysis sheet is shown in Figure A.4. On a blank Miscue Analysis sheet as provided in Figure A.5, list the student's miscues. Try to list at least ten miscues, but do not analyze any that are at or beyond the frustration level. Miscues can be chosen from the independent and instructional levels and from the zone between the instructional and frustration levels (91–94 percent word recognition). Also list the correct version of each error. Note whether the miscue fits the context. Also indicate corrected miscues with a check in the self-correction column. (A self-correction is a positive sign: it shows that the student is reading for meaning and is monitoring his reading.) Then note the graphic similarity of the miscue. Note whether the beginning, middle, or end of the miscue is similar to the beginning, middle, or end of the target word. It is similar if it contains at least half the sounds in the text word. Then indicate the student's needs in phonics. Note whether the student has difficulty with the beginning consonant, ending consonant, beginning cluster, ending cluster, short vowel, long vowel, *r*-vowel, or other vowel (/aw/, /oi/, /ow/, /$\overline{oo}$/, or /oo/). Tally each column (as shown in Figure A.4) and convert tallies to percentages. After tallying the columns, compare the tallies to see if the cues are being used in balanced fashion or if one is being overused or underused. The student may be overusing phonics and underusing semantic context, or vice versa. Draw tentative conclusions about the strategies that the student uses in his word recognition. Double-check these conclusions as you observe the student read in the classroom. As children struggle with difficult words, you may also want to conduct an on-the-spot mental miscue analysis. By closely observing miscues, you can infer whether students might need added instruction in using context, using phonics, or integrating the two.

ORAL READING CHECKUP

Students' decoding performance should be assessed on an ongoing basis. This can be done by readministering the Benchmark Passages Inventory or by a running record or an oral reading check. Similar to an informal reading inventory and based on the Goodmans' (Goodman & Goodman, 1994) theory of analyzing students' miscues to determine what strategies they are using to decode words, the running record is a popular device for assessing students' progress on a continuing basis. Like the Benchmark Passages Inventory, the running record is administered individually. However, only an oral-reading sample is obtained. The running record has two major purposes: to determine whether students' reading materials are on the proper level, and to obtain information about the word-recognition processes students are using. For detailed information about administering, analyzing, and interpreting running records, see Clay (1993a) or Johnston (1997).

As an efficient adaptation of the running record, administer an oral reading checkup. The oral reading checkup uses the same procedures and standards as those used in administering an informal reading inventory. However, since the student's level is known, only a passage on her instructional level is administered. And only an oral passage is read. To prepare an oral reading checkup, photocopy a passage of about 100 words from the student's basal reader or a children's book that is on her level. Give the student a copy of the book to read. Select a text in which the

Miscue Analysis | Semantic Similarity | Graphic Similarity | Word Analysis Needs

Name: Joseph M

Date: Nov. 15

Miscue	Text	Fits Context	Does Not Fit Context	Self-Correction	Beginning	Middle	End	Beginning Consonant	Ending Consonant	Beginning Cluster	Ending Cluster	Short Vowel	Long Vowel	R-Vowel	Other Vowel	Multisyllabic
cows	clowns		✓			✓				✓	✓					
circus	circuses	✓			✓	✓										✓
late	later	✓			✓	✓			✓							✓
ticks	tricks		✓			✓	✓			✓						
hoot	honk	✓			✓						✓				✓	
called	crawled		✓			✓	✓			✓						
ed	edge		✓		✓	✗					✓					
foat	float		✓			✓	✓			✓						
few	flew		✓		✓	✗	✓			✓						
saw	spotted	✓			✓				✓	✓		✓				✓
Column Total		4	6		6	8	10		2	6	3	1			1	4
Number of Miscues		10	10		10	6	4									
Percentage		40	60		60	75	40									

FIGURE A.4   Miscue Analysis Sheet Sample

Miscue Analysis

Semantic Similarity   Graphic Similarity   Word Analysis Needs

Name _____ Date _____		Fits Context	Does Not Fit Context	Self-Correction		Beginning	Middle	End		Beginning Consonant	Ending Consonant	Beginning Cluster	Ending Cluster	Short Vowel	Long Vowel	R-Vowel	Other Vowel	Multisyllabic
Miscue	Text																	
	Column Total																	
	Number of Miscues																	
	Percentage																	

FIGURE A.5   Blank Miscue Analysis Sheet

student knows about 95 percent of the words. If the student knows all the words, you won't obtain useful information about needs. If the student knows too few words, the student will be frustrated and won't be able to apply decoding skills and strategies. Use the photocopy to record the student's misreading. Use the same symbols that are used to record miscues on the Benchmark Passages Inventory.

Before administering the oral reading checkup, explain its purpose and put the student at ease. Tell the student that you want to get some information about the way she reads. Ask her to read the story out loud. Explain that you will be taking notes as she reads and that when she finishes reading, you will ask her to retell the story in her own words. As the student reads, mark her errors. Pay particular attention to strategies that she uses to decode difficult words. Note the processes that she seems to be using to decode the words she has difficulty with. After the student has read the passage, have her retell the story or ask a series of five to ten questions to assess the student's comprehension. An acceptable level of comprehension is 70 to 75 percent.

To get additional insight into the decoding processes the student is using, ask the student to tell you what she does when she encounters a difficult word. After a student has decoded a difficult word, ask, "How did you figure out that word?" or "How did you figure out that that word is *tent*?" Or "You read that word as *ten* first and then you went back and said *tent*. How did you figure out that that word is *tent* and not *ten*?"

It is important that you analyze a student's miscues in order to determine what strategies she is using. As you examine the student's miscues, ask the following questions:

- Is the student reading for meaning? Do the student's miscues make sense?
- Is the student self-correcting miscues, especially those that do not fit the meaning of the sentence?
- Is the student using meaning cues?
- Is the student using phonics cues? Are the student's miscues similar in appearance and sound to the target word?
- Is the student using picture cues?
- Is the student integrating cues? Is the student balancing the use of meaning and sound–symbol cues?
- Based on the student's performance, what strategies does she or he need to work on?

In addition to these formal oral reading checks, you might informally check students' reading as time permits. If possible, try to administer an oral reading check at least once a month. However, do not misinterpret oral reading checks as being an indication that all the students' reading should be oral. Excessive oral reading sends the message that reading is mostly a matter of getting the sounds right. The ultimate purpose of reading is to construct meaning. Most of the reading that students do should be silent. To determine whether or not students are able to handle the material, ask them to retell the selection or ask them questions. If they have a reasonable degree of comprehension, you can assume that they are able to read the words. To double-check, have them reread orally brief passages that help substantiate a response or clarify a confusing point. Students might also reread orally a passage that they found especially funny or interesting.

Benchmark Passages Inventory

Student Copy

The Cat

I am a cat. I have six kittens. My kittens like to play.

I can run. I can run fast. I can jump. I can jump fast. I can catch rats. I can catch big rats. And I can catch little rats. What can you do?

The Hen

I am a hen. I have a nest. My nest is big. I have six eggs in my nest.

I sit on the eggs. The eggs will hatch if I sit on them. Then I will not have six eggs. I will have six baby chicks. The chicks will run and play and have fun.

Sam's Dog

My name is Sam. I have a dog. My dog is brown. But she has a big white spot on her back. I call her Spot. Spot sleeps on a rug next to my bed. Spot likes to run and jump. It is fun to have a dog.

What Jan Likes to Do

Jan likes to read. Some days she reads two or three books. She likes books that have lots of pictures. She likes books about animals. She likes to read about cats and dogs. She likes books that tell about fish. But she likes books that tell about birds the best of all. What books do you like best?

A Big Bug

How big can a bug be? There is one bug that is bigger than your hand. The bug is white and black. It is a pretty bug. Its wings are brown. And its wings are very big. They are as big as a small bird's wings. When this bug flies, it looks like a strange bird.

You might never see the big bug. It lives in a place that is far, far away.

The Lost Hat

Jack was looking for his hat. He looked in his room. But it was not there. Jack looked in every room in the house. But he could not find his hat anywhere. "Will you help me find my hat?" he asked his big brother. "Yes," said Jack's brother. "Pat your head with your hand. I think you will find your hat."

Jack patted the top of his head. There was his hat. He forgot that he had put it on.

The Best Thing about the Circus

What do you like best about the circus? Many people like the clowns best of all. If you like clowns, go to the circus early. In many circuses, the clowns put on a show of their own 20 minutes before the circus begins. This is called a *come-in.* Later on, the clowns have another show of their own. They walk around doing funny things and playing tricks on each other. They also have fun with the people who have come to watch the circus. They might honk a horn at a person or sit in the person's lap. This show is called a *clown walk-around.* The clowns also come out and do tricks in between some of the circus acts. Clowns are a big part of the circus.

The Circus Comes to Town

Years ago, schools closed when the circus came to town. Stores and other places where people worked also closed. After feeding their animals, many farmers took the day off, too. That way everyone could go to the circus.

Years ago, there was no TV, and there were no movies. There wasn't even any radio. People got excited when the circus came to town. When the circus came to town, it gave people something special to do. The circus showed people things they had never seen. People saw elephants and camels for the first time at the circus. The first car that many people saw was in a circus parade. The circus also showed movies when movies first came out. The circus was a place for people to see new things and have fun.

The Ant and the Dove

One day an ant crawled to the edge of a pond. The ant was thirsty. It wanted to get a drink of water. But it slipped and fell in. "Help! Help!" called the ant. "I can't swim!"

A dove flying overhead heard the ant's call for help. It flew over to a tree and picked off a leaf. Then it flew to the ant and dropped the leaf on the pond. The ant climbed onto the leaf and floated to shore. "Thank you," said the ant to the dove. "You saved my life. Someday I will help you."

"I don't think so," said the dove. "How could a little ant help me?" And the dove flew away.

Not too long after that, the ant was walking in the woods. It spotted a hunter. The hunter was about to throw his net over the dove. The ant ran up to the man and bit him on the leg. "Ow!" yelled the man. Hearing the man yell, the dove flew away. Later, the dove thanked the ant. "I learned something," said the dove. "You don't have to be big to help others."

The Sun and the Wind

One day the Wind said to the Sun, "I am stronger than you are."

"No, you are not," answered the Sun.

"Yes, I am," said the Wind. "And I can prove it. We will have a contest." The Wind pointed to a man walking along the road. "See that man. I bet I can make him take his coat off faster than you can."

The Wind began to huff and puff and blew cold air onto the man. The man pulled his coat around him. The Wind blew harder. But the harder the Wind blew, the tighter the man pulled his coat. At last, the Wind gave up.

Now it was the Sun's turn. The Sun began to shine a little brighter. The day grew a little warmer. The man unbuttoned his coat. The Sun became a little warmer still. The day grew hotter and hotter. At last the man took his coat off. The Sun had won.

What Is It?

Looking out the kitchen window, Fred saw some kind of animal in the tree in the backyard. But he wasn't sure what it was. It was too big to be a squirrel. And it was too small to be a bear. Besides, this was a city. Bears don't live in the city. Could it be a large cat? No, it wasn't a cat. It was swinging from branch to branch. Cats don't swing from branch to branch. That's something that monkeys do. "Wow!" Fred said out loud. It must be a monkey.

Just then Fred's mom called to him. "Hey Fred," she called. "I just heard on the news that a monkey escaped from the zoo. Do you believe that?"

"Yes, I do," Fred replied. "By the way, Mom, could you come here for a minute? I want to show you something."

The Biggest Nose

Which animal has the biggest nose? Can you guess? The elephant does. The elephant's trunk is really its nose. The elephant smells with its trunk, so its trunk is its nose. A full-grown elephant's trunk is about six feet long and weighs anywhere from 300 to 400 pounds. In a way the elephant's trunk is like an arm and a hand, too. Although its trunk is very large, the elephant can pick up an object as small as a peanut. The elephant also uses its trunk to cool off. When it is hot, the elephant draws water up into its trunk. Then it lifts its trunk up and squirts water all over itself. When it is thirsty, it squirts water into its mouth. Some elephants even use their trunks to do work. These elephants help men who are cutting down trees in the forests. After the trees have been cut into logs, the elephants pick up the heavy logs and carry them away.

The Hatchet Fish

The hatchet fish is a strange-looking sea creature. It has a thin, hatchet-shaped body. But the strangest thing about the hatchet fish is its eyes. One type of hatchet fish has large eyes that point upwards. This hatchet fish lives deep in the water. Because they point upwards, the eyes of the deep-water hatchet fish help it to spot fish or bugs swimming above it. The hatchet fish's unusual eyes help it to hunt down other sea creatures.

Even stranger than the deep-water hatchet fish is the flying hatchet fish. Flying hatchet fish live near the surface of the water and feed on insects. If an insect tries to fly out of their reach, they chase it. Speeding through the water, they shoot up into the air. Then, by flapping their large fins, they glide through the air. They can't fly very far. But often they fly far enough to catch a meal.

Buddy

Frank Morris was totally blind. He couldn't see shapes and he couldn't tell the difference between light and dark. One day he went for a swim in a small lake. The warm sun felt good and so did the cool water, but suddenly, Frank felt tired. Frank's legs and arms had grown heavy. "I'd better head for shore," Frank said to himself. Then a frightening thought struck him. He didn't know which way shore was. Frank was sorry now that he had gone swimming alone. He wished that he had brought a friend along. But then Frank remembered that he wasn't really alone. "Buddy!" he called.

Soon Buddy was by his side leading him to shore. Buddy was Frank's guide dog and was always with Frank. Being rescued by his guide dog made Frank feel very thankful. He gave his faithful guide dog a big hug when they reached shore. "How lucky I am to have Buddy!" Frank thought to himself.

The Dust Bowl

The Dust Bowl sounds like a dirty dish, but it isn't. The Dust Bowl is a large piece of flat land. It is a dry, dusty place in the southwestern part of the United States. The first settlers there didn't take very good care of the land. After cutting down trees and plowing tall fields of grass, they planted crops everywhere they could. High winds picked up dust from the plowed fields and tossed it around. As time passed, more dust was blown away. And once in a while, dust storms would start up. Then dust blanketed everything. In the fierce dust storms of the 1930s, even homes that were locked up tight were full of dust inside. Powerful winds forced grains of dust through the tiniest openings. Often people used shovels instead of brooms to clean up the dust. There were also times when people couldn't tell day from night. Thick clouds of flying dust darkened the skies so that midday looked like midnight.

Today the Dust Bowl is not as dusty as it was. Trees and grass have been planted in many places. They help keep the wind from carrying away the soil.

Food for Life

The ship's captain was worried. A deadly but mysterious sickness had struck his crew. At first, the sailors' teeth would hurt and then their gums would start bleeding. They would lose their appetites and, after a while, their teeth fell out. They would then become very ill and die.

During the voyage, the captain lost 100 out of 160 men. Even the 60 who lived were sick, but after reaching shore, they soon recovered.

This strange illness struck sailors on a number of other ships that were taking long voyages. The illness came to be known as scurvy. Later, it was found that fruit juices kept people from getting scurvy. Fruit juices also helped those who already had scurvy.

In time, scientists found that people get scurvy if they don't get enough vitamin C. Vitamin C is found in oranges, limes, and some other fresh fruits. It is also found in green vegetables and some other foods.

The sailors weren't getting fresh fruits or vegetables. That is why they got scurvy. In 1795, the English Navy provided each sailor with a lime every day. The limes didn't taste that great, but they put an end to scurvy.

TEACHER MARKING COPY OF THE BENCHMARK PASSAGES INVENTORY

■ ORAL SELECTION

Introduction: Do you have a cat? Do you know anyone who does? Read about a cat and what it can do.

The Cat (46 words)

I am a cat. I have six kittens. My kittens like to play.
I can run. I can run fast. I can jump. I can jump fast. I can catch rats.
I can catch big rats. And I can catch little rats. What can you do?

1. What does the cat have? (kittens)
2. How many kittens does the cat have? (six)
3. What do the kittens like to do? (play)
4. What can the cat do? (any two of the following: run, jump, catch rats)
5. How do you know the cat is a good runner and jumper? (either answer: can run and jump fast; can catch rats)

Word Recognition Table

Errors	1	2	3	4	5
Percentage Correct	98	96	94	92	90

Teacher Marking Copy: Easy first-grade level

▪ SILENT SELECTION

Introduction: What is a hen? What are some things a hen might do? Read about a hen and some of the things a hen does.

The Hen (55 words)

I am a hen. I have a nest. My nest is big. I have six eggs in my nest. I sit on the eggs. The eggs will hatch if I sit on them. Then I will not have six eggs. I will have six baby chicks. The chicks will run and play and have fun.

1. What does the hen have? (nest)
2. What is in the hen's nest? (eggs)
3. What is the hen doing with the eggs? (sitting on them)
4. Why do you think the hen is sitting on the eggs? (either answer: to keep them warm; so they will hatch)
5. What will happen to the eggs? (either answer: they will hatch; baby chicks will come out of them)

Teacher Marking Copy: Easy first-grade level

▬ ORAL SELECTION

Introduction: Do you have any pets? Read about a boy and his pet dog. Find out what his pet is like.

Sam's Dog (47 words)

My name is Sam. I have a dog. My dog is brown. But she has a big white spot on her back. I call her Spot. Spot sleeps on a rug next to my bed. Spot likes to run and jump. It is fun to have a dog.

1. What is the boy's name? (Sam)
2. What is the dog's name? (Spot)
3. Why is the dog called Spot? (She is brown but she has a big white spot on her back.)
4. Where does Spot sleep? (on a rug next to Sam's bed)
5. What does Spot like to do? (run and jump)

Word Recognition Table

Errors	1	2	3	4	5
Percentage Correct	98	96	94	92	90

Teacher Marking Copy: Middle first-grade level

■ SILENT SELECTION

Introduction: What do you do during your free time? Read about a girl and find out what she does.

What Jan Likes to Do (50 words)

Jan likes to read. Some days she reads two or three books. She likes books that have lots of pictures. She likes books about animals. She likes to read about cats and dogs. She likes books that tell about fish. But she likes books that tell about birds the best of all. What books do you like best?

1. What does Jan like to do? (read)
2. How many books does Jan read some days? (two or three)
3. What does she like books to have lots of? (pictures)
4. What books does Jan like to read best? (books about birds)
5. What other kinds of animals does Jan like to read about? (cats, dogs, fish)

Teacher Marking Copy: Middle first-grade level

■ ORAL SELECTION

Introduction: What is the biggest bug that you have ever see? Read to find out what the world's biggest bug is like.

A Big Bug (73 words)

How big can a bug be? There is one bug that is bigger than your hand. The bug is white and black. It is a pretty bug. Its wings are brown. And its wings are very big. They are as big as a small bird's wings. When this bug flies, it looks like a strange bird.

You might never see the big bug. It lives in a place that is far, far away.

1. How big is the bug? (bigger than your hand)
2. What color is the bug's body? (white and black)
3. What color are the bug's wings? (brown)
4. How big are the bug's wings? (as big as a small bird's wings)
5. What does the bug look like when it flies? (like a strange bird or like a bird)

Word Recognition Table

Errors	1	2	3	4	5	6	7
Percentage Correct	99	97	96	95	93	92	90

Teacher Marking Copy: Ending first-grade level

▦ SILENT SELECTION

Introduction: Have you ever lost anything? What did you lose? Did you find it? Read the story. Find out what the boy in the story lost and how he found it.

The Lost Hat (78 words)

Jack was looking for his hat. He looked in his room. But it was not there. Jack looked in every room in the house. But he could not find his hat anywhere. "Will you help me find my hat?" he asked his big brother. "Yes," said Jack's brother. "Pat your head with your hand. I think you will find your hat."

Jack patted the top of his head. There was his hat. He forgot that he had put it on.

1. What did Jack lose? (hat)
2. Where did he look for his hat? (his room, every room in the house)
3. Whom did he ask to help him? (his brother)
4. What did his brother tell him to do? (pat his head)
5. Why do you think Jack's brother told him to pat his head? (He would feel that the hat was on his head.)

Teacher Marking Copy: Ending first-grade level

◼ ORAL SELECTION

Introduction: What do you think is the best thing about the circus? Read and find out what the author believes is the best thing about the circus and why.

The Best Thing about the Circus (129 words)

What do you like best about the circus? Many people like the clowns best of all. If you like clowns, go to the circus early. In many circuses, the clowns put on a show of their own 20 minutes before the circus begins. This is called a *come-in.* Later on, the clowns have another show of their own. They walk around doing funny things and playing tricks on each other. They also have fun with the people who have come to watch the circus. They might honk a horn at a person or sit in the person's lap. This show is called a *clown walk-around.* The clowns also come out and do tricks in between some of the circus acts. Clowns are a big part of the circus.

1. If you like clowns, why should you go to the circus early? (In many circuses, the clowns put on a show before the circus starts.)
2. How many minutes before the show starts do the clowns put on a show? (20)
3. What is this special show called? (come-in)
4. Later on, the clowns put on another show. What is this show called? (clown walk-around)
5. Besides, the come-in and clown walk-around, when else do clowns come out? (between some acts)

Word Recognition Table

Errors	1	2	3	4	5	6	7	8	9	10	11	12	13
Percentage Correct	99	98	98	97	96	95	95	93	93	92	92	91	90

Teacher Marking Copy: Second-grade level

▪ SILENT SELECTION

The Circus Comes to Town (128 words)

Years ago, schools closed when the circus came to town. Stores and other places where people worked also closed. After feeding their animals, many farmers took the day off, too. That way everyone could go to the circus.

Years ago, there was no TV, and there were no movies. There wasn't even any radio. People got excited when the circus came to town. When the circus came to town, it gave people something special to do. The circus showed people things they had never seen. People saw elephants and camels for the first time at the circus. The first car that many people saw was in a circus parade. The circus also showed movies when movies first came out. The circus was a place for people to see new things and have fun.

1. Why did schools close when the circus came to town? (so children could go to the circus)
2. What else closed besides schools when the circus came to town? (stores and other places where people worked)
3. What did farmers do before they took the day off? (fed their animals)
4. How was life different many years ago? (There was no TV and no movies.)
5. What animals did many people see at the circus for the first time? (elephants, camels)

▤ ORAL SELECTION

Introduction: Have you ever helped anyone? How? Read this story to find out how an ant helped a dove. A dove is a bird.

The Ant and the Dove (191 words)

One day an ant crawled to the edge of a pond. The ant was thirsty. It wanted to get a drink of water. But it slipped and fell in. "Help! Help!" called the ant. "I can't swim!"

A dove flying overhead heard the ant's call for help. It flew over to a tree and picked off a leaf. Then it flew to the ant and dropped the leaf on the pond. The ant climbed onto the leaf and floated to shore. "Thank you," said the ant to the dove. "You saved my life. Someday I will help you."

"I don't think so," said the dove. "How could a little ant help me?" And the dove flew away.

Not too long after that, the ant was walking in the woods. It spotted a hunter. The hunter was about to throw his net over the dove. The ant ran up to the man and bit him on the leg. "Ow!" yelled the man. Hearing the man yell, the dove flew away. Later, the dove thanked the ant. "I learned something," said the dove. "You don't have to be big to help others."

1. Why did the ant crawl to the pond? (It was thirsty and wanted to get a drink of water.)
2. What happened to the ant? (It slipped and fell in the water.)
3. What did the ant do when it fell in the water? (It called for help.)
4. Why did the ant call for help? (It couldn't swim.)
5. How did the dove help the ant? (The dove got the ant a leaf to float on.)
6. What did the ant promise the dove? (It would help the dove someday.)
7. Why didn't the dove think that the ant would help it? (It said the ant was too small to help it.)
8. How did the ant help the dove? (It saved it from a hunter by biting the hunter's leg.)

Word Recognition Table

Errors	1	2	3	4	5	6	7	8	9	10	11	12	13	14	15	16	17	18	19	20
Percentage Correct	99	99	98	98	97	97	96	96	95	95	94	94	93	93	92	92	91	91	90	90

Teacher Marking Copy: Third-grade level

■ SILENT SELECTION

Introduction: What is a contest? Have you ever been in a contest? Read and find out about a contest between the wind and the sun.

The Sun and the Wind (157 words)

One day the Wind said to the Sun, "I am stronger than you are."

"No, you are not," answered the Sun.

"Yes, I am," said the Wind. "And I can prove it. We will have a contest." The Wind pointed to a man walking along the road. "See that man. I bet I can make him take his coat off faster than you can."

The Wind began to huff and puff and blew cold air onto the man. The man pulled his coat around him. The Wind blew harder. But the harder the Wind blew, the tighter the man pulled his coat. At last, the Wind gave up.

Now it was the Sun's turn. The Sun began to shine a little brighter. The day grew a little warmer. The man unbuttoned his coat. The Sun became a little warmer still. The day grew hotter and hotter. At last the man took his coat off. The Sun had won.

1. What did the Wind say to the Sun? (I am stronger than you are.)
2. Who was walking along the road? (a man)
3. What was the man wearing? (a heavy coat)
4. What kind of a contest did the Wind and the Sun have? (see who could make a man take off his coat)
5. How did the Wind try to get the man to take his coat off? (tried to blow it off)
6. What did the man do when the Wind blew at him? (pulled his coat tighter)
7. How did the sun try to get the man to take his coat off? (shone brighter or warmer and made the day hotter)
8. What did the man do when the Sun made it warmer? (unbuttoned his coat and then took it off)

Teacher Marking Copy: Third-grade level

■ ORAL SELECTION

Introduction: Fred was looking out his window and he saw something strange. Read the story to find out what he saw. What do you think he might have seen?

What Is It? (142 words)

Looking out the kitchen window, Fred saw some kind of animal in the tree in the backyard. But he wasn't sure what it was. It was too big to be a squirrel. And it was too small to be a bear. Besides, this was a city. Bears don't live in the city. Could it be a large cat? No, it wasn't a cat. It was swinging from branch to branch. Cats don't swing from branch to branch. That's something that monkeys do. "Wow!" Fred said out loud. It must be a monkey.

Just then Fred's mom called him. "Hey Fred," she called. "I just heard on the news that a monkey escaped from the zoo. Do you believe that?"

"Yes, I do," Fred replied. "By the way, Mom, could you come here for a minute? I want to show you something."

1. Why did Fred think the thing in the tree couldn't be a squirrel? (It was too big.)
2. Why did Fred think the thing in the tree couldn't be a bear? (It was too small or bears don't live in the city.)
3. Where did Fred live? (in the city)
4. What did Fred think the thing was? (a monkey)
5. What made Fred think the thing in the tree was a monkey? (It was swinging from branch to branch.)
6. Who called to Fred? (his mom)
7. What news did she have to tell him? (A monkey had escaped from the zoo.)
8. What do you think Fred is going to show his mother? (the thing in the tree)

Word Recognition Table

Errors	1	2	3	4	5	6	7	8	9	10	11	12	13	14
Percentage Correct	99	99	98	97	96	96	95	94	94	93	92	92	91	90

Teacher Marking Copy: Fourth-grade level

◼ SILENT SELECTION

Introduction: Which animal do you think has the biggest nose? Read to find out which animal has the biggest nose and how it uses its nose.

The Biggest Nose (164 words)

Which animal has the biggest nose? Can you guess? The elephant does. The elephant's trunk is really its nose. The elephant smells with its trunk, so its trunk is its nose. A full-grown elephant's trunk is about six feet long and weighs anywhere from 300 to 400 pounds. In a way the elephant's trunk is like an arm and a hand, too. Although its trunk is very large, the elephant can pick up an object as small as a peanut. The elephant also uses its trunk to cool off. When it is hot, the elephant draws water up into its trunk. Then it lifts its trunk up and squirts water all over itself. When it is thirsty, it squirts water into its mouth. Some elephants even use their trunks to do work. These elephants help men who are cutting down trees in the forests. After the trees have been cut into logs, the elephants pick up the heavy logs and carry them away.

1. Which animal has the biggest nose? (elephant)
2. How long is the elephant's nose? (about six feet)
3. How much does the elephant's trunk weigh? (300 to 400 pounds)
4. Why is the elephant's nose like an arm and a hand? (can pick up things with its trunk)
5. How do you know that the elephant can pick up small objects? (can pick up a peanut)
6. How does the elephant use its trunk to cool off? (squirts water on itself)
7. How do elephants drink water? (draw up water in their trunks and squirt water in their mouths)
8. How do some elephants use their trunks to do work? (pick up logs and carry them away)

Teacher Marking Copy: Fourth-grade level

▥ ORAL SELECTION

Introduction: What is a hatchet? (Explain what a hatchet is if the student doesn't know.) Have you ever hear of a fish called a hatchet fish? Read the story to find what hatchet fishes are like.

The Hatchet Fish (152)

The hatchet fish is a strange-looking sea creature. It has a thin, hatchet-shaped body. But the strangest thing about the hatchet fish is its eyes. One type of hatchet fish has large eyes that point upwards. This hatchet fish lives deep in the water. Because they point upwards, the eyes of the deep-water hatchet fish help it to spot fish or bugs swimming above it. The hatchet fish's unusual eyes help it to hunt down other sea creatures.

Even stranger than the deep-water hatchet fish is the flying hatchet fish. Flying hatchet fish live near the surface of the water and feed on insects. If an insect tries to fly out of their reach, they chase it. Speeding through the water, they shoot up into the air. Then, by flapping their large fins, they glide through the air. They can't fly very far. But often they fly far enough to catch a meal.

1. How do you think the hatchet fish got its name? (It has a thin, hatchet-shaped body.)
2. What two kinds of hatchet fish did the article talk about? (deep-sea hatchet fish and flying hatchet fish)
3. What is strange about the hatchet fish's eyes? (They point upwards.)
4. What does the hatchet fish's unusual help it to do? (spot fish or bugs swimming above it)
5. What does the flying hatchet fish eat? (insects)
6. What does the flying hatchet fish do if an insect tries to fly out of its reach? (flies after it)
7. How does the flying hatchet fish fly? (by flapping its fins)
8. How far can the flying hatchet fish fly? (not very far but far enough to catch a meal)

Word Recognition Table

Errors	1	2	3	4	5	6	7	8	9	10	11	12	13	14	15
Percentage Correct	99	99	98	97	97	96	95	95	94	94	93	92	91	90	90

Teacher Marking Copy: Fifth-grade level

■ SILENT SELECTION

Introduction: How do friends help each other? Read to find out how a man was helped by his special friend.

Buddy (161 words)

Frank Morris was totally blind. He couldn't see shapes and he couldn't tell the difference between light and dark. One day he went for a swim in a small lake. The warm sun felt good and so did the cool water, but suddenly, Frank felt tired. Frank's legs and arms had grown heavy. "I'd better head for shore," Frank said to himself. Then a frightening thought struck him. He didn't know which way shore was. Frank was sorry now that he had gone swimming alone. He wished that he had brought a friend along. But then Frank remembered that he wasn't really alone. "Buddy!" he called.

Soon Buddy was by his side leading him to shore. Buddy was Frank's guide dog and was always with Frank. Being rescued by his guide dog made Frank feel very thankful. He gave his faithful guide dog a big hug when they reached shore. "How lucky I am to have Buddy!" Frank thought to himself.

1. Where was Frank? (in a small lake)
2. What frightened him? (He didn't know which way shore was.)
3. Why didn't he know where the shore was? (He was blind.)
4. Why was Frank sorry that he hadn't brought a friend along? (A friend could have guided him to shore.)
5. Whom did Frank call out to? (Buddy)
6. Who was Buddy? (Buddy was his guide dog.)
7. How did Buddy help Frank? (Buddy led Frank to shore.)
8. How did Frank thank Buddy? (Frank gave him a big hug.)

■ **ORAL SELECTION**

Introduction: What do you think an article called "The Dust Bowl" might be about? Read the article to find out about the Dust Bowl.

The Dust Bowl (195 words)

The Dust Bowl sounds like a dirty dish, but it isn't. The Dust Bowl is a large piece of flat land. It is a dry, dusty place in the southwestern part of the United States. The first settlers there didn't take very good care of the land. After cutting down trees and plowing tall fields of grass, they planted crops everywhere they could. High winds picked up dust from the plowed fields and tossed it around. As time passed, more dust was blown away. And once in a while, dust storms would start up. Then dust blanketed everything. In the fierce dust storms of the 1930s, even homes that were locked up tight were full of dust inside. Powerful winds forced grains of dust through the tiniest openings. Often people used shovels instead of brooms to clean up the dust. There were also times when people couldn't tell day from night. Thick clouds of flying dust darkened the skies so that midday looked like midnight.

Today the Dust Bowl is not as dusty as it was. Trees and grass have been planted in many places. They help keep the wind from carrying away the soil.

1. What is the Dust Bowl? (a large piece of flat land)
2. In what part of the United States is the dust bowl found? (the southwestern part of the United States)
3. Who is to blame for the Dust Bowl? (early settlers)
4. How did the early settlers cause the dust bowl? (Cut down trees and planted crops everywhere. Winds picked up dust from the plowed fields.)
5. When did some of the worst dust storms take place? (the 1930s)
6. How do you know there was a lot of dust inside people's homes? (They used shovels to clean up the dust.)
7. Why couldn't people tell night from day? (Flying dust kept the sky dark.)
8. What has been done to protect the land against dust storms? (Trees and grass have been planted to keep the winds from carrying away the soil.)

Word Recognition Table

Errors	1	2	3	4	5	6	7	8	9	10	11	12	13	14	15	16	17	18	19	20
Percentage Correct	99	99	98	98	97	97	96	96	95	95	94	94	93	93	92	92	91	91	90	90

Teacher Marking Copy: Sixth-grade level

▨ SILENT SELECTION

Introduction: What are your favorite foods? Read the story to find out about what happened to some sailors who weren't getting the right kinds of food.

Food for Life (196)

The ship's captain was worried. A deadly but mysterious sickness had struck his crew. At first, the sailors' teeth would hurt and then their gums would start bleeding. They would lose their appetites and, after a while, their teeth fell out. They would then become very ill and die.

During the voyage, the captain lost 100 out of 160 men. Even the 60 who lived were sick, but after reaching shore, they soon recovered.

This strange sickness struck sailors on a number of other ships that were taking long voyages. The illness came to be known as scurvy. Later, it was found that fruit juices kept people from getting scurvy. Fruit juices also helped those who already had scurvy.

In time, scientists found that people get scurvy if they don't get enough vitamin C. Vitamin C is found in oranges, limes, and some other fresh fruits. It is also found in green vegetables and some other foods.

The sailors weren't getting fresh fruits or vegetables. That is why they got scurvy. In 1795, the English Navy provided each sailor with a lime every day. The limes didn't taste that great, but they put an end to scurvy.

1. Why was the ship's captain worried? (A deadly but mysterious sickness had struck his crew.)
2. What was the first sign of scurvy? (The sailors' teeth would hurt.)
3. How many men did the captain lose? (100 men)
4. What happened to the 60 men who got sick but did not die? (After reaching shore, they recovered.)
5. What is the cause of scurvy? (not getting enough vitamin C)
6. In what foods is vitamin C found? (oranges, limes, and some other fresh fruits; green vegetables and other foods)
7. What food were the English sailors given each day? (a lime)
8. Why do you think the sailors were given limes? (Limes have vitamin C. The vitamin C kept the sailors from getting sick.)

Teacher Marking Copy: Sixth-grade level

■ Appendix B

FOLD-AND-READ BOOKS

Fold-and read-books are designed to provide added practice with beginning phonics patterns and high-frequency words. They have been created using a combination of clip art and art specially created for the booklet.

Fold-and-read books were deliberately designed so that no cutting is required. To create a booklet, follow these steps:

■ Tear the page from the book along the perforated line. The perforated page will be slightly narrower than a sheet of paper; therefore, when photocopying, center it side to side in the 8½"- by 11"-page area on your copying machine.

■ Fold the page in half vertically so that pages 4, 5, 6, and 1 are facing you.

■ Fold in half once more so that pages 1 and 6 are facing you.

■ Fold one last time so that only page 1 is facing you.

I see a lion.

1

I see a seal.

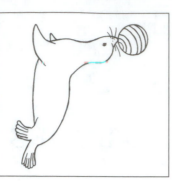

2

I see a fox.

6

I see a mouse.

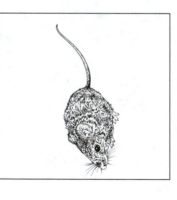

5

I see a horse.

4

I see a bee.

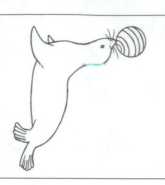

3

I see a cat.

I see a turtle.

Consonants: *n, c=/k/, r, g, t, d*

I see a gorilla.

I see a rabbit.

I see a dog.

I see a nest.

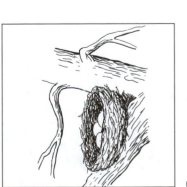

I like kangaroos.

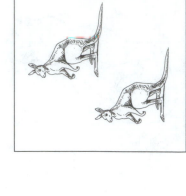

1

I like jackets.

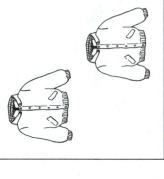

6

I like zebras.

2

I like pens.

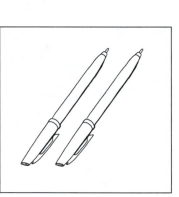

5

I like yo-yos.

3

I like watches.

4

I am a tiger.

1

I am a lamb.

6

I am a penguin.

5

I am a rabbit.

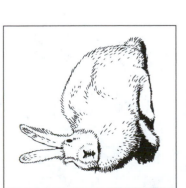

4

I am a seal.

2

I am a bee.

3

One cat sat
on the mat.

1

A rat sat on
the mat.

5

The cats ran
after the rat.

6

Two cats sat
on the mat.

2

Three cats sat
on the mat.

3

Four cats sat
on the mat.

4

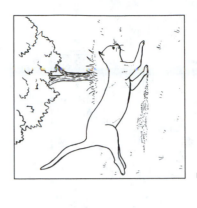

I am a cat.
I can run.

1

I am a frog.
I can jump.

2

I can run, jump,
swim, and hop.

6

I am Dan.

5

I am a fish.
I can swim.

3

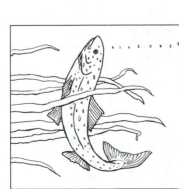

I am a rabbit.
I can hop.

4

1

Matt is sad.

2

Matt had a hat.

3

Pat is a cat. Pat has Matt's hat.

4

Pat ran with the hat.

5

Matt ran after Pat. He cannot catch that cat.

6

Matt is mad at Pat. "Bad cat!" Matt yells.

Ten hens are in
a pen.

1

Ben gets in the pen.
Ben is a bad cat.

2

The hens ran out
of the pen.

3

The bad cat is
in a pen.

6

Ben is in the pen.
He cannot get out.

5

Then the hens
shut the gate.

4

1

A puppy can be a pet.

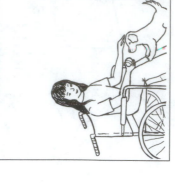

6

You bet. A pig can be a pet.

2

A cat can be a pet.

5

Can a pig be a pet?

3

A goat can be a pet.

4

A horse can be a pet.

This bird is little.
But it has a big bill.

2

A bird can be little.

This bird has big legs. It can run fast.

Short *i*: -*ig*, -*it*, -*ing* patterns

This bird cannot fly. It is too big.

This bird is big. It is bigger than a man.

3

This little bird has big wings.

A kangaroo
can hop.

1

The kangaroo rat
can hop a lot.

6

This is a kangaroo
rat.

This rat can hop.

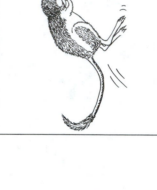

5

Can a rat hop?
This rat cannot hop.

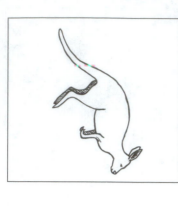

4

A kangaroo can
hop a lot.

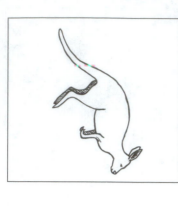

2

A rabbit can hop.
A rabbit can hop
a lot.

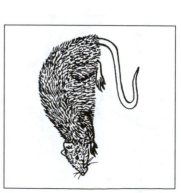

3

What is red?
A truck can be red.

A bus can be
yellow.

Short *u*: *-ug, -un, -us* patterns

A tiger can be
yellow with black
stripes.

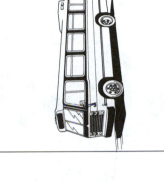

This bug is red.
And it has black
spots.

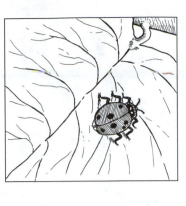

A rug can be red.

What is yellow?
The sun can be
yellow.

How many bugs
can you see?
___

1

How many drums
can you see?
___

6

Short *u*: *-ug, -um, -un* patterns

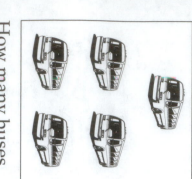

How many buses
can you see?
___

2

How many rugs
can you see?
___

5

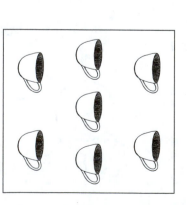

How many cups
can you see?
___

3

How many puppies
can you see?
___

4

References

Aaron, I. E., Artley, A. S., Goodman, K. S., Huck, C. S., & Jenkins, W. A. (1971). *Reading systems.* Glenview, IL: Scott, Foresman.

Adams, M. J. (1990). *Beginning to read: Thinking and learning about print.* Cambridge, MA: MIT Press.

Bear, D. (1995). Word study: A developmental perspective based on spelling stages. Paper presented at the annual meeting of the International Reading Association, Anaheim, CA.

Bear, D., & Barone, D. (1989). Using children's spellings to group for word study and directed reading in the primary classroom. *Reading Psychology, 12,* 275–292.

Bear, D., Invernizzi, M., Johnston, F., & Templeton, S. (1996). *Words their way: Word study for phonics, spelling, and vocabulary development.* Upper Saddle River, NJ: Merrill.

Blocksma, M. (1989). *Yoo hoo! Moon.* New York: Bantam.

Bryant, N. D., Kelly, M. S., Hathway, K., & Rubin, E. (l981). *A summary of directions for the "LD-Efficient" teaching manual.* New York: Research Institute for the Study of Learning Disabilities, Teachers College, Columbia University.

Buchanan, C. D., & Sullivan, C. (1973). *Programmed reading.* New York: McGraw-Hill.

Carle, E. (1987). *Have you seen my cat?* New York: Oxford.

Chall, J. S. (1967). *Learning to read: The great debate.* New York: McGraw-Hill.

Chall, J. S. (1996). *Stages of reading development* (2nd. ed.). Fort Worth, TX: Harcourt Brace.

Clarke, L. K. (1988). Invented vs. traditional spelling in first graders' writings: Effects on learning to spell and read. *Research in the Teaching of English, 22,* 281–309.

Clay, M. M. (1993a). *An observation survey of early literacy achievement.* Portsmouth, NH: Heinemann.

Clay, M. M. (1993b). *Reading recovery: A guidebook for teachers in training.* Portsmouth, NH: Heinemann.

Cunningham, P. M. (1978). Decoding polysyllabic words: An alternative strategy. *Journal of Reading, 21,* 608–614.

Cunningham, P. M. (1992). What kind of phonics instruction will we have? In C. K. Kinzer & D. J. Leu (Eds.), *Literacy research, theory, and practice: Views from many perspectives* (pp. 17–31). Chicago: National Reading Conference.

Cunningham, P. M., & Allington, R. L. (1999). *Classrooms that work: They can all read and write* (2nd ed.). New York: Longwood.

Cunningham, P. M., & Cunningham, J. W. (1992). Making words: Enhancing the invented spelling–decoding connection. *The Reading Teacher, 46,* 106–115.

Durrell, D. D. (1980). Letter name value in reading and spelling. *Reading Research Quarterly, 16,* 159–163.

Education Department of Western Australia. (1994). *Writing resource book.* Melbourne, Australia: Longman.

Ehri, L. C. (1983). A critique of five studies related to letter-name knowledge and learning to read. In L. Gentile, M. Kamil, & J. Blanchard (Eds.), *Reading research revisited* (pp. 143–153). Columbus, OH: Merrill.

Ehri, L. C. (1994). Development of the ability to read words: Update. In R. B. Ruddell, M. R. Ruddell, & H. Singer (Eds.), *Theoretical models and processes of reading* (4th ed., pp. 323–358). Newark, DE: International Reading Association.

Ehri, L. C., & McCormick, S. (1998). Phases of word learning: Implications for instruction with delayed and disabled readers. *Reading and Writing Quarterly: Overcoming Learning Disabilities, 14,* 135–163.

Elkonin, D. B. (1973). Reading in the USSR. In J. Downing (Ed.), *Comparative reading* (pp. 551–579). New York: Macmillan.

Fernald, G. M. (1943). *Remedial techniques in basic school subjects.* New York: McGraw-Hill.

Fitzgerald, J. (1951). *The teaching of spelling.* Milaukee, WI: Bruce Publishing.

Flesch, R. (1955). *Why Johnny can't read.* New York: Harper & Row.

Fries, C. C., Wilson, R. G., & Rudolph, M. K. (1966). *Merrill linguistic readers.* Columbus, OH: Merrill.

Gaskins, I. W., Ehri, L. C., Cress, C., O'Hara, C., & Donnelly, K. (1996–1997). Procedures for word learning: Making discoveries about words. *The Reading Teacher, 50,* 312–327.

Gaskins, R. W., Gaskins, J. C., & Gaskins, I. W. (1991). A decoding program for poor readers—and the rest of the class, too! *Language Arts, 63,* 213–225.

Gentry, J. R. (1997). *My kid can't spell.* Portsmouth, NH: Heinemann.

Gentry, J. R., & Gillet, J. W. (1993). *Teaching kids to spell.* Portsmouth, NH: Heinemann.

Gibson, E. (1969). Learning to read. *Science, 148*, 1066–1072.

Glass, G. G., & Burton, E. H. (1973). How do they decode? Verbalizations and observed behaviors of successful decoders.*Education, 94*, 58–65.

Goodman, K. S. (1967). Reading: A psycholinguistic guessing game. *Journal of the Reading Specialist, 3*, 126–135.

Goodman, Y. M., & Goodman, K. S. (1994). To err is human: Learning about language processes by analyzing miscues. In R. B. Ruddell, M. R. Ruddell, & H. Singer (Eds.), *Theoretical models and processes of reading* (4th ed., pp. 104–123). Newark, DE: International Reading Association.

Goswami, U., & Bryant, P. (1990). *Phonological skills and learning to read.* East Sussex, UK: Lawrence Erlbaum.

Gunning, T. (1975). A comparison of word attack skills derived from a phonological analysis of frequently used words drawn from a juvenile corpus and an adult corpus. Unpublished doctoral dissertation, Temple University, Philadelphia.

Gunning, T. (1988, May). Decoding behavior of good and poor second grade students. Paper presented at the annual meeting of the International Reading Association, Toronto.

Gunning, T. (1995). Word building: A strategic approach to the teaching of phonics. *The Reading Teacher, 48*, 484–488.

Gunning, T. G. (1998a). *Best books for beginning readers.* Boston: Allyn & Bacon.

Gunning, T. G. (1998b). *Assessing and correcting reading and writing difficulties.* Boston: Allyn & Bacon.

Gunning, T. G. (1999, December). Word analysis knowledge and processes of second graders. Paper presented at the annual meeting of the National Reading Conference, Orlando.

Gunning, T. (2000). *Creating literacy instruction for all children* (3rd ed.). Boston: Allyn & Bacon.

Hanna, P. R., Hodges, R. E., Hanna, J. S., & Rudorf, E. (1966). *Phoneme–grapheme correspondences as cues to spelling improvement.* U.S. Department of Health, Education, and Welfare, U.S., Department of Education, Bureau of Research. Washington: U.S. Government Printing Office.

Hardy, M., Stennett, R. G. F., & Smythe, P. C. (1973). Word attack: How do they figure them out? *Elementary English, 50*, 99–102.

Henderson, E. H., & Templeton, S. (1986). A developmental perspective of formal spelling instruction by alphabet, pattern, and meaning. *Elementary School Journal, 56*, 305–316.

Hooks, W. H. (1992). *Feed me.* New York: Bantam.

Hughes, M., & Searle, D. (1997). *The violent "e" and other tricky sounds: Learning to spell from kindergarten through grade 6.* York, ME: Stenhouse.

Hughes, M., & Searle, D. (2000). Spelling and "the second r." *Language Arts, 77*, 203–208.

Iverson, S., & Tunmer, W. W. (1993). Phonological processing skills and the Reading Recovery program. *Journal of Educational Psychology, 85*(1), 112–126.

Johnston, F., Juel, C., & Invernizzi, M. (1998). *Book buddies: Guidlines for volunteer tutors of emergent and early readers.* New York: Guilford Press.

Johnston, P. (1997). *Constructive evaluation of literacy* (2nd ed.). New York: Longman.

Juel, C., & Roper/Schneider, D. (1985). The influence of basal readers on first-grade reading. *Reading Research Quarterly, 23*, 134–152.

Liberman, A. M., & Mattingly, I. G. (1991). A specialization for speech perception. *Science, 243*, 489–494.

Liberman, I. Y., & Shankweiler, D. (1991). Phonology and beginning reading: A tutorial. In L. Rieben & C. A. Perfetti (Eds.), *Learning to read: Basic research and its implications* (pp. 3–18). Hillsdale, NJ: Lawrence Erlbaum.

Liberman, I. Y., Shankweiler, D., Fischer, F. W., & Carter, B. (1974). Explicit syllable and phoneme segmentation in the young child. *Journal of Experimental Child Psychology, 18*, 201–212.

Lopshire, R. (1960). *Put me in the zoo.* New York: Random House.

Moats, L. C. (1995). *Spelling: Development, disability, and instruction.* Timonium, MD: York Press.

Moore, I. (1991). *Six dinner Sid.* New York: Simon & Schuster.

Morris, D. (1983). Concept of word and phoneme awareness in the beginning reader. *Research in the Teaching of English, 17*, 359–373.

Morris, D. (1992). Concept of word: A pivotal understanding in the learning-to-read process. In S. Templeton & D. Bear (Eds.), *Development of orthographic knowledge and the foundations of literacy: A memorial festschrift for Edmund H. Henderson* (pp. 53–77). Hillsdale, NJ: Erlbaum.

Morris, D. (1998, December). Preventing reading failure in the primary grades. Paper presented at the annnual meeting of the National Reading Conference, Austin, TX.

Morris, D. (1999). *The Howard Street tutoring manual: Teaching at-risk readers in the primary grades.* New York: Guilford Press.

Peek, M. (1980). *Roll over! A counting song.* Boston: Clarion.

Pinnell, G. S., & Fountas, I. C. (1998). *Word matters.* Portsmouth, NH: Heinemann.

Read, C. (1971). Pre-school children's knowledge of English phonology. *Harvard Educational Review, 41*, 1–34.

Samuels, S. J. (1967). Attentional processes in reading: The effect of pictures in the acquisition of reading responses. *Journal of Educational Psychology, 58*, 337–342.

Santa, C. & Høien, T. (1999). An assessment of Early Steps: A program for early intervention. *Reading Research Quarterly, 34*, 54–79.

Schade, S. (1992). *Toad on the road.* New York: Random House.

Seuss, Dr. (1988). *Green eggs and ham.* New York: Random House.

Singer, H., Samuels, S. J., & Spiroff, J. (1973–1974). The effect of pictures and contextual conditions on learning responses to printed words. *Reading Research Quarterly, 9*, 555–567.

Snowball, D., & Bolton, F. (1999). *Spelling K–8: Planning and teaching.* York, ME: Stenhouse.

Stadler, J. (1985). *Snail saves the day.* New York: Crown.

Stahl, S., Stahl, K. A., & McKenna, M. (1998, December). How do phonological awareness, spelling, and word recognition relate to each other? Paper presented at the annual meeting of the National Reading Conference, Austin, TX.

Stahl, S. A., Osborne, J., & Lehr, F. (1990). *Beginning to read: Thinking and learning about print: A summary.* Urbana, IL: Center for the Study of Reading, University of Illinois at Urbana-Champaign.

Temple, C., Nathan, R., Temple, F., & Burris, N. A. (1993). *The beginnings of writing* (3rd ed.). Boston: Allyn & Bacon.

Treiman, R. (1992). The role of intrasyllabic units in learning to read and spell. In P. B. Gough, L. C. Ehri, & R. Tremain (Eds.), *Reading acquisition* (65–106). Hillsdale, NJ: Lawrence Erlbaum.

Tremain, R. (1993). *Beginning to spell: A study of first-grade children.* New York: Oxford University Press.

Tunmer, W. E., & Chapman, J. W. (1999). Teaching strategies for word identification. In G. B. Thompson & T. Nicholson (Eds.), *Learning to read: Beyond phonics and whole language* (74–102). Newark, DE: International Reading Association.

Venezky, R. L. (1965). A study of English spelling-to-sound correspondences on historical principles. Unpublished doctoral dissertation, Stanford University, Stanford, CA.

Wilde, S. (1992). *You kan red this! Spelling and punctuation for whole language classrooms.* Portsmouth, NH: Heinemann.

Zeno, S. M., Ivens, S. H., Millard, R. T., & Duvvuri, R. (1995). *The educator's word frequency scale.* Brewster, NY: Touchstone Applied Science Associates.

Index